Twenty-Three Minutes to Eternity

Twenty-Three Minutes to Eternity

The Final Voyage of the Escort Carrier USS *Liscome Bay*

JAMES L. NOLES JR.

THE UNIVERSITY OF ALABAMA PRESS
Tuscaloosa

Manufactured in the United States of America

Typeface: Goudy and Goudy Sans

Library of Congress Cataloging-in-Publication Data

Noles, James L.
Twenty-three minutes to eternity : the final voyage of the escort carrier U.S.S. Liscome Bay / James L. Noles, Jr.
p. cm.
Includes bibliographical references and index.
ISBN 0-8173-1369-9 (cloth : paper) ISBN 978-0-8173-5603-3 (pbk. : paper) ISBN 978-0-8173-8214-8 (electronic)
1. Liscome Bay (Escort Carrier : CVE 56) 2. World War, 1939–1945—Naval operations, American. 3. World War, 1939–1945—Campaigns—Kiribati. I. Title. D774.L57 N65 2004
940.54′26681—dc22

2003018416

To James B. Gooch, PFC, United States Army, and his late wife, Ethel, and to Dennis A. Noles and his wife, Grace—my grandparents and members of America's greatest generation

Contents

Illustrations

Abbreviations

ACV	auxiliary aircraft carrier or tender
AE	ammunition ship
AH	hospital ship
AP	transport ship
AV	seaplane tender
AVG	aircraft tender, general purpose
A-V(G)	USNR aviation officers holding designations as naval aviators, qualified for general detail afloat or ashore
A-V(N)	USNR aviation flight officers, detailed to active duty in the aeronautic organization of the navy immediately following their completion of training and designation as naval aviators
A-V(S)	USNR aviation officers, commissioned and warrant, including gunners, radio electricians, machinists, aerographers, and photographers, qualified for specialist duties
A-V(T)	USNR aviation officers, former civil aviation pilots or aviators of the army, navy, marine corps, or coast guard, qualified for specialist duties
BB	battleship
CA	heavy cruiser
ChC-V(G)	USNR commissioned chaplains qualified for general detail afloat and ashore
CL	light cruiser
CV	aircraft carrier
CVE	aircraft carrier, escort
CVL	aircraft carrier, small

C-V(G)	USNR communication officers, commissioned and warrant, including radio electricians, qualified for general duty afloat and ashore
C-V(S)	USNR communications officers, commissioned and warrant, including radio technicians, qualified for specialist duties
DD	destroyer
DE	destroyer escort
DE-V(G)	USNR commissioned deck and engineer officers, qualified for general duty afloat and ashore
DE-V(S)	USNR commissioned deck and engineer officers qualified for specialist duties
D-M	USNR deck officers, merchant marine, commissioned and warrant, including boatswains, qualified for deck and other appropriate administrative duties
D-V(G)	USNR deck officers, commissioned and warrant, including boatswains, gunners, and torpedomen, qualified for general duty afloat and ashore
D-V(S)	USNR deck officers, commissioned and warrant, including boatswains and ships clerks, qualified for specialist duties
E-V(G)	USNR engineer officers, commissioned and warrant, including electricians, carpenters, and machinists, qualified for general duty afloat and ashore
E-V(S)	USNR engineering officers, commissioned and warrant, including electricians, radio electricians, and machinists, qualified for specialist duties
jg	junior grade
LCM	landing craft, motorized
LCP	landing craft, personnel
LCVP	landing craft, vehicle and personnel
LVT	landing vehicle, tracked (aka "water buffalo" or "amtrac")
LSO	landing signal officer
LST	landing ship, tank
MC	Medical Corps
MC-V(G)	USNR medical officers, commissioned and warrant, including pharmacists, qualified for general duty afloat and ashore
NA	Naval Aviator
NAS	Naval Air Station
NTS	Naval Training Station

SC	USN supply officer
SC-V(G)	USNR supply officers, commissioned and warrant, including pay clerks, qualified for general duty afloat and ashore
TBF	Avenger torpedo bomber (manufactured by Grumman)
TBM	Avenger torpedo bomber (manufactured by Eastern Aircraft)
USN	United States Navy, used to designate an officer commissioned in the "regular" navy as opposed to a commissioned reservist
USNR	United States Navy Reserve, used to designate an officer commissioned from the reserve ranks
VC	composite squadron
VF	fighter squadron
WAVES	Women Accepted for Volunteer Emergency Service (U.S. Navy Women's Reserve)

Preface

This story of the sinking of the escort carrier *Liscome Bay* (CVE-56) in November 1943 is lifted from the history of the U.S. Navy's epic conflict with the Japanese during World War II. In recounting the short history of this almost-forgotten carrier, I have aspired to breathe life into a sixty-year-old tale. One question that arose early on was how best to handle various portions of dialogue. I was tempted to take some poetic license and create dialogue and conversations for the crew, especially those who are no longer available for interviews. In the end, however, I stuck strictly to the facts as I could best discern them—these, I decided, were more than enough. Accordingly, anything in direct quotes was either recorded by me in an interview with the speaker—in person, over the telephone, or in the course of personal correspondence—or is quoted from the identified source.

I was, however, forced to take some poetic license in describing the order in which various groups of sailors abandoned the sinking *Liscome Bay*, since my research did not reveal the precise sequence. Consequently, to a large extent I described departures in the order that best fit my narrative flow. I hope that I have slighted no one in implying that he abandoned ship prior to any of his comrades.

Foremost among those who deserve credit for enabling me to tell *Liscome Bay*'s tale are the ship's survivors. Every man I contacted was extremely polite and helpful. Tim Woodham, Leonard Bohm, and Francis Daily deserve special credit for tolerating my phone calls, letters, and e-mails.

Starting in the 1990s, Tim Woodham spearheaded the collection of survivor statements from his shipmates—statements that proved crucial to me in telling this story. Leonard Bohm took my manuscript to the 2002 reunion of *Liscome Bay*'s survivors in Hannibal, Missouri, and shepherded their review of its pages. Francis Daily, Don Cruse, and James Beasley had the foresight to put their experiences down on paper in memoirs of remarkable detail, insight, and candor. Their accounts formed the backbone of my manuscript, which was in turn fleshed out by the military records held by the National Archives and the Naval Historical Center.

Robert Cressman of the Naval Historical Center kindly reviewed my manuscript and played an essential role in whipping it into shape. He also helped me with the biography of *Liscome Bay*'s executive officer, Commander Finley Hall, and assisted me in identifying medals awarded to members of the crew. Jeffrey Barlow, also of the Naval Historical Center, generously reviewed my manuscript and provided invaluable assistance. Sarah Churchill of the United States Naval Academy provided copies of *Lucky Bag* yearbook entries for many of the academy graduates who served on the *Liscome Bay*.

In Birmingham, Kara Till read the manuscript in its earliest stages and provided valuable encouragement. The same can be said for my father, James Noles Sr., former brigadier general, U.S. Army, who reviewed the manuscript and offered incisive and helpful critiques.

Thanks are also due to General Alfred Sanelli and Amy Tennison at the Valley Forge Military Academy, who provided me with the photographs of the academy's stained-glass windows, and to David Ireland, of the Friends of Borderlands, who provided the photograph of Lieutenant Commander Oliver Ames. I also owe debts of gratitude to Cheryl Belding, who placed me in touch with Maxsy Homec, and especially to Ronald Wiltsie and Ronald Wiltsie Jr., U.S. Navy veterans themselves and the sons of Captain Irving Wiltsie. They provided, among other items, the photographs of Irving Wiltsie. I have credited all sources of the photographs in this book, but I still want to emphatically thank everyone who helped me obtain them.

Of course, all of this work would have been in vain had it not been for the staff and editorial board of the University of Alabama Press, who believed in this project and in the need to tell the story of *Liscome Bay* and her crew.

As always, thanks to my wife, Elizabeth, who endured an unkempt lawn, unwashed cars, and my long nights at the keyboard as I worked to complete my manuscript. Nevertheless, she remained a rock of faith and a font of good nature throughout the entire project. And thanks to young James as well, who quietly and good-naturedly sat in his "pack-n-play" and high chair beside my desk throughout much of this project.

Prologue: Unbehagen's Dream

The hands on Seaman First Class James C. Beasley's wristwatch showed midnight. It was time for the midwatch on the quiet American escort carrier *Liscome Bay* (CVE-56)—midnight to 4 A.M. in civilian time, 0000 to 0400 in military time.

Leaving the darkened crew quarters, Beasley joined shipmate Signalman's Mate Third Class Peter E. Unbehagen and headed above decks. Both men, still shy of their twentieth birthdays, were signalmen assigned to *Liscome Bay*. Beasley hailed from North Carolina, where he had left his first year of college to join the navy, and Unbehagen was a native of Louisiana. Despite their different backgrounds, the two young men had become good friends. That was typical of the ship's signal shop. Led by capable officers, it was a taut, happy outfit.

The signal shack was located on the carrier's island, near the bridge. Once inside, Beasley and Unbehagen noted appreciatively that a fresh pot of coffee was brewing for them. They relieved the two sailors standing watch before them and signed in on the watch's log. Beasley and Unbehagen dated their signatures November 22, 1943, and settled in for what they hoped would be a quiet watch. As signalmen, they had been in a better position than most of the other enlisted men on board to follow the unfolding events of Operation Galvanic—the American invasion of the Gilbert Islands. As Beasley and Unbehagen stood watch, they knew the marines were still locked in a vicious struggle ashore at Tarawa, where the outcome was still in doubt, and that the army troops on Makin had almost completed the annihilation of the stubborn Japanese defenders there. To date, however, the navy's role in the waters of the Gilberts had been practically bloodless.

Despite the navy's—and *Liscome Bay*'s—run of good luck so far, Beasley noticed in the dim light of the signal shack that his friend Unbehagen looked unusually somber. Seeing Beasley looking at him, the Louisiana teenager stepped over to his fellow signalman.

"Sam," he said, using a nickname that Beasley had acquired aboard the carrier, "I want to talk."

Beasley could tell that Unbehagen was serious about something. "Sure, Pete," he said. "Go ahead."

"Sam, I'm scared and concerned about a ridiculous dream I had a couple of nights ago. It was so real I can't get it off my mind."

Beasley nodded for Unbehagen to continue.

"You and I had the midwatch, just as tonight," Unbehagen said. "We were standing about where we are now. The night seemed unusually dark and the seas were choppy with whitecaps. All the elements seemed very unusual, uneasy, and scary. Suddenly I looked up toward the radar mast and saw a strange white creature—shimmering and ghostlike—coming down the mast." Unbehagen was referring to the large mast extending above the carrier's island and bridge. It contained the ship's radar apparatus and the massive bullhorns that were used for barking orders over the noise of the flight deck. "I pointed to it and asked if you could see it. You said that you did see it."

"When it finally reached the bridge deck close to where we were, we stood there looking at it. It looked like a faceless man dressed in a shimmering white robe. You asked it, 'Who are you, and what do you want?'"

"The thing answered, 'I am the Grand [*sic*] Reaper; my name is Death. I have come for both of you.'"

Unbehagen spoke more quickly now. "Between the two of us we began arguing with the thing. We told him it was not time for us to go with him. Finally, you threatened the thing and told him we were not going, and he had better move away and out of sight. He began to move away and go back toward the mast. He began shimm[y]ing back up the mast, but as he was about halfway up he turned and said in a weird way, 'You wait and see, I will be back, and I will come down this mast.'"

With that said, Unbehagen ended his story.

"Ah, Pete, it was just a foolish dream," Beasley reassured him. "You probably ate too much supper—forget it."

Unbehagen agreed, but he remained somber. It was so real and so strange, he told Beasley, and it just would not go away. With that said, Unbehagen (whose name in German means, ironically, "to cause unease")—returned to his work.[1]

Elsewhere on the ship, as Beasley and Unbehagen settled into their watch, slightly over nine hundred other men either stood the midwatch or slumbered in their narrow bunks. In the quiet of the signal shack, broken only by the occasional radio transmission, the two signalmen had no idea that, in just over forty-eight hours, Unbehagen's Reaper would return once more. When he did, he would take 644 of their shipmates in less than half an hour. With the exception of the disastrous kamikaze strike on the aircraft carrier *Franklin* (CV-13) later in the war, the sinking of *Liscome Bay* would cause the heaviest loss of life on board an American aircraft carrier in U.S. naval history. Indeed, the number of casualties she suffered would be among the highest ever suffered by the service at sea.

Twenty-Three Minutes to Eternity tells the story of some of Beasley and Unbehagen's shipmates—both the quick and the dead. As the years have passed, some have called their ship the "forgotten flattop." It's time to remember her story.

1
The Baby Flattops

When dawn came on Monday, April 19, 1943, Americans awoke to their 497th day at war. The morning papers, whether purchased on a New York sidewalk or tossed onto a suburban lawn by a San Diego paperboy, brought reports of the widening and strengthening crusade against the Axis by the United States and its allies. That particular day, headlines proudly announced the interception and destruction over the weekend of nearly six dozen German air transports as they tried to ferry Afrika Korps troops to Sicily out of the tightening noose of Allied forces in Tunisia.

Other articles brought more war news: a massive air strike by British Lancaster, Halifax, and Stirling bombers on the Italian naval base at Spezia; U.S. Navy air raids on the Japanese-occupied Aleutian island of Kiska and on Japanese shipping in the Solomons; a smaller Japanese aerial sortie against U.S. Marines occupying Guadalcanal; heavy fighting between Japanese and Chinese forces near Ichang; an Allied air raid on the German U-boat pens at the occupied French port of Lorient; bitter battles between the Soviet Red Army and the German Wehrmacht in the Caucasus; Royal Air Force raids on enemy positions in the Arakan region of Burma; B-17 Flying Fortress bombing missions against Palermo, Sicily; and Dutch B-25 Mitchell bomber raids on the Penfoel Aerodrome in East Timor.

The new issue of *Life* hit the stands that same day. The cover photograph portrayed the tender farewell between a bespectacled army soldier and his wife. With one glance, readers were quickly reminded that the skies of Europe, the jungles of Guadalcanal and New Guinea, and the mountains of North Africa were only a draft notice, boot camp, and troop transport ship voyage away for their sons, fathers, and brothers.

The effort to support such far-flung military operations, as well as those of the United States' British, Chinese, and Soviet allies, stretched vulnerable maritime supply lines across every sea-lane on the globe. From the icy expanses of the North Atlantic to the sweltering ports of the Red Sea to the steamy islands of the South Pacific, Allied merchant ships had struggled for more than three years to keep their troops supplied with arms and ammunition.

Almost from the outset, that supply effort came at a painful cost. German submarines stalked the nearly defenseless Allied cargo ships, sinking dozens of them. Six months before the Japanese struck Pearl Harbor, the United States and Germany fought an undeclared war in the Atlantic. Today it is easy to remember the hundreds of lives lost at Pearl Harbor on December 7, 1941, aboard such battleships as *Arizona* (BB-39), *Oklahoma* (BB-37), and *West Virginia* (BB-48). Americans are not as quick to remember, however, the eleven sailors who died on board the American destroyer *Kearny* (DD-432) on October 17, 1941, following a German submarine attack, or the sinking of *Reuben James* (DD-245) that same month on Halloween, when 115 of 159 men aboard perished after a German torpedo ripped the American destroyer open in the bitter cold North Atlantic. The Japanese attack on Pearl Harbor was still more than a month away.

At least one could mark the demise of *Kearny* and *Reuben James* with some degree of stoic acceptance. After all, they were warships, tasked with the thankless mission of going into harm's way. Loss figures for the civilian merchantmen seemed even grimmer, especially after Hitler's declaration of war on the United States and the launching of the Paukenschlag submarine offensive the month after the Pearl Harbor attack. Within two weeks of the offensive's opening salvos, U-boats had torpedoed twenty Allied ships to the ocean's bottom.

As hostilities widened, the U.S. Navy faced an acute challenge. Escort destroyers and cruisers could only do so much to protect the merchant convoys. Naval air power seemed to be one of the obvious keys to beating back the submarine menace, but the vast stretches of sea tra-

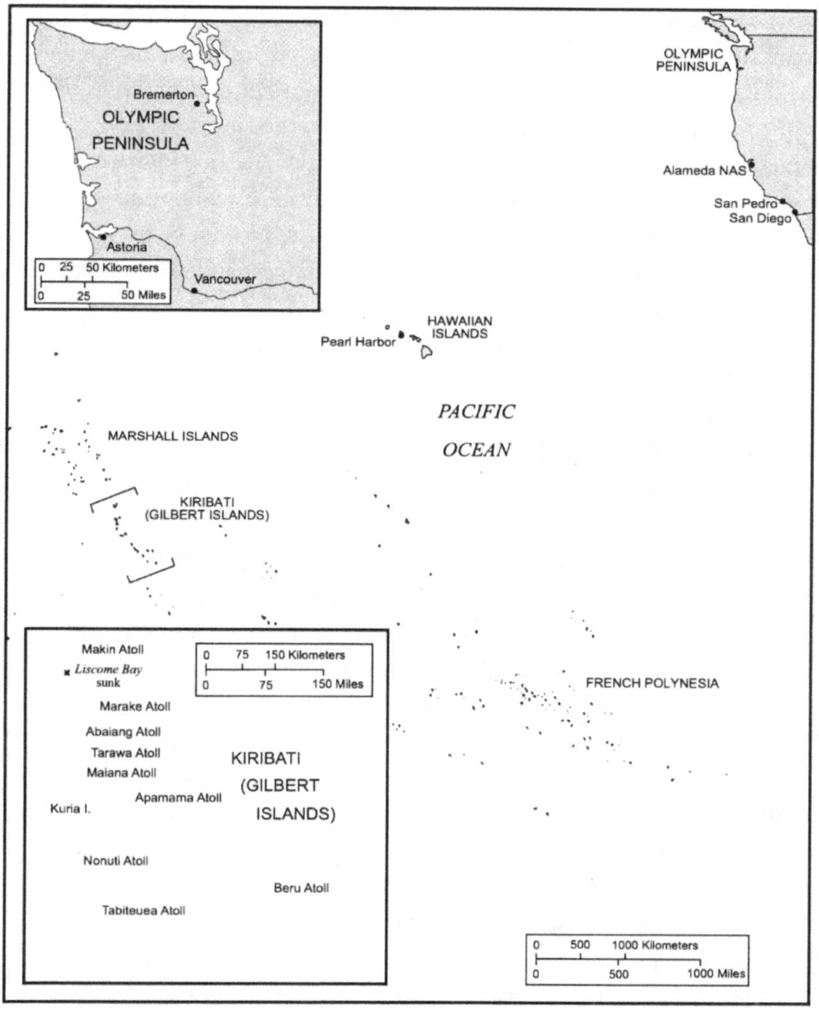

The Pacific, Gilbert Islands, and Olympic Peninsula

versed by the Allied cargo ships imposed limits on how far U.S. and British land-based warplanes could provide air cover.

Aircraft carriers seemed the obvious answer to the United States' dilemma. At the time of the attack on Pearl Harbor, however, the U.S. Navy boasted only seven large fleet carriers. As the Japanese attack had proven, such carriers were far too valuable to be relegated to escorting convoys or ferrying warplanes to the United States' allies or its various island outposts. More fleet carriers were already under construction, but it was typically at least eighteen months between the time a shipyard laid down a carrier's keel and the ship's commissioning. As the Japanese rampage across the Pacific and into Southeast Asia in December had vividly demonstrated, much could happen in thirty days. No doubt even more could happen in eighteen months. The U.S. Navy needed to solve its carrier problem, and quickly.

Fortunately, a possible solution had been in development as early as 1927. At that time, Lieutenant Commander Bruce G. Leighton, USN, a naval aviator and aide to the secretary of the navy, had authored a paper titled "Light Aircraft Carriers, A Study of Their Possible Uses in So-Called 'Cruiser Operations,' Comparison with Light Cruisers as Fleet Units." In his paper, Leighton forecast the use of light carriers in roles such as bombing enemy capital ships, support of fleet operations, scouting and reconnaissance, attacks on shore positions, and, importantly, antisubmarine missions. He concluded that the light carrier "might well be considered as a worthy substitute for the light cruiser, or even distinctly preferable to the cruiser."[1]

Leighton's idea survived the passing years. In 1939, Captain John S. McCain, USN, commander of the aircraft carrier *Ranger* (CV-4) and grandfather of the latter-day senator from Arizona, advocated building at least eight "pocket-size" carriers of cruiser speed. A year later, the navy's Bureau of Construction and Repair went so far as to begin drawing up plans for converting passenger ships to carriers.

In November 1940, however, the chief of naval operations halted further development of light carriers. "The characteristics of aircraft have changed," he reasoned, "placing more exacting demands upon the carrier. These demands are such that a converted merchant vessel will no longer make as satisfactory an aircraft carrier as was [formerly] the case."[2]

At that point, though, President Franklin D. Roosevelt weighed in on the matter. The chief executive, a former assistant secretary of the navy, was well attuned to the difficulties being encountered by the British as they struggled to keep supplies flowing to their war machine across the Atlantic in the face of relentless German submarine attacks. Through his naval aide, Roosevelt suggested pointedly that the navy acquire a merchant ship and convert her into an aircraft carrier that could provide escort service to the Atlantic convoys. Roosevelt even suggested that such a ship might accommodate eight to twelve of the newfangled helicopters under development at the time.[3]

Although it declined to adopt the use of the prototype helicopters, on January 7, 1941, the navy, under ever-increasing pressure from the president, agreed to convert two merchant ships, *Mormacmail* and *Mormacland,* to light carriers. On March 6, 1941, the navy acquired *Mormacmail* and began her $1.5 million conversion. Three months later she emerged from the shipyard as the auxiliary aircraft escort vessel *Long Island,* designated as AVG-1 and captained by Commander Donald B. Duncan, USN. The converted ship had a flight deck length of 362 feet, carried sixteen planes, was capable of reaching speeds of 17.6 knots, and berthed 190 officers and 780 sailors. Unlike contemporary carriers, she contained no island atop her flight deck to break her flat silhouette. Rather, a rectangular flight deck capped the length of the ship. Using diesel engines for power meant that *Long Island*'s flight deck was not obstructed by smoke pipes.

The speed of *Mormacmail*'s conversion to the carrier *Long Island* benefited from the president's personal attention and insistence on a three-month deadline for the project. *Mormacland*'s conversion took longer, but in November 1941 the United States turned her over to the Royal Navy as HMS *Archer.*

The U.S. Navy's operations with the ungainly *Long Island,* like those of the Royal Navy with *Archer,* proved the viability of the light carrier concept. Japan's raid on Pearl Harbor drove the point home. Accordingly, on December 26, 1941, the navy ordered the conversion of twenty-four merchantmen and *Cimmaron*-class fleet oilers to aircraft carriers. Those converted from merchantmen became known as the *Bogue* class, named after the first carrier to be converted in that class, while the four ships converted from the faster and larger fleet oilers were designated the *Sangamon* class. Carriers of this group relied on a steam turbine power plant rather than diesel engines, boasted a small island like the larger carriers, and enjoyed longer flight decks and more hangar deck space.

The four *Sangamon* carriers—*Sangamon* (AVG-26), *Suwannee* (AVG-27), *Chenango* (AVG-28), and *Santee* (AVG-29)—demonstrated their value in November 1942 during Operation Torch, the Allied invasion of North Africa. Fighters and bombers from *Sangamon*, *Suwannee*, and *Santee* complemented those of the carrier *Ranger* and lashed at the Vichy French defenses in Morocco. Following Operation Torch's success, the commander in chief of the navy's Atlantic force commented that the escort carriers "proved to be a valuable addition to the Fleet. They can handle a potent air group and, while their speed is insufficient, they can operate under most weather conditions and are very useful ships."[4]

After Operation Torch, the navy dispatched escort carriers to the Pacific. The pilots stationed on board *Chenango*, *Suwannee*, and *Sangamon* saw action in the Solomon Islands. Their clashes with Japanese aircraft and warships, while seldom decisive, played an important role in helping to develop the United States' small-carrier doctrine. The relative success of these ships' operations off the North African coast and in the South Pacific encouraged the navy to pursue an ambitious building program in partnership with Henry J. Kaiser.

Kaiser, a longtime political supporter of President Roosevelt's, had risen from humble beginnings as a photographer and hardware salesman to control one of the largest construction companies in the country. During the 1930s his workers were responsible for such structures as the Bonneville, Grand Coulee, and Shasta Dams as well as the Oakland–San Francisco Bridge. As war approached, Kaiser shifted his focus and remarkable energy to shipbuilding. On January 20, 1941, he rolled his bulldozers into Richmond, California, to build his first shipyard. Less than ninety days later, it laid down its first keel.[5]

The heavy-set, sixty-year-old Kaiser and his shipbuilding operations personified Roosevelt's philosophy that "energy was more efficient than efficiency." Kaiser embraced on-the-job training for his workers, relied on prefabricated bulkheads, decks, and hulls to speed ship construction, and utilized welding rather than the slower but more commonly accepted riveting as his preferred means of slapping ships together. His methods paid off. By early 1942 his company was capable of completing a so-called Liberty ship in less than sixty days.

Regardless of his revolutionary pace, however, Kaiser was not satisfied with building merchant ships. The navy clearly needed aircraft carriers, and Kaiser approached his friend Roosevelt with a bold proposition—his shipyards would build fifty escort carriers within a year.

Roosevelt and the navy accepted Kaiser's proposal and awarded him a contract for the next class of escort carriers, to be constructed under the supervision of the U.S. Maritime Commission. Although Kaiser's team pushed its own design for the carriers, the navy interceded. In the end, the naval architectural firm of Gibbs and Cox designed Kaiser's carriers, but serious questions remained regarding the combat-readiness of the proposed design. In the eyes of many naval officers, the final product bore too many similarities below the waterline to a merchant ship. Merchant ships, for example, didn't need excessive watertight compartmentalization or thickened hulls to withstand torpedo strikes; warships did. Despite the navy's misgivings, Kaiser's shipyards sprang into action. This time the work would be focused in his new shipyard in Vancouver, Washington, a small town nestled a hundred miles inland from the Pacific on the banks of the Columbia River.

Before Kaiser arrived, Vancouver had been a quiet Pacific Northwest riverfront town, home to about eighteen thousand residents. With his arrival, however, the face of Vancouver changed forever. Kaiser had begun acquiring property for the Vancouver yards in January 1942. Eventually, twelve massive shipways lined the Columbia River. The first Kaiser-built ship slipped down one of those ways that June, built by workers who had poured into Vancouver from every corner of the nation. The town's population almost tripled in two years under the rush of wartime ship production, and its streets rang with accents ranging from Brooklyn to New Orleans. Thousands of workers—male and female—swarmed over skeletal steel hulks as they welded steel plating on the slowly materializing ships. Blowtorches glowed and sparks flew day and night as Kaiser's workers applied American industrial assembly-line operational concepts to the task of creating ships for a growing navy.

As the pace of shipbuilding at the Vancouver yards accelerated into the autumn of 1942, a piece of unsettling news arrived. Two weeks into November 1942, a Royal Navy escort carrier, HMS *Avenger*, had sailed into the sights of a German U-boat off the coast of Gibraltar. The German skipper planted a torpedo into the middle of the British ship, detonating its bomb magazine and literally blowing the vessel in half. More than five hundred British officers and sailors died; only about a dozen survived. The remnants of the broken ship sank beneath the waves in less than three minutes.

Shaken by the dramatic loss, the British Admiralty Delegation wrote to Admiral Howard L. Vickery of the U.S. Maritime Commission. "I know it is late to start talking about modifications in design," the letter began, "but the thought of sending these ships to sea as at present designed quite frankly fills me with dismay, particularly after the recent experience we . . . had when [*Avenger*] sank practically with all hands after one torpedo hit near the bomb-room. These auxiliary carriers are such valuable ships, have such valuable equipment and, above all, invaluable trained personnel, that if it is humanly possible I think we would be amply justified in any reasonable improvements which will help them to keep afloat when damaged."[6]

The Admiralty's warning, however, didn't arrive until January 1943, by which time Kaiser had laid down the first keels of the U.S. Navy's new class of escort carriers. Within three months the Vancouver yards launched what would become the *Casablanca* (CVE-55), the navy's first all-welded carrier, on April 5, 1943. Before thousands of excited onlookers, First Lady Eleanor Roosevelt broke a bottle of champagne over the ship's bow. The ceremonial smashing sent the ship slipping down the ways into the Columbia River, and the *Casablanca* class was born.

Even as Eleanor Roosevelt was launching *Casablanca*, Kaiser Shipyards was putting the finishing touches on the first of *Casablanca*'s sister ships. Like *Casablanca*, they would be designated by the navy with the letters CVE, meaning "aircraft carrier, escort." Naval officers referred to these ships as simply escort carriers. Skeptical sailors, noting the thin welded hulls and seemingly inadequate compartmentalization of the new ships, and less than enthusiastic about sailing on a vessel that was essentially a floating aviation fuel and ammunition dump, agreed that "CVE" was the appropriate moniker for the small carriers but claimed that the letters stood for "combustible-vulnerable-expendable." Others called them "Kaiser's coffins" or "two-torpedo carriers." One torpedo, the sailors reasoned derisively, would be the one that would sink it, and the second would simply pass over the sinking ship's flight deck.[7] The

British, with perhaps a greater understanding of the need for Kaiser's new brand of ship and their slapdash method of production, labeled them "Woolworth carriers" after the chain of U.S. department stores.[8]

Despite the sailors' skepticism, the public and press quickly took to calling the escort carriers "jeep carriers" or "baby flattops." The reasons for these nicknames were readily apparent. The *Casablanca* class boasted "islands" above the flight deck and resembled miniature versions of their bigger *Yorktown*- and *Essex*-class carrier cousins. Whereas the length of those warships ranged from 809 to 872 feet, the diminutive *Casablanca*-class carriers measured only 512 feet. That meant a pilot would have only a 477-foot flight deck, layered in wooden planking, upon which to land.

In many ways the *Casablanca* class represented a major improvement over the *Bogue*- and *Sangamon*-class carriers. The escort carriers had a longer hangar deck, which meant they could carry more aircraft. They also possessed a longer flight deck than the *Bogue*-class ships. It was small in comparison to that of the decks of the larger fleet carriers, but it was still an improvement. The *Casablanca*-class ships had twin screws and propellers, separate machinery spaces, and a propeller race that acted upon the large, balanced rudder so as to make the carriers very maneuverable.[9] They were also a few knots faster than *Bogue*-class ships—an important consideration, since an aircraft carrier typically needed 30 knots of relative wind across its flight deck to launch a fully loaded torpedo bomber. In the soft winds of the Pacific, coaxing every extra knot out of the ships' engines would prove critical.

Despite these advantages, ships of the *Casablanca* class were not without their deficiencies. Because of the wartime shortage of turbines and diesel engines, they relied on two old-fashioned Uniflow reciprocating steam engines. These engines used superheated steam, which stressed the boilers and made it difficult for engine room personnel to maintain cylinder lubrication and filtering systems, especially during prolonged combat operations.[10] Furthermore, although the 4,500-horsepower engines were designed for operations at 161 rpm, skippers frequently pushed them to perform at 178 to 182 rpm or higher. These operations in turn led to such problems as excessive piston wear and exorbitant stress on the brick walls and decks of the boilers as well as on the associated auxiliary machinery. Less apparent, but always lurking in the back of the crews' minds, was the recognition that these ships had been built in great haste by relatively inexperienced welders. Nevertheless, as all readily admitted, there was a war to be won. As President Roosevelt himself reasoned, a fleet of makeshift ships in 1943 was preferable to a fleet of faster, more graceful, more durable ships after the war was lost.[11]

Makeshift ships, however, came with their own set of risks, as evidenced by the *Avenger* disaster. In a prescient report, Captain Calvin T. Durgin, USN, who had commanded the aircraft carrier *Ranger* during Operation Torch and would eventually rise to command the navy's Pacific Escort Carrier Force, commented on escort carrier operations during the North African invasion in 1942. Escort carriers, Durgin noted, could "be used to advantage, and [are] capable of inflicting substantial damage to the enemy in assault where the enemy air and sea opposition is negligible or when it is being contained by other superior forces." He added an important caveat, however, which echoed the Royal Navy's concerns: "Due to their low speed, lack of protection, and light armament, it is considered hazardous to employ a CVE group in operation where there is likely to be an effective enemy opposition."[12]

Whether or not the U.S. Navy properly employed the new escort carriers was beyond the immediate concern of Kaiser Shipyards. Kaiser's workers were racing to meet his promise of fifty *Casablanca*-class carriers within a year. In 1943 the rallying cry in the shipyard was "Eighteen or more by '44." Answering the call, West Coast shipyards spit out new escort carrier hulks "as rapidly as a drunk emitting burps."[13]

One such ship was Maritime Commission hull no. 1137, whose keel had been laid on December 12, 1942. Later, as work progressed, the shipyard labeled the infant vessel Kaiser Shipyards hull no. 302. Her eventual owner was to be Great Britain's Royal Navy, which decided to christen its soon-to-be-acquired carrier the HMS *Ameer*. On April 19, 1943, *Ameer* slid down the ways into the Columbia River with a loud crash of spray, becoming the second of the *Casablanca*-class carriers to make it into the water. At the time her flight deck wasn't completely finished, but this did little to diminish the festivities, as the wife of Admiral Ben Moreell, USN, the navy's chief of yards and docks, performed the obligatory champagne honors. James MacDonald, the British consul in Portland, no doubt watched the proceedings with satisfaction, pleased that another carrier would soon be joining the Royal Navy's fight against Hitler's U-boats.

A skeleton crew soon boarded the powerless *Ameer* and supervised her gentle tow to the nearby Vancouver Shipyards for the completion of her fitting out. But as dozens of workers clambered aboard and began their noisy work, the United States was already rethinking its decision to provide the carrier to Britain. As the spring of 1943 passed into summer, word was sent to the shipyard: *Ameer* would stay in American hands, and her new name would be *Liscome Bay*, with the designation CVE-56. She was named after a small body of water on the south coast of Dall Island, off the southern coast of Alaska. Embarrassingly, the navy first named the carrier *Liscombe Bay*, a spelling error that was later caught by a yeoman preparing a newspaper article on the carrier.[14] After a flurry of official correspondence, the spelling was corrected.

The story of *Liscome Bay*'s crew, however, does not start with the launch of hull no. 1137. It begins in nearby Tacoma, with the launching and fitting out of the escort carrier *Glacier*.

2
A Crew for the "Listing Lizzie"

On June 15, 1943, Ensign Francis X. "Frank" Daily Jr., SC-V(G), USNR, arrived at the Puget Sound Navy Yard in Bremerton, Washington. In his hands were orders assigning him to the precommissioning detail for the *Bogue*-class escort carrier *Glacier* (ACV-33). The navy had a somewhat schizophrenic protocol regarding escort carrier names, christening the ships either after North American bays and sounds (Bogue is a sound off the North Carolina coast, Glacier a bay in southern Alaska) or in commemoration of World War II battles (as was the case with the *Casablanca* class's namesake).

The twenty-one-year-old Daily had graduated the previous year from St. Joseph's College in Overbrook, Pennsylvania. With the nation at war, he soon found himself applying for a commission at the Office of Naval Officer Procurement. His degree in accounting warranted a billet in the navy's Supply Corps, and his next stop was Harvard, Massachusetts, for Supply Corps School. Once Daily completed the course at Harvard, he headed west for Puget Sound. Back in Pennsylvania, his college sweetheart, Gloria, watched his departure with trepidation.

Upon arriving at Puget Sound, Daily reported in at an old loft building at the shipyard. He soon learned that three other supply officers had preceded him for assignment to *Glacier*. Lieutenant George Pettengill III, SC-V(G), was head of the ship's supply department, and he oversaw two assistant supply officers, Lieutenant (jg) Albert C. Strong Jr., SC-V(G), and Ensign Severine J. Robben, SC, USN. Pettengill informed Daily that he would be the ship's disbursing officer—essentially the carrier's paymaster. To old navy hands, Daily would be simply known as "Pay."[1] Like all officers, Daily also had secondary duties. His main second duty was that of the division officer of the ship's supply division. As such, he bore responsibility for all of the division's military duties. The division's battle stations, drills, leaves, and disciplinary actions all came under the young ensign's purview.

The Seattle-Tacoma Shipbuilding Company had launched *Glacier* on September 7, 1942. By the time Daily arrived in June 1943, the precommissioning activities of the new carrier were already well under way. The navy had scheduled the ship's commissioning for July, so mail addressed to the ship's disbursing officer sat piled high waiting for Daily's sorting and distribution. Fortunately, Daily's main enlisted assistant, Chief Storekeeper Frederick L. Sheppard, arrived at the shipyard almost simultaneously with Daily. The two men quickly went to work responding to correspondence, setting up files, developing working relationships with the ship's other departments, and preparing to move into their small office aboard *Glacier*.

Shortly after arriving, Daily met his commanding officer, Captain Irving D. Wiltsie, NA, USN. The forty-one-year-old skipper had wavy brown hair and big ears, but his penetrating eyes were his most distinctive features. "He was very stern (but fair), very involved and dedicated to his job, and very much in command," recalled one sailor who served under Wiltsie. "In a relatively short period of time I acquired a great deal of respect for him."[2]

Daily didn't know it at the time, but he would have been hard pressed to find a more experienced skipper to serve under. Born in Hartford, Connecticut, Wiltsie had attended high school in Plainfield, New Jersey, and then entered the United States Naval Academy at Annapolis in 1917. A year later, the academy's traditional summer "youngster" cruise placed Wiltsie aboard the battleship *Missouri* (BB-11). His time there gave the young midshipman an early taste of wartime operations at sea.

Wiltsie graduated from the Naval Academy in 1921 and served briefly on the battleship *Arizona* (BB-39) before orders sent him to *Wyoming* (BB-32), where he spent nearly two years before reporting to Quincy, Massachusetts, for duty fitting out the light cruiser *Raleigh* (CL-7). In

1924 he transferred to another light cruiser, *Cleveland* (CL-21), which operated primarily in the Caribbean during his short time with her. His tour of duty lasted long enough, however, for him to witness *Cleveland*'s role in quelling an uprising of Kula Indians in Panama in 1925.

That summer, orders arrived directing Wiltsie to flight school in Pensacola. Catching one of the Panama Railroad Steamship Line's steamers, he returned to the States and earned his wings. Now a naval aviator, he went to sea once again to serve in the catapult-launched seaplane units based on board the light cruisers *Milwaukee* (CL-5) and *Memphis* (CL-13) and the battleship *Texas* (BB-35). After that sea duty, Wiltsie returned for a tour at Naval Air Station (NAS) Pensacola. While there, he married Helene M. Barry, whom he had met several years earlier on a blind date at a Naval Academy hop. Three years as the senior aviator flying scout planes off the cruiser *Louisville* (CL-28) followed the Pensacola assignment. Helene gave birth to their first child, Ron, during Wiltsie's time on board *Louisville*.

In 1935, Wiltsie took command of the Naval Reserve Aviation Base in Minneapolis, Minnesota. The following year, after fifteen years in the navy, he was promoted to lieutenant commander. That fall, Wiltsie found himself performing unusual duty for a naval officer—providing air support to the Department of the Interior to fight forest fires near Houghton, Michigan.

Wiltsie left Minnesota to command scouting and bombing squadrons aboard the carrier *Saratoga* (CV-3) from 1937 to 1939. While serving on board *Saratoga* during the Fleet Problem XIX war games in the spring of 1938, he helped lead a surprise air attack on the U.S. naval base at Pearl Harbor—a lesson in the viability of such a raid apparently forgotten less than four years later.

Following his service with *Saratoga*, Wiltsie served ashore as the head of the Assembly and Repair Department at North Island NAS in Coronado, California. By then the Wiltsie family included a second child—a daughter named Barbara. But Wiltsie spent only two years with his family in San Diego before heading to sea once again—this time as the navigation officer for the carrier *Yorktown* (CV-5). The navy moved *Yorktown* to the Atlantic to assist in the United States' "Neutrality Patrols"; she arrived on the East Coast in May 1941. Helene, Ron, and Barbara followed Wiltsie east and made a home in New York City.

Upon the successful completion of a fourth patrol, *Yorktown* stood into Norfolk on December 2, 1941. Once ashore, Wiltsie, who now held the rank of commander, raced to New York to rejoin his family. That Sunday, while he and his young son were listening to a football game on the radio, an excited announcer broke in with news of the attack on Pearl Harbor. Within the hour, Wiltsie had made his farewells and was on a train heading for Norfolk. Nine days later, *Yorktown* was on her way to the Pacific.

As *Yorktown*'s navigator, Wiltsie participated in the United States' initial actions against the Japanese in the central and south Pacific. The carrier's fliers struck at Japanese bases in the Gilbert Islands and later raided New Guinea. Then, from May 4 to May 8, 1942, *Yorktown* and *Lexington* (CV-2) foiled a Japanese invasion of Port Moresby in the Battle of the Coral Sea. During the fighting *Yorktown* suffered grievous damage from attacking Japanese dive-bombers. If not for Wiltsie's work in her conning tower, the damage may have been far worse. According to the letter of commendation the navy awarded Wiltsie two months later, "as Officer-of-the-Deck in battle on May 8, while under heavy bombing and torpedo attack from enemy carrier aircraft, [Wiltsie], under the Captain's direction, controlled the ship calmly and expertly from his battle station in the conning tower so that the ship was able to avoid all enemy torpedoes and all except one of the many accurately aimed bombs."[3]

Following that engagement, *Yorktown* steamed back to Pearl Harbor, where a hurried repair job in late May made her seaworthy for her critical role during the Battle of Midway the first week in June. In the initial stages of that fight, Wiltsie showed "outstanding professional ability" as he provided "such complete and accurate navigational information that the *Yorktown* Air Group Units achieved complete success in making contact with their objectives."[4] The Japanese also had competent navigation officers, though, and their pilots soon located *Yorktown*.

First a force of eighteen Aichi D3A dive-bombers, escorted by a similar number of Mitsubishi A6M fighters, rolled in to attack Wiltsie's wildly maneuvering ship. Three of the bombers scored hits, and by midafternoon the battered carrier lay dead in the water. Repair crews worked frantically to restore power, knowing that at any moment more enemy planes might appear on the horizon. After an hour, their efforts paid off. With propellers churning, *Yorktown* was soon making 20 knots.

And not a moment too soon. A force of Japanese torpedo planes roared in to attack. From his battle station in the conning tower, Wiltsie maintained "expert control of the ship under the Captain's direction [and] was directly responsible for avoiding two of the enemy's torpedoes."[5] But despite his efforts, two other torpedoes smashed into the carrier's port side. Once again the wounded *Yorktown* slowed to a stop, keeling ever more severely to port, and this time she seemed beyond hope. Her skipper, Captain Elliott Buckmaster, USN, ordered the crew to abandon ship. Wiltsie, one of the last men to leave the stricken carrier, slipped down a line on the starboard side into the water below.

At dawn, however, *Yorktown* was still afloat. Buckmaster conferred with Rear Admiral Frank J. Fletcher, USN, and decided to send back a salvage party. He selected Wiltsie to lead the team of 29 officers and 141 men. By midafternoon, with the assistance of the destroyer *Hammann* (DD-412), Wiltsie's team seemed to have matters well in hand. By pushing planes overboard, pumping water out of *Yorktown*'s flooded compartments, and counter-flooding others, they had reduced the carrier's twenty-six-degree list to a mere two degrees. Meanwhile, the tug *Vireo* (AT-144) took *Yorktown* under tow. But then fate intervened.

A Japanese submarine, *I-168*, managed to slip within range of the lame American carrier and unleashed a salvo of four torpedoes. Two plunged into *Yorktown*'s side and a third broke *Hammann*'s back, sinking her within four minutes. As she sank, her depth charges exploded, further damaging the carrier and killing many of the destroyer's crew still floating in the water. The torpedo blasts caught Wiltsie standing on an aircraft elevator that had been lowered to the hangar deck. The force of the explosions hurled him straight up into the air. He landed on his feet, but the jolt seriously injured his back muscles.

In pain, Wiltsie surveyed this latest catastrophe. Unfortunately, the choice seemed clear—it was time to abandon ship once again. "Facing the probability of further torpedo attacks, [Wiltsie] coolly and efficiently directed the transfer of the salvage party and wounded personnel who had been rescued from the water."[6] The following morning *Yorktown* sank, leaving Wiltsie in search of a new ship. While he was back onshore the navy awarded him the Silver Star for his "outstanding gallantry and heroic devotion to duty" at Midway, lauding it as "characteristic of a fine seaman and an exemplary leader."[7]

Four months after *Yorktown*'s sinking, Wiltsie found a new ship—on the East Coast—the seaplane tender *Albemarle* (AV-5). Under his command, she shuttled vital aviation fuel and ammunition between Norfolk, Cuba, San Juan, Trinidad, and Bermuda. But in June 1943, after only eight months, Wiltsie—now a captain—relinquished command of *Albemarle* and took on a new assignment: supervising the fitting out of *Glacier* at the Seattle-Tacoma Shipbuilding Company's Puget Sound shipyards.

It was there, in Bremerton's cool summer of 1943, that the paths of Ensign Daily and Captain Wiltsie crossed. One was a young man fresh out of the navy's Supply Corps School, the other a steady, decorated combat veteran, and for a moment it seemed they would soon be going their separate ways.

Only two weeks after Daily reported for duty, a decidedly unwelcome piece of news arrived for *Glacier*'s infant crew. The navy had decided to transfer the ship to Britain's Royal Navy. For the officers and men who had worked so hard to get "their" ship ready for commissioning—and who were only two weeks from commissioning her—it was a frustrating time. Then, to add insult to injury, civilian yard workers descended on the carrier to bring *Glacier* up to Royal Navy specifications. They ripped out the ship's dentist's office and, in its place, put in the officers bar. "At least the Brits have their priorities straight," the dispossessed sailors muttered to one another.[8] They didn't know it at the time, but the former *Glacier* would soon be commissioned in the Royal Navy as the HMS *Atheling* and head for duty in the Indian Ocean.

New orders also arrived for Wiltsie, directing him to take command of the *Casablanca*-class escort carrier *Natoma Bay* (CVE-62), still under construction at Kaiser's Vancouver yards. She wouldn't even be launched for nearly another three weeks. The navy had her commissioning scheduled for October—three months later than *Glacier*'s. For an officer like

Wiltsie who had expected to be going out to sea again soon, this was bitter news. Something had to be done.

Commander Finley E. "Fee" (also "Pete") Hall, NA, USN, *Glacier*'s executive officer, sensed that an alternate plan was afoot. Hall, a native of Tupelo, Mississippi, had graduated from the Naval Academy in 1929. His description in the academy's yearbook, the *Lucky Bag*, goes a long way in describing the athletic and fun-loving southerner: "After brief sojourns at most of the prep schools in Dixie, 'Pete' joined the Navy to settle down, bringing with him the jargon of the Mississippi swamps and a sense of the ludicrous that has helped to make many a tedious hour more bearable for us. . . . Often unforeseen circumstances kept him from social functions, but at those which he attended, he could always be found working his persuasive powers on some fair damsel, and usually with victorious results."[9]

The *Lucky Bag* also itemized Hall's extracurricular activities. That list included a cryptic reference to the "Black N," which may have accounted for the "unforeseen circumstances" that kept Midshipman Hall from social functions. To earn a Black N—an unofficial award frowned upon by the administration but conferred by a secret society of renegade midshipmen—required disciplinary lapses at the academy that flirted with expulsion. Hall and the academy's discipline, it seemed, enjoyed a relationship that was strained at best.

Hall attended flight school in Pensacola within a year after graduating from the academy. He spent the next ten years on constant flying duty with *Tennessee* (BB-43), VP Squadron 1-F, *Ranger* (CV-4), *Yorktown* (CV-5), and the seaplane tender *Owl* (AM-2). He eventually took command of the seaplane tender *Swan* (AVP-7) on July 8, 1941. *Swan* was in Pearl Harbor's Marine Railway Dock on December 7 when the Japanese attacked. Despite being high and dry, her 3-inch antiaircraft battery gunners claimed at least one of the attacking enemy aircraft. By that afternoon *Swan* was out of the dry dock and ready to assist with the numerous salvage operations in the wrecked harbor.

In the seven months after the attack on Pearl Harbor, Hall and his ship supported seaplane operations out of American Samoa and Wallis Island. By September 1942, Hall was back in the States training new naval aviators. Then, in the summer of 1943, he received orders for *Glacier*. Like Wiltsie, Hall soon found that the navy had changed his assigned ship to *Natoma Bay*.

Hall was no happier than Wiltsie about the change in orders. He was also eager to get back out to sea. Still, the executive officer retained his characteristically unruffled demeanor. He sensed Wiltsie was not about to sit out three more months of the war. "Don't panic," the commander drawled to Daily and the other officers. "Things might turn out okay. Captain Wiltsie is trying to take care of it for us."[10]

Events soon proved Hall correct. Through a bit of bureaucratic legerdemain, Wiltsie managed to get his entire ship's company transferred en masse to a new escort carrier—the Royal Navy's former *Ameer*, now the U.S. Navy's *Liscome Bay*. Kaiser Shipyards had launched *Liscome Bay* three months earlier in Vancouver. Tugs had then towed her down the Columbia River to Astoria, Oregon, to finish her fitting out. She needed a crew, and *Glacier*'s orphaned crew needed a ship. It looked like a perfect fit.

Meanwhile, for Daily, a new ship wasn't the only change in his life. He coaxed his college sweetheart out to the West Coast, where he wasted no time in slipping a wedding ring on her finger. On July 3, 1943, he and Gloria married in a simple ceremony. Ensign Leonard F. Black Jr., D-V(G), USNR, stood in for him as best man. Black was, like fellow *Liscome Bay* ensign William C. Schmidt, D-V(G), USNR, one of Wiltsie's nephews—a fact both ensigns intended to keep hidden from their fellow officers.

Unfortunately, the exigencies of war permitted no honeymoon for Daily and Gloria. She returned to the East Coast, and he immediately plunged back into his work transitioning the ship's company from *Glacier* to *Liscome Bay*.

The crew's move to their new ship culminated on the evening of Friday, July 30, when they assembled at the Puget Sound Navy Yard's baseball field. Shouldering their seabags, they marched through the yard, through the town of Bremerton outside the yard's front gates, and then onto a ferry for Seattle. Once aboard the ferry, the men enjoyed a brief respite. On the other side of Puget Sound, they were on the march once again. Trudging through the darkness, the company finally reached Seattle's rail yards and boarded a decrepit train for the overnight ride to Astoria.

Upon arriving in Astoria, the tired and hungry crew faced further disappointment. They had expected to go on board *Liscome Bay* immediately, but instead they learned that she had developed boiler trouble during her final acceptance trial the day before and had been temporarily rejected by the navy while her engines were modified. Grumbling and cursing, the exhausted sailors dropped their seabags and plopped heavily on them to wait for their officers to sort out this latest mess.

In the end, the delay proved to be an unexpected benefit. Wiltsie and Hall secured the company billets at nearby Tongue Point NAS. The navy had first developed its Tongue Point facilities in 1921, constructing a submarine and destroyer base there on the shores of Cathlamet Bay. In the 1930s the base became a naval air station and home to a collection of seaplanes and navy blimps. In the summer of 1943, for the homeless men, formerly of *Glacier* and soon of *Liscome Bay*, Tongue Point became a veritable oasis. The docile deer wandering among the station's wooden buildings only added to the base's tranquillity.

Daily, like his men, was impressed with their accommodations. After seeing that his division's sailors were adequately quartered and fed, the pay officer headed for the base's bachelor officers' quarters. Finding his room, the tired ensign collapsed and slept for twenty hours straight.

The week that followed their arrival at Tongue Point was, as Daily recalled, "simply idyllic."[11] Officers and sailors wandered the shores of the Columbia River, visited the nearby resort of Seaside, played baseball, fed the brown bears that were kept penned up on the station, enjoyed excellent chow, and caught up on lost sleep. Every other night, the officers were released for an evening of leave. Daily and Lieutenant (jg) Thomas W. Roche, E-V(G), USNR, looked up one of Roche's friends who resided in the area and spent a pleasant afternoon playing golf at his country club.

The crew's sojourn at Tongue Point ended the following Saturday, August 7, 1943. That morning, to the shouts of the ship's petty officers, the crew tumbled out of their temporary quarters. Lugging their seabags, they formed up behind their officers for a final shore muster. Once they found their places beside their shipmates, the sailors and officers stood in neat, linear formations. Only the occasional cough broke the silence as the men waited for Captain Wiltsie to give the order to move out to their new shipboard home.

That morning's formation contained men from every walk of life and every corner of America. Among them was Lieutenant (jg) Robert H. Carley, ChC-V(G), USNR. As a junior at Occidental College in Los Angeles, Carley had spent hours working at the city's YMCA. He found the work there so satisfying that he decided to enter the ministry when he graduated from college.[12]

Carley finished college at Occidental, making the All-Southern basketball team in his final year. He then traveled east to attend Princeton Theological Seminary. Upon graduation from the seminary, Carley joined the navy as a chaplain. Young, blond, and handsome, he was a recruiting officer's dream prospect. Now he was charged with tending to the souls of the 948 men who would soon sail in *Liscome Bay*.[13] Wiltsie had underscored the importance of Carley's position when the chaplain first reported on board. "Next to my own," he warned Carley, "yours is the most important job aboard this ship."[14]

Fifty-nine other officers shouldered more temporal responsibilities for the ship and her crew. Lieutenant Gardner Smith, C-V(S), USNR, from Cazenovia, New York, had been a radio announcer before the war. Now he would serve as the ship's communications officer. Lieutenant (jg) Glenn E. Hunt, C-V(S), USNR, from Albuquerque, New Mexico, stood beside Smith as signal officer.

Twenty-one-year-old Ensign William H. Davis, NA, USNR, had completed two years of prelaw studies at the University of Denver before receiving a naval commission and attending flight school. In Denver he had read law casebooks; now, as one of the ship's landing signal officers, he would have the difficult task of reading the lines of an incoming aircraft's approach. Davis had a wife and a two-month-old son back in Colorado.

Ensign William J. Woodward Jr., D-V(G), USNR, was, along with Daily, one of the most senior ensigns assigned to *Liscome Bay*. Woodward had left behind a civilian life of comfort and ease in New York. His family owned the famed Belair Stables in Maryland, one of the nation's oldest horse farms. Woodward had traded that life for the crowded wardrooms, sleepless nights, and hard bunks of *Liscome Bay*.

Lieutenant Commander Oliver Ames, NA, A-V(T), USNR, could have boasted of an even more illustrious family tree. Ames's father was Harvard professor Oakes Ames, a nationally renowned expert in orchids and director of Harvard's Botanical Museum. His mother, Blanche Ames, was a Smith College graduate, artist, and noted suffragist. The couple's forebears included industrialists who financed the Union Pacific's transcontinental railroad, governors of Massachusetts and of Reconstruction-era Mississippi, a congressman, and two Civil War generals, one of whom received the Medal of Honor for his service at the First Battle of Bull Run. Oliver Ames, born in 1903, was the pair's first son.

Lieutenant Commander John R. Bodler, D-M, USNR, hailed from Wellsboro, Pennsylvania. As the carrier's gunnery officer, he would be responsible for both the 5-inch gun mounted on her fantail and, more importantly, the bevy of 20- and 40-millimeter antiaircraft guns ringing the flight deck. Once aboard *Liscome Bay*, the pipe-smoking Bodler gained a respected reputation for almost always being on the bridge. If he wasn't there, he could likely be found on the flight deck, épée in hand and mask on his face, fencing with another officer. The bouts always presented an incongruous sight—two naval officers slashing and lunging at one another with bladed weapons on one of the most modern ships in the navy's inventory.

Lieutenant Commander Spencer A. Adams, NA, USN, was another colorful officer, albeit in the more classical "flyboy" sense. Adams had served in the South Pacific during the Guadalcanal campaign and was rumored, according to Daily, to be the inspiration for the "handsome, blond, cocky" pilot Bus Adams in James Michener's *Tales of the South Pacific*. "He came from nowhere in particular and wasn't sure where he would settle when the war was over," Michener had written about Bus.[15] It was a description that could have fit many of the aviators who would soon be flying off *Liscome Bay*'s small deck.

Lieutenant Commander Wells W. "Buzz" Carroll, D-V(S), USNR, had sailed into hostile waters before—during World War I. Standing six feet tall and weighing two hundred pounds, Carroll was described by one shipmate as "a big, tough, fighting Irishman."[16] Now approaching fifty, he had left Notre Dame University in 1914 in order to enlist in the navy, eventually rising in rank to command the tugboat *Leopold Adler* during World War I. After the war he left the navy and settled on Long Island, only to rejoin the service in 1942. This time he was commissioned as a lieutenant commander and assigned to the Office of Naval Advisors attached to the War Production Board.

Unhappy behind a desk, Carroll agitated for sea duty and eventually received orders for *Liscome Bay* to serve as her first lieutenant, leaving a wife and daughter back home on Long Island. In a short time he won the respect and affection of the sailors serving under him, most of whom were close to the same age as his son serving in the U.S. Army Air Corps.

Thirty-year-old Lieutenant Commander John B. Rowe, MC, USNR, would be the senior medical officer aboard *Liscome Bay*. Rowe, of Gary, Indiana, graduated from the University of Chicago's School of Medicine in 1939 and then interned at the University of Iowa. He joined the navy in April 1941 and eighteen months later found himself serving as a flight surgeon with Marine Air Group 23, the first marine air group to be based at Guadalcanal's beleaguered Henderson Field. According to the letter of commendation he earned for his service on Guadalcanal, "During this time he . . . repeatedly administered first aid and medical treatment while under actual enemy aerial bombardment and artillery fire without regard for his personnel safety."[17] Rowe was, in short, no stranger to tough situations. A Louisiana native, Lieutenant (jg) Louis A. Ensenat, MC, USNR, assisted Rowe as the ship's junior medical officer.

Liscome Bay's sailors were as diverse as the officers. Fireman Third Class James L. King, for example, was a long way from his hometown of Birmingham, Alabama, where he had enlisted in the navy six months earlier. Like many of his new shipmates, he had carefully analyzed the pros and cons of the life in the army compared to that of the navy. Known alternately as "Alabama" or "Red," King was destined to be assigned to the ship's "black gang"—the group of sailors responsible for tending to the carrier's two engines. He had his sights set higher, however; he was apprenticing, or "striking," to be an electrician.

Seaman First Class William L. Fisher, a muscular youth from Quincy,

California, had been in the navy for only five months. He had obtained a job as a fireman with the Western Pacific Railway after graduating from high school, but in March 1943 he, his best friend, and his cousin decided to enlist in the navy. They all had decided that a military stint aboard a ship was infinitely preferable to spending the war in a foxhole as an infantryman.

Together the teenagers trooped down to the town's post office to enlist, where they joined a line of would-be recruits that extended into the street. Fisher's friend took a place in line in front of him; his cousin stood behind him. As they waited impatiently, a recruiter appeared and began counting down the line. He reached Fisher's friend, and then Fisher, and then stopped. "Okay, you guys," the recruiter announced. "Everyone from here forward is navy. The rest of you guys are going in the army." Fisher's disappointed cousin, as it turned out, was destined for a military career in the paratroops.

Once Fisher successfully enlisted in the navy, orders sent him to boot camp at Farragut Naval Training Station (NTS). Nestled at the foot of the Coeur d'Alene Mountains in Idaho's Bitteroot Range, Farragut sat on the southwestern shore of Lake Pend Oreille. The navy, seeking a secure inland training base, had placed the training station in Idaho. By the end of the war nearly 300,000 recruits had passed through it. Fisher jovially remembered the eight weeks of "invigorating exercise and workouts" he spent there, after which he was sent to Bremerton and then Astoria.[18] He had hopes of "striking" for a quartermaster rating.

Seaman First Class Richard L. Abbott Jr. enlisted in the navy in October 1942. At thirty-four, the square-jawed Abbott was considerably older than most of the young carrier's crew. He was a widower with a nine-year-old son, Robert. Abbott was originally from Pawtucket, Rhode Island, where he had worked for a local transportation company. Following his enlistment, he had attended boot camp at Farragut. His parents followed him to the West Coast with his young son in an effort to keep Robert close to his father.

Seaman Second Class Leonard J. Bohm, a resident of Concordia, Kansas, had joined the ship's crew just days before this early-morning muster. The nineteen-year-old had enlisted in the navy in Kansas City, Missouri, six months before. He would work as one of *Liscome Bay*'s shipfitters. Also from Kansas was Seaman Second Class Raymond J. Bergquist, who reported to *Liscome Bay* following eight weeks of boot camp at Farragut. Bergquist was promptly assigned to the ship's First Division, which was responsible for various deck operations, including "clean up, mooring, casting off lines, refueling, gunnery, anchoring, [and] taking on ammunition."[19]

Seaman First Class James C. Beasley came from Mount Airy, North Carolina, a small hometown he shared with television star Andy Griffith. Beasley had completed high school and was already enrolled in Elon College when he turned eighteen and decided to enlist in the navy. The young sailor had just finished four months of signalman school at Farragut when orders and train tickets arrived directing him to report to *Liscome Bay*. With orders in hand, Beasley and his best friend from the signalman course, Seaman First Class Wallace R. Andrews, had eagerly headed west to join the crew of the new flattop.

Fireman First Class Phelan E. Allee, originally from Houston, Texas, had enlisted in the navy three days after he turned twenty, taking his oath of service exactly one year after the Japanese attack on Pearl Harbor. A day later he had left Houston for boot camp in San Diego. Three months of machinist's mate school followed before he graduated with a rating of fireman first class. Like many of his shipmates, Allee arrived in Bremerton expecting to serve in *Glacier*. Now, however, he would tend *Liscome Bay*'s Uniflow steam engines. Fireman Third Class Robert E. Haynes, from Cedar Ridge, Colorado, was another fireman bound for *Liscome Bay*.

Among the ship's company stood at least one pair of brothers—Seamen Second Class Maxsy T. Homec and Frank E. Homec. The Homec brothers were farm boys from Hudson, Wyoming, a small town nestled in the Wind River Valley where the Big Popo Agie and Little Popo Agie Rivers meet. War and the closing of Poposie Coal Mine no. 2, the town's main employer, came to Hudson at about the same time. As 1942 wore on, Hudson's young men slipped off into the armed forces and left an increasingly ghostly town behind. The navy drafted Frank when he was nineteen; Maxsy, though only seventeen, wasted no time in enlisting as well.

The brothers reported for boot camp at Farragut NTS, where they were pleased to see Seaman Second Class John T. Cristando, another hometown youth, handing out uniforms to the new recruits. "Everything just seemed to be falling into place," Maxsy recalled.[20] After eight weeks of boot camp they headed west, eventually ending up in Astoria. It was the first time Maxsy and his brother had seen the ocean. "We were just young, dumb kids."[21] Once again, they linked up with Cristando, who had also landed a berth in *Liscome Bay*.

Storekeeper First Class Clovis M. Roach, a thin, wispy Texan, claimed a rare distinction among the young sailors formed up to his left and right: he was one of the ship's few combat veterans. Roach had previously served aboard the cruiser *San Francisco* (CA-38) when it participated in the naval fighting in support of the Guadalcanal landings in October and November 1942 at such clashes as the Battle of Cape Esperance and the Naval Battle of Guadalcanal. In the latter conflict, *San Francisco* served as the flagship for Rear Admiral Daniel J. Callaghan. The brutal shelling it endured during that brawling night fight not only left the task group commander, the ship's captain, and seventy-five other men dead but also convinced Roach, who had survived the confused battle entombed in the bowels of the cruiser, that he was not going to spend any more time below than was necessary. After Guadalcanal he even went so far as to sleep topside when weather permitted. It was a habit to which he intended to adhere while aboard his thin-skinned new escort carrier home.

Like Roach, Seaman First Class Edward Jonas had seen action in the waters off Guadalcanal. In fact, his date of this muster was almost exactly one year after his former ship, the heavy cruiser *Quincy* (CA-39), had been sunk in the disastrous Battle of Savo Island. Now Jonas was going back to sea once more, this time as ship's tailor.

With only a few exceptions, all of *Liscome Bay*'s officers and the overwhelming majority of her sailors were white. The carrier's crew included roughly two dozen stewards. Although the ship's muster rolls do not identify sailors by race, one can assume, based on the established navy policies of the day, that these stewards were—with the apparent exception of Steward's Mate First Class Irineo Almazan, of Salinas, California—exclusively black.

At the time of the Pearl Harbor attack, the navy's ranks contained slightly more than four thousand African Americans. Other than six black sailors who had enlisted prior to segregationist regulations re-implemented following the World War I demobilization, all black sailors served as mess stewards. Stewards manned the officers' mess, maintained the officers' billets aboard ship, and occasionally planned menus and purchased supplies.

Even after war broke out, the navy fought ferociously to keep black sailors relegated to steward or mess duties. But a remarkable display of heroism by a black mess steward—one who would eventually count himself among *Liscome Bay*'s sailors—had gone a long way in changing the navy's mind. That man was Doris "Dorie" Miller.

The twenty-three-year-old Miller hailed from the dusty streets of Waco, Texas. The third of four brothers, he was positively supposed to have been, according to the family's midwife, a girl. Accordingly, the Millers named their yet-unborn infant "Doris." Miller's entry into the world on October 12, 1919, as a bouncing baby boy proved the midwife wrong, but the name stuck. Twenty years later, Miller enlisted for a six-year tour with the navy. His first set of orders sent him to boot camp in Norfolk, Virginia. After two months of training, he joined the crew of the ammunition ship *Pyro* (AE-1) before being transferred to the battleship *West Virginia* (BB-48) on January 2, 1940. While aboard *West Virginia*, Miller, who stood over six feet, three inches tall and weighed more than two hundred pounds, claimed the ship's heavyweight boxing title.

December 7, 1941, dawned with *West Virginia* lying serenely at her quays alongside Pearl Harbor's Ford Island. She was one of seven battleships moored on "Battleship Row"—an inviting target for the Japanese air attack that erupted shortly before 0800. Within the first few minutes of the attack, a series of torpedoes smashed into *West Virginia*'s side. An attack by enemy dive-bombers quickly followed, and soon the "Wee Vee" was afire and listing.

In the ensuing chaos, Miller, with his battle station out of commission, joined a pair of officers in going to the aid of Captain Mervyn S. Bennion, USN, *West Virginia*'s commanding officer. Bennion, though severely wounded, was still on the bridge directing his ship's defense and damage control efforts.

Before they could move Bennion, another group of Japanese warplanes appeared in the sky over Pearl. This time, thirteen dive-bombers screamed down at the nearby *Maryland*. Miller, although he had never fired the ship's Browning .50-caliber machine guns, manned one of the guns and began blasting at the attacking Japanese planes. When asked about manning a weapon on which he had never been trained, Miller commented modestly, "It wasn't hard. I just pulled the trigger and she worked fine."[22]

Although the press subsequently emphasized Miller's role in the manning of the machine gun, he rendered greater—and more dangerous—service trying to save his captain and other shipmates. Threatened by a raging oil fire, he helped drag Bennion to temporary safety. Although the captain succumbed to his wounds on the ship's deck moments later, Miller quickly turned his attention to pulling sailors out of the harbor's oily, burning water and onto the deck. But for Miller's work, the battleship's death toll of 130 men would have been higher.

In the days following the defeat at Pearl Harbor, as an angry navy licked its wounds, the first recommendations for medals began arriving at the Navy Department. Although an "unknown Negro" mess attendant was mentioned in the dispatches, it was not until March 1942 that the navy identified Miller as the heroic steward.

Miller quickly became a symbol of black America's fighting pride. When he joined the heavy cruiser *Indianapolis* (CA-35) for combat operations in the South Pacific, the nation's black community agitated with increasing stridency for Miller to receive adequate recognition for his deeds aboard *West Virginia*. George Schuyler, writing in a front-page column in the *Pittsburgh Courier*, a newspaper serving the city's black population, reflected the growing sense of impatience with the navy's treatment of Miller. "The Navy," he complained, "finds Dorie Miller too important waiting tables in the Pacific to return home so that his people might see him."[23] As word of Miller's exploits aboard *West Virginia* spread, some members of Congress even introduced legislation calling for him to receive the Medal of Honor.

Meanwhile, the *Pittsburgh Courier* continued its efforts to ensure that Miller was properly recognized. It initiated a mail-in campaign to send Miller to the all-white Naval Academy. "To President Franklin D. Roosevelt," the newspaper's clip-out coupons began, "as Commander-in-

Chief of the Army and Navy of the United States, as a token of national appreciation, Colored America urges you to send Dorie Miller, messman hero of Pearl Harbor, to the Naval Academy for training."[24] It was a bold call given Miller's eighth-grade education, and ultimately it was unsuccessful.

Nearly six months after the attack on Pearl, the navy finally relented to the public's demand. On May 27, 1942, back at Pearl Harbor and on the flight deck of the carrier *Enterprise,* Admiral Chester W. Nimitz, USN, presented Miller with the Navy Cross for "distinguished devotion to duty, extraordinary courage and disregard for his own personal safety" in aiding Captain Bennion and manning a machine gun in the face of the Japanese attack.[25] When Nimitz pinned the bronze medal and blue ribbon to Miller's chest, it was the first time the decoration had ever been worn by a black sailor. Commenting to a group of reporters, Nimitz remarked: "This marks the first time in this conflict that such high tribute has been made in the Pacific Fleet to a member of his race and I'm sure that the future will see others similarly honored for brave acts."[26]

The month before Miller received his Navy Cross, the navy had finally capitulated to the pressure to open all its branches to black sailors. Accordingly, Miller, while back in the States on a war bonds tour, was eventually able to speak at the ceremony marking the first class of black sailors to graduate from Camp Robert Smalls at the Great Lakes NTS. These men still labored under a segregated assignment policy, but they played an important role in the service's eventual integration in 1948.

Once he completed his war bonds tour, Miller—by then a cook third class—reported for duty at Puget Sound Navy Yard and soon found himself assigned to *Liscome Bay.* Many of his fellow enlisted sailors didn't know that the towering cook preparing their stews, steaks, and eggs wore the Navy Cross. Nor were they aware of the role he had played in the advancement of the cause of African Americans in the navy.

The ship's officers, however, were well aware of their distinguished cook. Miller fell under the command of Ensign Daily. "He was a big guy," Daily recalled, "but tender as a deer."[27] Miller's primary duty station was the ship's galley, but during general quarters he manned one of the ship's 20-millimeter antiaircraft guns.

All told, nearly six hundred men formed up at Tongue Point that morning. They didn't constitute the entire complement for an escort carrier's crew, but more men were filtering in every day. Daily's pay records showed that their hometowns dotted every corner of the nation. Some came from America's coastal cities—New York, Seattle, Miami, Los Angeles, New Orleans, Portland, and San Diego. Others arrived from the heartland—Birmingham, Cleveland, Omaha, Topeka, Minneapolis, Chicago, Dallas, Detroit, and Salt Lake City. But for every New York there was a Sleepy Eye, Minnesota, a St. Maurice, Louisiana, a Spur, Texas, or a Pine Hill, Alabama. Some claimed just rural route numbers.

Some hometowns were not even in the United States. Cook Third Class Gabriel M. Mansapit hailed from Guam, while Seaman Paul P. Rocha's parents lived in Nueva Laredo, Mexico. But regardless of their hometowns, accents, or color of skin, they were all prepared to close ranks to face a common foe somewhere over the western horizon.

Shouted orders sent the crew's formation peeling off the field and onto a roadway. With seabags balanced on their shoulders, the crewmen of *Liscome Bay* headed for Astoria and the new floating home that awaited them. Once pierside, they formed into long, snaking lines to board the carrier towering above them. Picking their way through unfamiliar passages, they found their quarters, broke open their bags, donned their dress uniforms, and then headed topside to the flight deck.

On the flight deck, the ship's company fell into formation again as the navy formally commissioned *Liscome Bay* and welcomed her into the Pacific Fleet. A scant eight months had passed since her keel had been laid in Vancouver. On the other side of the Pacific, in Japanese shipyards, it would almost be another year before the carriers intended to replace Japan's losses at Coral Sea, Midway, and Guadalcanal would hit the water. From his signal station at the ship's bridge, Beasley watched the ceremonies. "Very impressive," the North Carolina native later wrote.[28]

Despite their new home, the crew of *Liscome Bay* quickly found out that they were little closer to sea than they had been at Tongue Point. For nearly four weeks the ship remained dockside as its crew transformed the carrier into a veritable floating city. Its officers and sailors loaded stores, opened galleys and mess halls, started up the ship's laundry room, post office, barbershop, and ship's store, and stocked and prepared the carrier's operating room and sick bay for its first patients. Constructed as only the second vessel in a brand-new class of warship, *Liscome Bay* and her interior compartments and passageways represented uncharted territory for each member of her crew. Though a relatively small carrier, she was still a new ship, and it took several days for her officers and sailors to find their way around.

Atop her flight deck, three-fourths of the way to the ship's bow and on the starboard side of the deck, stood the carrier's island. This four-story structure housed *Liscome Bay*'s bridge, fly control station, and steering station, essentially doubling as a flight control tower. Below the flight deck lay the gallery deck. It ran for only approximately the front quarter of the carrier but was packed with such stations and compartments as the ship's air plot, radar plot, radio rooms, coding room, captain's and executive officer's staterooms and cabins, junior officers' bunk room, and catapult machinery room. The upper deck, located beneath the gallery deck, was home to "officers' country," where the ship's officers lived. The hangar deck, which provided covered storage for the aircraft of the ship's aircraft squadron and a maintenance area for their crews, was located aft as well as below the upper deck. The shipfitters' shop was also found on this deck.

Below the hangar deck lay the so-called second deck, sitting just barely above the waterline. This was home to the crew's quarters, the sick bay, the medical officer's office, the damage control office, the officers' wardroom, and the chief petty officers' mess. The first platform deck lay below the second deck—beneath the waterline. More officer wardrooms, the electricians' workroom, the generator room, the steering gear, the ammunition magazine for the 5-inch gun, and the forward machinery spaces were found on this deck. Finally, at the very bottom of the ship lay the tank top deck, which housed the aircraft bomb stowage, the machine shop, the forward machinery space (extending down from the deck above), tanks for fresh water, fuel, oil, and gasoline, and the boiler rooms.

As the first men on board worked to make *Liscome Bay* ready for operations, new crewmen continued to filter in. Among the new arrivals was Warrant Officer Lyle D. Blakley, who would serve as the ship's aerographer, or weatherman. Blakley's role was an important one, since the decision of whether to send *Liscome Bay*'s aircraft squadron aloft each day would often hinge on his weather reports and prognostications. Accompanying Blakley were Aerographer's Mates Third Class Williard L. "Bob" Pinder and Russell J. "Jack" Mahood. They occupied the aerology office and weather balloon inflation room on the ship's gallery deck, on her port side just abaft a 40-millimeter gun tub. Directly above them lay the carrier's noisy catapult track.

As Blakley, Pinder, and Mahood settled into their new home, the ship's chief cook, Cook First Class Robert C. Smith, supervised the installation of the new coffee urns in the wardroom's galley. With much fanfare, Smith's sidekick, Cook First Class Homer Lambert, prepared the initial batch of the wardroom's coffee. In a show of exaggerated formality, he dolloped carefully measured amounts of sugar and cream into the dark liquid and stiffly presented Smitty with the first steaming cup. Smith, in turn, sought out Daily and passed the ensign the cup for his tasting and approval.

Daily took a careful sip and almost gagged.

A look of concern flashed across the chief cook's face. "Mr. Daily, is it that bad?"

"It's pretty bad, Smitty. Want to try again?"

Smith took back the cup and disappeared into the gallery. Five minutes later he returned.

"I'm going to kill that Lambert!" he sputtered. "He put salt in there instead of sugar!"[29]

After a second, untainted, cup, Daily pronounced the wardroom's coffee acceptable.

Meanwhile, the outfitting of the ship continued. As the day of departure approached, the old hands began to warn the young sailors under their wings of their impending bouts of seasickness. With a certain amount of glee, they speculated that the ship's first dinner at sea would feature a main entrée of cruel tradition—greasy pork chops. It was a grim prospect for the 80 percent or so of the crew who had never been to sea. Daily was among them. He wondered how he would weather his first days at sea.

The first week of September brought his answer. On September 7, *Lis-*

come Bay cast off her lines from Astoria's docks, slipped out into the Columbia River's shipping channel, and followed the river's flow into the nearby Pacific. From there the carrier headed north, pitching and bobbing through the long groundswells that marked that particular stretch of coast. The long-awaited moment was at hand.

Near the end of the war, famed war correspondent Ernie Pyle would pen a famous dispatch describing the aircraft carrier *Cabot* (CVL-28). His words could have just as easily been written for *Liscome Bay* as she rolled awkwardly through the swells of the North Pacific. "An aircraft carrier," Pyle wrote, "is a noble thing. It lacks almost everything that seems to denote nobility, yet deep nobility is there. A carrier has no poise. It has no grace. It is top-heavy and lopsided. It has the lines of a well-fed cow. It doesn't cut through the water like a cruiser, knifing romantically along. It doesn't dance and cavort like a destroyer. It just plows. You feel it should be carrying a hod, rather than wearing a red sash. Yet a carrier is a ferocious thing, and out of its heritage of action has grown its nobility."[30]

Such esoteric thoughts were beyond the vast majority of *Liscome Bay*'s crew at that moment. Most of them were just excited to finally be at sea. For many, however, excitement soon gave way to another feeling. When Daily made his way to the wardroom for dinner, he found that nearly half the chairs in the wardroom were empty—their missing occupants apparently the victims of seasickness. When the plates of greasy pork chops arrived, the number of officers in the wardroom shrank even further. By the end of the meal, the only officers remaining were "Fee" Hall, who had presided over a champagne party for the other officers the night before; Daily; and six others. Daily later learned that over five hundred of the ship's crew were seasick that evening.

The next day, September 8, *Liscome Bay* dropped anchor off Bremerton, across Puget Sound from Seattle. The smoking lamp went out from 0800 to 1700 for two days as the crew loaded the carrier's ammunition. With careful hands, under the watchful eyes of their officers and petty officers, the sailors loaded a deadly array of ordnance. They carried on board crate after crate of ammunition for the 20- and 40-millimeter antiaircraft guns, in addition to boxes containing thousands of rounds of .50-caliber aircraft machine-gun ammunition. Even more delicately, the sailors loaded nine 2,000-pound general-purpose (GP) bombs, nine 1,600-pound armor-piercing (AP) bombs, twenty-four 1,000-pound AP bombs, thirty-six 1,000-pound semi-armor-piercing (SAP) bombs, eighteen 1,000-pound GP bombs, ninety-six 500-pound GP bombs, one hundred and twenty 100-pound GP bombs, and ninety-six 350-pound depth-charge bombs in the bomb stowage area on the starboard side of the ship's lowest level. The sailors stacked the smaller 100-pound GP bombs and the 350-pound depth-charge bombs on the outboard side of the ship's stowage area, where they almost touched the thin walls separating the stowage area from the surrounding seawater.[31]

Once the ammunition and bombs were safely on board, it was time for the ship to be electrically depermed, which the crew accomplished by passing electric cables completely around the ship. Following this procedure, *Liscome Bay* headed for Puget Sound's degaussing range, where she spent eight hours passing back and forth over a series of huge underwater magnets. Like the deperming, the degaussing was intended to keep the steel ship from attracting magnetic mines. Daily didn't know if the deperming and degaussing technology would successfully foil enemy mines, but he knew one thing for sure—his "antimagnetic" wristwatch was never the same again.

These procedures finished, Wiltsie's crew was ready to take to sea and test the ship's guns. After sailing into the nearby Strait of Juan de Fuca, *Liscome Bay* began her gunfire tests. Officers evaluated each gun position and then, as the final test, ordered that every gun on the carrier be fired at once. The noise was deafening. Many of the gunners simply closed their eyes, gripped their weapons, and blasted away blindly as the roar of gunfire enveloped the ship.

On September 15, *Liscome Bay* moored in Seattle. Before stepping down the gangplank on liberty with his friends from the ship's signal shop, Seaman Beasley scrawled a quick letter to his father back in North Carolina detailing the past few days' activities. "After leaving Astoria and the Puget Sound," he wrote, "we returned to Bremerton for additional work on the ship. After a couple of days there we went back into the Sound for additional shakedown runs. During the day of September 14, we went out a bit further for our first gunnery practice—that was exciting. We returned to Seattle. Dad, I am really happy to be where I am and doing the things I am doing."[32]

In the course of these and other sea trials, the ship's officers noted two problems with the ship. First, a crack developed in the steel upper sheathing on the port side. Starting at the catwalk level amidships, the crack ran down toward the waterline about fifteen feet. Numerous attempts to weld the crack shut failed. In the end, since the siding wasn't critical for structural support, Wiltsie and his engineering officers decided to simply leave it alone. The second problem was more drastic. For some unknown reason, the carrier developed a permanent five-degree list to starboard. Despite the crew's best efforts and numerous conferences among the officers, the list couldn't be corrected. Faced with the permanent list, the crew soon irreverently christened their carrier the "Listing Lizzie."[33]

Throughout these operations, new sailors continued to filter aboard the young carrier. Twenty-two-year-old Parachute Rigger First Class James E. Gibbons from Seattle was among the new arrivals. Gibbons set foot on his new home with some trepidation. Previously he had served on the carrier *Lexington* (CV-2). On May 8, 1942, Japanese air attacks in the Battle of the Coral Sea had mortally wounded *Lexington*, causing Gibbons and his shipmates to abandon the flaming carrier hurriedly. Gibbons knew from firsthand experience that the navy's carriers were prime targets of the Japanese navy. He could only hope that a smaller carrier like *Liscome Bay* would be less inviting.

Armed, fueled, and with the initial shakedown under her belt, *Liscome Bay* was almost ready to begin operations. On September 17, Wiltsie took her to sea once more and turned her bow south. This time the destination was San Francisco's Alameda NAS.

Shortly after *Liscome Bay* set out from Puget Sound, Wiltsie began running the ship through gunnery practices. During these drills the carrier's crew released fat helium balloons to serve as targets for the carrier's gunners, who would then dutifully plug away at them with their 40-millimeter "pom-pom" guns and 20-millimeter antiaircraft machine guns. In all, *Liscome Bay* carried sixteen 40-millimeter guns and twenty 20-millimeter guns to aid the carrier in warding off enemy aircraft. She also carried a single 5-inch gun mounted in a gun tub overhanging her square stern, but most sailors disparaged this weapon's value. According to one sailor on a *Casablanca*-class carrier, the only real purpose of the 5-inch piece was "to keep the ship's rudder in the water."[34]

Perhaps not surprisingly for a man of his accomplishments, Dorie Miller manned one of the ship's 20-millimeter guns. The first time he and his loader, Steward's Mate First Class Theodore R. Harris of East Orange, New Jersey, took their position at their gun, they attracted a gaggle of curious spectators. Aware of Miller's exploits at Pearl Harbor, Daily and about a dozen of his fellow officers gathered behind Miller and Harris, eager to see the hero of Pearl Harbor in action. Miller, perhaps drawing from his experience as a Texas squirrel hunter, didn't disappoint. It only took three or four blasts of the 20-millimeter gun for his red tracers to explode the target balloon. Miller and Harris quickly gained a reputation as the ship's best gun team. Their deadly aim was a valuable asset on a ship destined to sail in harm's way.

The 20-millimeter guns of Miller and his fellow gun crews were merely defensive weapons for the escort carrier. As Captain Wiltsie well knew, it was through her warplanes that *Liscome Bay* would carry the fight to the Japanese. Those awaited in California.

3

Wildcats, Avengers, and a Rear Admiral

Liscome Bay stood into San Francisco Bay on September 18, 1943. Captain Wiltsie mustered the ship's company, resplendent in their dress uniforms, on the flight deck to mark their arrival. For most of the crew, it was their first sight of the Golden Gate and the city of San Francisco.

When the carrier slipped past the rocky island of Alcatraz to port, her crew contemplated the infamous island prison with unabashed curiosity, wondering if any of the penitentiary's unseen prisoners were staring back at them. "Take a good look off the port bow," Wiltsie advised his ship's supply department from the bridge. "Get a good view of your future home," he added with a sly grin, referring to silent Alcatraz.[1] An experienced officer like the captain knew the department probably contained more than its share of scroungers, hustlers, and midnight-requisitions artists. *Liscome Bay*'s storekeepers smiled knowingly in response to the skipper's warning.

Leaving Alcatraz in the carrier's wake, *Liscome Bay*'s quartermaster guided the ship southward. She sailed deeper into the bay, sliding underneath the San Francisco–Oakland Bridge. (The bridge, like *Liscome Bay*, was an iron-and-steel product of Henry Kaiser's construction companies.) Once clear of the bridge, the carrier stood into a berth at nearby Alameda NAS, where she refueled and, for the next day and a half, carefully loaded approximately sixty aircraft for delivery to San Diego. It was an exercise that underscored one of the reasons the navy needed its jeep carriers—to ferry aircraft between ports. From Alameda, a two-day sail took *Liscome Bay* further south to San Diego, where she arrived on September 22 with every available square foot of her flight and hangar decks crowded with airplanes.

After unloading the cargo, Wiltsie took his carrier to sea once more for drills and shakedown activities. The carrier also practiced her night gunnery skills—"like fireworks at the county fair back home," Seaman Beasley reported in a letter to his father.[2] *Liscome Bay* conducted this training off California's coast in fits and spurts of two to three days each. Fog interrupted the training, sending the carrier back to San Diego for days at a time. Standing back into San Diego harbor, especially at night with a fog rolling in, provided the officers on duty and their quartermaster with an opportunity to share in some of the anxiety experienced by their flying brethren during their carrier landings. The narrow channel at San Diego presented a particularly stern navigational challenge.

The San Diego shipping channel proved so difficult to negotiate that it was reportedly the only harbor on the Pacific Coast to require the use of a civilian pilot to navigate its waters. This meant that whenever *Liscome Bay* left the harbor for her drills at sea, Ensign Daily went through a familiar drill as the ship's paymaster. His day would start at 0530, when one of the ship's boatswains would shine a flashlight in his face, waking him to handle the payment to the civilian harbor pilot. Wiping the sleep from his eyes, Daily would climb to the bridge, pick up the pilot's bill (calculated based on the ship's draft and displacement), hasten to the ship's cramped disbursing office, cut the pilot a check, and slip him the payment before he disembarked.

During this stretch of training, heavy fog frequently socked in the ship's company. For several days the ship anchored off Point Loma, where her crew could hear a nearby foghorn and the clanging of ships' bells. With visibility reduced to less than one hundred feet, they were out of sight of the rest of the world. It was a boring, lonely stretch of days for the crew. A bit of excitement came, however, when Wiltsie learned that the ship had dropped anchor a scant twenty yards from a submarine telephone cable. The captain, a former navigation officer himself, "was not amused," and he "exchanged pleasantries" with *Liscome Bay*'s navigation officer regarding the narrowly averted disaster.[3]

Wiltsie's frustration likely peaked with the arrival of a particular set of orders which informed him that the navy had appointed *Liscome Bay* as the flagship of Carrier Division 24. The division would also include two sister ships, *Coral Sea* (CVE-57) and *Corregidor* (CVE-58). As flagship, *Liscome Bay* would be responsible for housing the division's commander, Rear Admiral Henry M. Mullinnix, USN, and his staff. Like any self-respecting ship's captain, Wiltsie did not look forward to having his every move come under the scrutiny of an embarked flag officer. Nevertheless, orders were orders, and *Liscome Bay* spent several days moored at the San Pedro Naval Base as construction crews installed quarters and work areas for Mullinnix and his staff.

By October 11, all was ready. Back in San Diego, under Wiltsie's watchful eye, the carrier ceremoniously piped aboard Rear Admiral Mullinnix and his staff. The fifty-one-year-old Mullinnix, a native of Spencer, Indiana, had first attended Purdue University but then moved on to Annapolis. He graduated from the Naval Academy in 1916 at the top of his class and soon found himself aboard the destroyer *Balch* (DD-50) matching wits with German U-boats in the North Atlantic in World War I. Later assignments included service on board the destroyers *Gridley* (DD-92) and *Brooks* (DD-232).

Mullinnix earned a master's degree in aeronautical engineering from the Massachusetts Institute of Technology in 1923 and then received flight training at Pensacola during 1923 and 1924. He subsequently served in the Engine Section of the Navy Department's Bureau of Aeronautics, where he eventually earned the credit of being one of the officers primarily responsible for the development of radial engines later found in such aircraft as the Wildcat fighter.

After three years at the Bureau of Aeronautics, Mullinnix reported to the brand-new carrier *Saratoga* (CV-3) in 1927. He served as her assembly and repair officer and assistant air officer. At the time, his boss as the ship's air officer was Commander Marc A. Mitscher, USN, who would become the navy's premier carrier admiral in World War II. Mullinnix later commanded *Saratoga*'s Bombing Squadron 2. Subsequent service included more staff assignments and sea duty at various times in the seaplane tender *Wright* (AV-1).

In the fall of 1940, Mullinnix commanded the navy's newest seaplane tender, *Albemarle* (AV-5), during her fitting out. Upon completion of those duties, he commanded a patrol wing in the Atlantic Fleet and then served as the air officer for the Eastern Sea Frontier during the difficult and tense days of German U-boat attacks on Allied merchant shipping throughout most of 1941 and 1942. During this time, the navy promoted Mullinnix to captain. Shortly thereafter, on November 13, 1942, he was again promoted, this time to rear admiral. He also commanded *Saratoga* briefly, from February to August 1943. August brought Mullinnix his orders to leave *Saratoga* and take command of Carrier Division 24.

By the time he broke out his flag on board *Liscome Bay*, Mullinnix could rightly be called one of the "air admirals"—naval officers who had cut their teeth during the interwar years of naval aviation and who were destined to make their mark in the unprecedented carrier raids and battles of the Pacific theater. In the prewar fleet problems and in the skies over Pensacola, they had helped to forge U.S. naval air doctrine. Their experience in supporting the complex amphibious assaults that would characterize the United States' advance across the Pacific, however, was decidedly limited. In the end, Mullinnix and his staff officers would have to learn on the job.

Fortunately, Mullinnix's staff included a number of seasoned naval aviators. Captain John G. Crommelin, USN, NA, his chief of staff, had previously served as the air officer and executive officer aboard the carrier *Enterprise* (CV-6) in the desperate fighting in the Solomons in 1942. Crommelin's excellent reputation from his time on *Enterprise* followed him to *Liscome Bay*. "He was as fine a man as the admiral," one sailor said of the Alabama-born Crommelin. "You could talk to him about any problem you had."[4] Beasley agreed, writing that "Captain Crommelin was a great leader and commanded respect."[5]

Mullinnix's operations officer, Commander Charles H. "Whitey" Ostrom, USN, NA, was, like Mullinnix and Crommelin, a Naval Academy graduate. Hailing from Miami, Florida, Ostrom had previously commanded Fighter Squadron 21 (nicknamed the Blackjacks) in the summer of 1943, flying Wildcats out of Guadalcanal's Henderson Airfield. On one day alone, June 30, 1943, Ostrom's squadron downed thirty Japanese aircraft in an aerial melee of almost unheard-of proportions.

Only orders for staff duty succeeded in pulling Ostrom out of his cockpit and back to the West Coast.

In total, the admiral's staff contained ten officers. Also on his staff was the bespectacled twenty-seven-year-old Quartermaster First Class Percy W. "P. W." Rairden Jr. from Seattle, Washington. Rairden had enlisted in the navy four years earlier. He accompanied the rear admiral on board *Liscome Bay* with the Carrier Division 24 staff to serve as Mullinnix's flag quartermaster.

A few days later, on October 14, *Liscome Bay* finally received her raison d'être: the composite squadron of naval aircraft that would make up VC-39. Swinging back and forth, dockside cranes placed eleven FM-1 Wildcats, five F4F-4 Wildcats, and nine TBM-1 and three TBM-1C torpedo bombers onto the escort carrier's flight deck. Once the planes were securely on board and their wings folded neatly back, crewmen pushed them to either of the ship's two elevators and struck them below to the hangar deck.

The aircraft in VC-39's inventory were typical of those carried by a *Casablanca*-class escort carrier. Fighter duties were fulfilled by the single-seat Wildcat, built by one of two manufacturers—Grumman or General Motors—in slightly different versions. But regardless of manufacturer, the Wildcat would come to occupy a hallowed place in the annals of American naval aviation.

In the 1930s, when the navy elected to switch from biplanes to monoplanes, it let out contracts for prototype monoplane carrier fighters. Brewster Aeronautical Corporation submitted one prototype, the XF2A-1, which first flew in 1937. Its competitor's design, Grumman Aircraft Engineering Corporation's XF4F-2, also completed its maiden flight that year. In the end, though, the navy elected to use Brewster's fighter, which became known as the Buffalo officially or, disparagingly and unofficially, the "Peanut Special" or the "Flying Barrel."[6]

Although Brewster won the initial contract, production problems plagued the company's manufacture of the F2A. Encouraged by their rival's difficulties, Grumman's engineers revamped their design and resubmitted their fighter as the XF4F-3. Impressed with the plane's increased performance thanks to a two-stage, two-speed supercharger, in 1939 the navy ordered fifty-four of the F4F-3s, which it would eventually christen Wildcats. The first ones rolled off the assembly line in 1940, and for a time the navy's fighter pilots were flying both Brewster F2As and Grumman F4F-3s.

Brewster's factories, however, continued to suffer from production difficulties and struggled to deliver the requisite numbers of aircraft on schedule. Furthermore, efforts to upgrade the F2A while increasing its range only worsened the aircraft's speed, maneuverability, and climb rate. At high altitudes, its single-stage supercharger delivered only mediocre performance; on flight decks, the fighter's landing gear had a distressing tendency to fail catastrophically with the hard carrier landings. Accordingly, the navy's pilots shed few tears when they learned that January 1941 marked the last order of F2As from Brewster. The sturdy F4F-3 became the navy's preferred aircraft for its fighter squadrons.

Even as it was providing the navy with F4F-3s, Grumman continued to tinker with the aircraft's design. In particular, both the U.S. Navy and the Royal Navy wanted a fighter with folding wings, since this freed up storage space on the decks of aircraft carriers—space that could be used for more planes. Grumman obliged with a new variant of the Wildcat, the F4F-4, and delivered the first model for testing in 1941. By the time *Liscome Bay* loaded VC-39's aircraft on board, the F4F-4 design had been in service with the navy for nearly two years.

The F4F-4, like the earlier Wildcats, was a short, stubby, wide-winged aircraft whose appearance caused one pilot to describe it as a "little beer bottle of a plane."[7] Underneath a fat fuselage, it sported spread-eagled main landing gear that had to be cranked up by hand once the aircraft was in flight. The tail wheel simply remained fixed in the extended position while in flight.

With their armor plating, self-sealing fuel tanks, and wing-mounted batteries of six .50-caliber machine guns, the squat F4F-4s weighed in at nearly eight thousand pounds—a figure that many pilots viewed with alarm, especially after experiencing the aircraft's sluggish flight characteristics. With all that weight, the fighter's air-cooled 1,200-horsepower Pratt and Whitney radial engine, accompanied by a two-stage, two-speed supercharger, could only coax the Wildcat up to a maximum speed of 320 miles per hour. The Wildcat's maneuverability and climb rates also left a great deal to be desired, especially when compared with its typical opponent in the Pacific—the Japanese Mitsubishi A6M Zero. Faster, lighter, and possessing the nimbleness of a sparrow in flight, the Zero was considered by many aviation experts one of the best aircraft designs in the world at the time.

To some extent, Lieutenant Colonel Harold W. "Indian Joe" Bauer, a U.S. Marine Corps pilot who had gained fame in the skies over Guadalcanal, had echoed those sentiments. "A Zero can go faster than you can, it climbs faster than you can, and it can outmaneuver you. Aside from those things, you've got a better aircraft," he told some of his newly arrived pilots at Guadalcanal's muddy and shell-pocked Henderson Airfield in 1942.[8] Bauer made a good point—and one that had likely been driven home to the young pilots who would be flying *Liscome Bay*'s Wildcats during their flight training. Their fighter was a rugged aircraft, capable of absorbing an enormous amount of punishment. Indeed, its pilots labeled the factories that produced it "the Grumman Ironworks." In addition, certain of the Wildcat's characteristics, such as its dive speed, surpassed those of the Zero. Finally, superior tactics, such as coordinated formation flying and tight wingman support, could quickly tip the balance aloft in favor of a group of the American fighters.

Lieutenant Commander James H. Flatley Jr., a renowned naval aviator, took a similarly realistic view of the Wildcat's strengths and weaknesses. "Our planes and pilots," he wrote, "if properly handled, are more than a match for the enemy. What the F4F-4 lacks in climb and maneuverability is more than compensated by its excellent armament, protective armor, protected fuel system, and greater strength. Add to this the inherent superior ability of the [U.S.] navy pilot, particularly as regards to using his armament, and the outlook is very favorable."[9] By the end of 1942 that outlook was so favorable that Wildcat pilots were downing nearly six enemy aircraft for each of their own fighters lost.[10]

Most of *Liscome Bay*'s Wildcats were the FM-1 variant. By 1943, Grumman had begun focusing its manufacturing efforts on its second-generation naval carrier fighter, the F6F Hellcat. There was still, however, a role to be played by the smaller Wildcats, especially on board the rapidly proliferating escort carriers, and Grumman licensed its design for the little fighter to General Motors. General Motors, in turn, converted five of its East Coast automobile factories to aircraft production, created a subsidiary called Eastern Aircraft, and began churning out its own version of the Wildcat, the FM-1. General Motors' design was essentially identical to Grumman's sturdy work on the F4F-4, with the exception that the General Motors version carried four, rather than six, .50-caliber machine guns in its wings.

Among the aircraft of VC-39, the F4F-4 and FM-1 Wildcats shared the hangar and flight deck with another aircraft originally designed by Grumman: the Avenger torpedo bomber. First built in 1940, the Avenger was a longer and larger aircraft than the Wildcat. It sported a fifty-four-foot wingspan as compared to the Wildcat's thirty-eight-foot span. But like the F4F-4 and FM-1, the Avenger's wings could be folded for storage in the tight confines of its carrier home. And as with the Wildcat, Grumman had licensed the design of the Avenger to General Motors' Eastern Aircraft division. Grumman-built Avengers were designated TBFs, the General Motors version TBMs.

Three men crewed each Avenger—a pilot, a radioman-bombardier, and a turret gunner manning a .50-caliber machine gun in the Avenger's electric-powered gun turret. The pilots were officers, typically products of the Naval Academy or, as the war wore on, one of America's college Naval Reserve Officer Training programs. The public might call them "flyboys," but in navy slang they were known as "brownshoes."

The vast majority of the squadron's pilots, while reasonably well trained by the standards of most of the world's militaries, were painfully inexperienced. A typical new pilot with gold naval aviator wings of a 1943 vintage had likely logged thirteen weeks of ground school and about two hundred hours in the cockpit during his seven-month flight training at naval air stations located in such places as Pensacola, Jacksonville, Corpus Christi, and Miami. If he was lucky, he logged another seventy-five hours at one of the navy's advanced carrier training groups (ACTGs) for further work in tactics, navigation, gunnery and bombing, field carrier land practice, carrier qualification, night flying, and instruments. With a shortage of carriers on which to actually practice landings, the training opportunities available in the ACTGs were limited, and experienced naval aviation officers felt that an additional one hundred hours of on-the-job gunnery and team tactics training was usually necessary before a young pilot was ready for combat.[11] Time for such training prior to the first set of combat operations, however, was a luxury the carrier squadrons did not always enjoy.

The Avengers' radiomen-bombardiers and rear turret gunners were enlisted men. They led a hazardous life, entrusting their fate to the pilots. The 50 percent increase in base pay that they enjoyed, coupled generally with a freedom from standing watch aboard ship, must have been some consolation to them in that regard.

An Avenger could carry either a torpedo or two thousand pounds of bombs in its internal bomb bay. Easy to handle at low speeds, possessing the good lift demanded of a carrier aircraft, powered by a reliable Wright 2600 radial engine, and capable of absorbing a heavy amount of punishment, the Avenger was generally well liked by its pilots. Equipped with radar and capable of a range of approximately one thousand miles, it provided the fleet with a valuable scouting aircraft as well.

Once at sea, the aircraft of VC-39 were intended to play a variety of roles. The Wildcats would fly combat air patrol to screen *Liscome Bay* and her fellow ships from enemy air attack. The Avengers would typically complement the Wildcats' screen by flying antisubmarine patrol or scouting for enemy shipping. When the carrier switched over to the offensive, the Avengers would lash at enemy shipping and ground positions while the Wildcats escorted them to their targets or conducted strafing attacks of their own.

Liscome Bay carried two types of Avengers. Nine were TBM-1s, the earliest version of the torpedo bomber to be built by Eastern Aircraft. Three, however, were TBM-1Cs. These aircraft benefited from modifications that included replacing the pilot's single fuselage-mounted .30-caliber machine gun with two wing-mounted .50-caliber machine guns. An internal fuel tank in the bomb bay and two additional wing tanks more than doubled the TBM-1C's fuel capacity.

Accompanying the squadron's twenty-eight Wildcats and Avengers were the thirty-six officers and forty-one enlisted men of VC-39. They were all under the authority of Lieutenant Commander Marshall U. Beebe, USN. Just barely thirty years old when he reported aboard *Liscome Bay*, Beebe was a native of Anaheim, California, and like Chaplain Carley, a graduate of California's Occidental College. He had joined the navy in 1936, earned his aviator wings at Pensacola, and served in the Pacific Fleet. Beebe was in Washington, D.C., assigned to the Navy Department's Bureau of Aeronautics, when the Japanese attacked Pearl Harbor. This was his first combat command.

Beebe was VC-39's only regular navy officer—all the others were products of the Naval Reserve. One such officer was Lieutenant John G. "Pete" Piegari, A-V(N), USNR, of New York, the squadron's executive officer and Beebe's second-in-command. Another was Ensign Frances J. "Dutch" Polman, A-V(N), USNR, a native of New Orleans, Louisiana. Polman didn't so much take his seat in his Wildcat cockpit as mold his bulk into it. Despite the cramped quarters in flight due to Polman's girth, the ensign's flying skills were so steady that Beebe made him his wingman.

More than half of the squadron's officers were ensigns, fresh from flight school and hailing from towns all across America. Willard H. Youtz, A-V(N), USNR, for example, came from Burns, Wyoming; John C. Moore, A-V(N), USNR, from Bell, California; Harold E. Porter, A-V(N), USNR, from Beckley, West Virginia; and Grover J. "Jake" Marvin, A-V(N), USNR, from Lincoln, Nebraska. Happy-go-lucky Marvin cheerfully peppered his speech with so many profanities that even seasoned naval officers blushed. During one squadron meeting liberally laced with Marvin's foul language, even Beebe's patience reached its end. After the meeting, Beebe reprimanded the young ensign for such unbecoming behavior.

Subdued but not defeated, Marvin assured Beebe that he would work on the problem: "I'm damned sorry, Captain, that my f——g profanity is so G-d-d——ed obnoxious, but I'll sure as hell see that it is corrected immediately."[12]

Another ensign, Eugene Tornquist, A-V(N), USNR, had been a varsity football star and wrestler at Cornell University and had spent a season with the Cincinnati Bengals before leaving the team to join the navy. Tornquist's wife of six months had followed him to the West Coast but would soon be returning to Mitchellville, Iowa, to wait out his war cruise with Tornquist's parents.[13]

In VC-39, most of the aircrew, like most of the pilots, had never been assigned to a carrier, much less sailed into combat aboard one. Shard W.

"Jack" Wells, an aviation machinist's mate second class, was an exception. "Tall, trim, and as handsome as a movie star," according to a hometown paper in Oklahoma, Wells had enlisted in the navy at the age of seventeen on September 1, 1941.[14] Following boot camp and aviation machinist's mate school in Seattle, Wells headed for Pearl Harbor, arriving two weeks after the Japanese attack. He immediately shipped out in *Lexington* and, like Parachute Rigger James Gibbons, survived her sinking in the Battle of the Coral Sea. Aboard *Liscome Bay*, Wells was assigned to one of the Avenger torpedo bombers.

Seaman Second Class Lloyd D. Whalen, a draftee from a small town forty miles east of Lubbock, Texas, also joined *Liscome Bay* with VC-39. Whalen was one of the squadron's alternates awaiting orders for radio operator school so he could eventually help man one of the squadron's TBM Avengers. After watching a string of crashes of the torpedo bombers as the novice pilots struggled to master their new aircraft, and noting that the radio operators seldom survived such incidents, Whalen had decided that radio operator school could wait indefinitely.

Seaman First Class James D. Honold, one of the squadron's parachute riggers, had joined the navy on February 23, 1943. Because Honold was only seventeen at the time, his parents had to sign his enlistment papers for him at the recruiting station in Little Rock, Arkansas. After boot camp in San Diego, he served as a plane captain at Alameda NAS before completing three months of a parachute rigger course. He joined VC-39 to pack and rig parachutes for the squadron's pilots and aircrews. Soon after he came aboard *Liscome Bay*, Honold encountered a pleasant surprise. One of his first cousins, Seaman Second Class Clayton C. Rucker, was also on the carrier. As with Wiltsie's nephews and the Homec brothers, the first combat voyage of the ship was destined to be a family affair for Honold.

With the pilots and aircrews safely aboard, *Liscome Bay* steamed out to sea once again, this time to qualify the pilots and train the ship's launch, landing, and rescue teams. The qualifying exercises made for many anxious moments aboard the small escort carrier. With an overall ship's length well short of two football fields, there was literally no room for error. According to Ensign Daily's recollection, two or three planes were lost during the violent takeoffs from and landings on *Liscome Bay*.

He later commented, "We began to learn about death during those qualifying flights. Life as a pilot or plane crew was not for the faint of heart."[15]

It certainly wasn't. During aircraft launches, the flight deck crews, often called "airedales," presided over a scene of controlled chaos. While some manhandled airplanes into position for takeoff, others fueled and armed the aircraft. Scrambling maintenance men would clamber onto wings, tear open and slap shut cowlings, and leap clear just before the catapults hurled the aircraft aloft. All the while, the flight deck crew kept a careful eye out to avoid being decapitated or blown overboard by a whirling propeller blade. Looking back on their activities, a pilot from another carrier recalled that "a flight deck would not be, could not be, worth taking to sea without them."[16]

Takeoffs from *Liscome Bay* held plenty of excitement for the pilots as well. Positioned on the hydraulic catapult mechanism that ran along the port side of the flight deck, they would signal they were ready for takeoff with a quick thumbs-up. Then they would be blasted into the air at seventy miles per hour, fighting to keep control of the plane as they cleared the flight deck at the bow of the ship.

The real challenge, however, came when the pilot tried to return to his shipboard home. First, he would enter the ship's racetrack landing pattern. Dropping his flaps and lowering his landing gear (cranking them down by hand if he was flying a Wildcat), he would drop down to approximately sixty to seventy feet above the water and bring his air speed down to just above stall speed. It was a delicate moment—a stall at that altitude, with no altitude to recover, would likely be fatal.

Flying the traffic pattern was only a prelude to the excitement that was to come. Circling around to come in over the carrier's stern, the pilot had to rely on directions from the ship's landing signal officer (LSO) for the last three hundred feet of the approach. Signaling with handheld paddles from the carrier's deck, the LSO would guide the incoming pilot in. If all looked good, he would signal "cut" and the pilot would cut power for the landing. If the approach was unacceptable, however, the LSO would desperately signal a "wave-off," sending the aircraft around for another attempt.

Assuming he received the coveted "cut" signal, the pilot would cut power and execute what was really little more than a controlled crash landing. Ideally, one of the arresting cables stretched across the flight deck would catch the plane's tail hook and pull the speeding aircraft to a stop. If the tail hook failed to catch, however, the aircraft would continue down the deck and smash into the crash barrier. Needless to say, snagging a cable with one's tail hook was the preferred method of coming to a halt. Fireman James King took a dim view of the ongoing carrier landing training. "We sure did tear up some airplanes," he recalled.[17]

Lieutenant Robert E. Ries Jr., A-V(N), USNR, VC-39's flight operations officer, kept a careful eye on the proceedings and likely shared King's opinion. Ries knew from firsthand experience the importance of having a well-trained squadron. Previously he had served in the South Pacific with the navy's fabled Torpedo Squadron 8. Half of the squadron, assigned to the carrier *Hornet* (CV-8), had been virtually wiped out during the Battle of Midway when gallantly pressing home an attack on the enemy carriers without fighter support. Ries was among the fortunate ones who had not flown that mission. He and the survivors later saw plenty of action, however, when the remnants of the squadron were transferred to the carrier *Saratoga* (CV-3) and fought in the various engagements to secure Guadalcanal in the late summer and autumn of 1942. Ries earned a Navy Cross and Distinguished Flying Cross while flying an Avenger in those engagements.

Not all of Ries's attention, however, was focused on the young carrier's air operations. On September 25, his wife, Helen, had given birth to their second child, Robert E. Ries III. During this time Helen was back in Decatur, Illinois, with Ries's brand-new son and their young daughter, hoping for the best and anxiously scanning every mail delivery as Ries and his shipmates put *Liscome Bay* through her paces off the Pacific coast.

Despite the best efforts of Beebe and Ries, accidents happened—sometimes with tragic results. On October 16, Lieutenant Joseph W. Castello, USN, guided in his Wildcat toward the flight deck. The LSO signaled "cut," but Castello's angle was too high. His Wildcat slapped down on the deck but missed catching its tail hook on the arresting cables. Veering to port, Castello brought the squat fighter back down again, only to strike the port stanchions anchoring the no. 2 and no. 3

crash barriers. His port landing gear sheared off, his starboard gear buckled, and the fighter slipped over the final cable. Skidding diagonally to starboard, Castello's Wildcat plunged over the starboard side.

The fighter dropped into the water with a heavy splash. At the time, Beasley was on the bridge performing signaling duties, and he ran over to the starboard side of the superstructure. Looking down, Beasley recognized Castello. He had first seen the lieutenant back on the dock in San Diego a little over a week ago and had, in the meantime, seen him often on the ship's flight deck. In a flash, Beasley remembered Castello kissing his wife and small child good-bye just before boarding *Liscome Bay*.

Now, however, Castello was struggling frantically to extricate himself from his cockpit. In the end, he simply didn't have enough time. With a rapidity that astonished the men aboard the carrier, the Wildcat sank beneath the waves, taking Castello with it. He had been a relatively experienced aviator, with no previous accidents and over 550 hours of flying under his belt. His death delivered a painful reminder to VC-39 of the dangers of their duties.[18]

A somber *Liscome Bay* completed that lethal set of carrier qualifications and returned to San Diego to load a wide range of military supplies destined for the Hawaiian Islands. The ship's hangar deck became an improvised warehouse, stacked fifteen feet high and end to end with crates of all shapes and sizes. The carrier's aircraft, wings folded, were relegated to the exposed flight deck. The war in the Pacific beckoned, and *Liscome Bay* needed a full complement of crew. Over the past several days, with a growing sense of urgency, the navy had scoured the naval bases and shore-based aviation squadrons of the West Coast for men to fill her ranks.

Aerographer's Mate First Class Donald A. Cruse was one such man. He and Aerographer's Mate Second Class Perry L. Bruce Jr. had been sitting in the pool of aerographer's mates at Alameda NAS when orders arrived sending them to *Liscome Bay*. As an aerographer's mate—the navy's version of an assistant weatherman—Cruse was familiar with carrier operations. He had enlisted in the navy in 1940, graduated from the ninety-day Primary Aerographer School at NAS Lakehurst, New Jersey, and then served on the carrier *Ranger*. Naval aviation was still a small, close-knit community in those pre–Pearl Harbor days, and the community of weather-watching aerographers and mates was smaller still. It seemed they all knew one another. As Cruse came aboard *Liscome Bay*, he saw a familiar face in charge of the ship's aerology office—Warrant Officer Lyle Blakley, a former *Ranger* shipmate.

Cruse and his fellow new arrival, Bruce, shared an even tighter bond. Both had served in the carrier *Wasp* (CV-7) during the dark days of the Guadalcanal campaign. In fact, if anyone had reason to feel anxiety while stepping onto the small carrier, it was Cruse and Bruce. They knew firsthand that there were few targets more sought-after by Japanese submarine skippers than an American flattop like *Liscome Bay*. Only a little over a year earlier, on the afternoon of September 15, 1942, off San Cristóbal Island, Cruse and Bruce had barely made it off the burning *Wasp* after a Japanese submarine put a pair of torpedoes into its starboard side. Cruse's scarred arms reminded him of the risks shared by all of a carrier's crew—not just the aviators.

Aviation Machinist's Mate Third Class Tim E. Woodham Jr., a dark-haired eighteen-year-old with bright eyes and a ready smile, was another sailor who embarked in San Diego. A native Californian, Woodham had left home at the age of fourteen and gone to work at the Monrovia County Airport in 1939. Living in a hangar, he attended school four hours a day and then worked as one of the airport's "line boys" for another eight. The airfield's owner, Al Blackburn, looked to Woodham to fulfill a variety of tasks—washing planes, cranking props, fetching cushions, helping passengers in and out of aircraft, securing seat belts, and moving planes into hangars at night. Later in his tenure, Woodham progressed to more skilled work, such as re-covering the canvas skin of fabric-covered aircraft, welding steel tubing, and rebuilding wooden wings. He also began taking flying lessons from Blackburn, at a cost of two dollars an hour.

Woodham was at the airfield when word of the Japanese strike on Pearl Harbor arrived. It was a typical Sunday afternoon at the airport. On Sundays, Blackburn would take Ralph Wiggins, a stunt jumper, up in a Waco F-2 biplane for a parachute jump in front of what was always a large crowd. Blackburn would then entertain the crowd with an hour of stunt flying.

Blackburn had rigged up a speaker system at the airfield so the crowd could enjoy music from the local radio station between bouts of flying. Shortly before noon, the radio announcer broke in with news that the Japanese had attacked the Pacific Fleet in Pearl Harbor. The gathered crowd quickly forgot the day's flying at Monrovia. Blackburn's plane bounced in for a landing, and he, his spectators, and sixteen-year-old Woodham crowded around the radio to listen to the incoming news reports.

Woodham turned seventeen the following June, and he enlisted in the navy on October 2, 1942, at a recruiting station in a Los Angeles post office. Boot camp in San Diego followed, after which Woodham volunteered for airplane mechanics school. He was one of seven men sent to Norman, Oklahoma, for the six-month course.

While in Norman, Woodham volunteered for navy flight school. "I lasted thirty minutes into the eye exam, and out the door," he recalled later. "Too much astigmatism."[19] He finished the mechanics course in Norman and then, as a newly designated aviation machinist's mate, attended a two-month aerial gunnery course in Purcell, Oklahoma. Following his sojourn in Oklahoma, it was back to San Diego, where he reported to North Island NAS. There he joined Headquarters Squadron (HEDRON) 14.

Woodham was with HEDRON-14 for two months, serving as a flight engineer for PBY Catalina flying boats with that training unit. His responsibilities included training line mechanics to assume duties as plane captains. It was an enjoyable billet for Woodham, allowing him to log flying time while putting to use the skills he had first begun to develop at Monrovia Airport three years earlier.

On October 21, however, fate dealt Woodham a bad hand. He was summoned that afternoon to the personnel office overlooking San Diego harbor, where the base's personnel officer directed Woodham's attention to the new escort carrier moored down at the pier.

"See that, Woodham?" the officer asked. "That's *Liscome Bay,* your new home," he explained as the office's typewriters clicked and chattered. "We're cutting your orders now. Report on board today before 1700."

"Aye, aye, sir," Woodham responded glumly.[20] He returned to his barracks, packed his seabag, and, that evening, climbed the gangway to his new billet. After he reported on board, one of the chiefs directed Woodham to his new bunk.

Later that night, as Woodham and his fellow airedales slumbered, Wiltsie ordered his crew to prepare to cast off. The time had come for the young carrier and her untried crew to join the war in the Pacific. As sailors prepared *Liscome Bay* to get under way, Daily and fellow ensign Warren A. Schafer, USNR, D-V(G), stepped out on the catwalk below the carrier's bridge for a last glimpse at San Diego. By now, Daily's wife had returned to Philadelphia, and Schafer's wife was home in Galena, Illinois.

As the two ensigns stood on the catwalk, quietly lost in their thoughts, their eyes caught a lone woman standing on the dock. Only the glow of a small lamp illuminated the dock, but Daily recognized the slender woman as Mrs. Helene Barry Wiltsie, the skipper's wife. Daily instinctively looked up at the bridge, where he saw Captain Wiltsie standing above them. As the last line from the carrier fell away into the water, *Liscome Bay*'s captain raised his hand in a final salute to his wife of a dozen years. She waved softly in response.

The carrier's propellers began to churn the dark water. Mrs. Wiltsie remained rooted to the dock, impervious to the evening's chill, as *Liscome Bay* carried her husband away from her and into harm's way. Daily had no doubt that she intended to stand there until the carrier disappeared into the darkness of the bay.

Below the bridge, the two ensigns turned away from each other, neither one wanting the other to see his eyes filling at the poignant farewell they had just witnessed. As *Liscome Bay* drew away from the dock, they were both well aware that they and their captain might never see their spouses again. With lumps in their throats, Daily and Schafer hurried below for a hot cup of coffee and the warm fellowship of the carrier's wardroom.

4
Into the Breach

With Rear Admiral Mullinnix and the staff of Carrier Division 24 aboard, *Liscome Bay* slipped out of San Diego and set a course for Pearl Harbor. Running without an escort, the carrier zigzagged westward at top speed in an effort to foil enemy submarine attacks. Her lookouts sighted no enemy periscopes or torpedoes—just limitless vistas of blue Pacific water and fluttering schools of flying fish. The run to Pearl took only four and a half days. *Liscome Bay* arrived at sunset on October 27, 1943, and since entry into the harbor after dusk was prohibited, the carrier dropped anchor and waited out the anxious night offshore the island of Oahu.

The next morning, *Liscome Bay* stood into Pearl. The sailors crowded on her flight deck and catwalks viewed an unforgettable sight. They marveled at the coral beaches, blue waters, and towering green volcanic mountains of Oahu—a scene of tropical beauty few had seen before—but the island's beauty couldn't hide the carnage left from the Japanese attack twenty-three months earlier. Sailing past the army's Hickam Field, the sailors could still see burned buildings, shattered palm trees, and scorched hulks of mangled planes that had been carted off to the side of the base's revetments and taxiways.

The carrier tied up at Ford Island, and her officers and men went ashore for their first taste of Hawaiian hospitality and a closer look at the damage. They left behind them, on the carrier's flight deck, crowded rows of Wildcats and Avengers. Before *Liscome Bay* had left San Diego, dockworkers had stuffed the hangar deck with crates of all shapes and sizes. As the U.S. military built up its forces in the central Pacific, every westbound ship was being crammed with supplies. *Liscome Bay* was no exception, and her voyage to Hawaii had doubled as a supply run. Captain Wiltsie likely wasn't happy with the conversion of his carrier into a cargo ship, even for five days, so he headed for the Pearl Harbor Officers Club that evening with a sense of relief that dockworkers would begin unloading the crates and returning *Liscome Bay* to a fighting warship.

Wiltsie's satisfaction evaporated in a flash of anger, however, when he returned to the darkened *Liscome Bay* at 0100 the next day. Peering into the shadows of the hangar deck, he realized that not a single crate had been removed from his ship. As a veteran of the early fighting in the Pacific, Wiltsie was aware of how badly American forces needed the supplies in those crates, whether they were in Alaska's frigid Aleutians or the fetid jungles of the Solomons and New Guinea.

"All hands on deck," he ordered grimly.

Within minutes, the ship's company, officers and enlisted, formed up on the dark carrier's deck. Tension hung as thick as one of the California fogs they had left behind them as Wiltsie seethed on the bridge. Finally, he spoke.

"I want all this material off our ship and placed on the dock," Wiltsie snapped at the crew, his anger at the dockworkers boiling over.[1]

The ship's tired officers and sailors quickly turned to work. Although ill-equipped for such stevedore work, they located two or three forklifts and soon put them into action. Other men jury-rigged slings, slides, and skids to start moving the crates out of the hangar deck. It was hot, sweaty work, but by 0430 the hangar deck was clear of the offending crates. Bone-tired, *Liscome Bay*'s weary crewmen hit their bunks. Remarkably, the shared challenge of clearing the hangar deck had cemented crew camaraderie in a way that few other events could have done. "A great team was made that night," Ensign Daily observed.[2]

Liscome Bay remained at Pearl for the next week as stores were loaded for her upcoming operations. Meanwhile, other crewmen continued to filter on board as Wiltsie and Hall worked to bring the carrier up to full combat strength. Aviation Machinist's Mate Second Class John T. Beymer was once such late addition. In early 1943, Beymer had been assigned to NAS Memphis to undergo training in ordnance, radio operations, instrument repair, and meteorology. The fleet, however, needed aerial gunners to man its swelling inventory of Avenger torpedo bombers and to replace men lost in the fighting at Midway and in the Solomons, as well as in accidents and other operational mishaps. Eager to get into action, Beymer volunteered for gunnery training.

By the late summer of 1943, with his instruction complete, Beymer found himself on board one of three LSTs (landing ship, tanks) wallowing their way through Pacific swells with a draft of seasick reinforcements bound for Hawaii. The seas were so rough that one LST turned back. Beymer's ship made it, however, and he quickly received orders to report on board *Liscome Bay*.

Meanwhile, crewmen like Beasley and his comrades in the ship's signal shop continued to marvel at Hawaii's natural beauty. In letters that spoke in vague generalities designed to satisfy the military censors, they wrote home. In a letter to his father, Beasley reported on his arrival at "this place in the South Pacific [*sic*]. I cannot tell you where, but it is nice, sunny, and warm."[3]

But even the comforts of Hawaii couldn't mask the unsettling reality of *Liscome Bay*'s impending combat operations. The day after her crew unloaded the cargo on Pearl Harbor's docks, the carrier stood out of the harbor and rendezvoused with her sister ships *Coral Sea* (CVE-57) and *Corregidor* (CVE-58). Together the trio would make up the ships of Carrier Division 24. The three carriers spent three days at sea, practicing running in their standard triangular steaming formation. They then moved across the Kauai Channel to the nearby island of Molokai, where they supported simulated amphibious landings. By now *Liscome Bay*'s sailors had deduced that they were bound for an island assault somewhere. But where?

Throughout the preparations, the five men in Warrant Officer Blakley's aerology office—Blakley, Cruse, Pinder, Mahood, and Bruce—carried on business as usual. Bruce and Mahood worked together as one duty section, while Cruse and Pinder formed the other. Several times a day they would step out onto the ship's port-side catwalk and into the ship's thermoscreen—a small instrument shelter enclosed by louvered wood. There they could consult various instruments and record the day's temperature, dewpoint, and humidity. Every morning they would launch a helium-filled weather balloon from the balloon inflation room adjacent to the aerology office. By allowing the balloon to rise into the air for three or four minutes and then tracking its drift, they could judge the various wind speeds aloft. Their various weather and wind readings would factor into the critical flying forecasts that Blakley incorporated into his weather briefings to Captain Wiltsie, Lieutenant Commander Beebe, and the Carrier Division 24 staff. It was not an enviable position. With regard to the weather, the skipper always wanted "a definite answer, and he wanted it *now*. On a carrier, the weather guy earns his pay."[4]

Seaman William Fisher, who had told his chief that he wanted to strike for a quartermaster rating, was also busy during this time. As part of his training he logged time in the carrier's wheelhouse at the helm of the baby flattop, guiding it through the inter-island waters. His other responsibilities included winding the carrier's chronometer and updating the various navigational charts. None of the charts Fisher had seen gave him any indication of the eventual destination of Carrier Division 24.

The pilots of VC-39 kept busy during this time as well, honing the combat skills that they knew would soon be put to the test. Beebe put his men through their paces in an effort to meld together a coordinated fighting force before they would have to face Japanese Zeros and antiaircraft guns. The frantic training pace stretched the squadron's nerves, and one day, when confronted with a misting spell of rain, Beebe's officers complained about the condition of the flight deck.

"Some of the pilots are grumbling this morning," Beebe told Captain Crommelin, the chief of staff of Carrier Division 24. "They say the flight deck is wet and slick, and could be dangerous." Beebe's mistake was uttering that warning within earshot of Wiltsie and Rear Admiral Mullinnix. As Wiltsie quickly ordered the carrier to turn into the wind for launch, Crommelin let loose a string of profanities.

"Order a plane ready and to the flight deck," Crommelin snapped as he left the bridge to go to his quarters. Moments later, he appeared on the wet flight deck in his flight gear and climbed into a Wildcat. With a roar of his engine and the clacking rush of the ship's catapult, Crommelin vaulted into the air. Banking back around, he made two low passes around the carrier. "Now, Beebe, get those planes into the air," the chief of staff ordered, punctuating the radioed command with another burst of profane comments. Back on the carrier, the chastened pilots sprinted to their aircraft while Rear Admiral Mullinnix chuckled his approval.[5]

Seaman Honold and his fellow parachute riggers were also busy. Because of the humidity, they had to inspect and repack each chute at least once every fifteen days. *Liscome Bay* had no parachute rigging room, so the riggers had to wait until the mess hall emptied after meals. They would then push the tables together, inspect and pack the chutes, and haul them back to the parachute storage room next to the pilots' ready room. From there, Honold would issue chutes to aircrew as necessary.

By the end of the intense training period in the Hawaiian waters—which, on its last day, had included another fatal FM-1 training accident—*Liscome Bay*'s crew was dog-tired. With bleary eyes, they watched the carrier stand into Pearl Harbor once again. There was no liberty that night, however, and the tired crew hit their bunks with heavy heads. Later that evening, Hawaii's air defenses detected an incoming aircraft. Its identity was unknown, and when it failed to correctly respond accurately to the IFF (identification, friend or foe) signals flashed by the island's nervous defenders, they didn't hesitate to sound the alarm. General quarters sounded across the harbor and on the numerous vessels within it. On board *Liscome Bay*, the crew's exhaustion was so complete that the blare of the alarm succeeded in raising only about 10 percent of them. Fortunately, the incoming aircraft turned out to be an American plane.

On November 10, 1943, *Liscome Bay* sortied from Pearl Harbor once more. A final load of supplies, including dozens of Thanksgiving turkeys, provided a subtle indication that the escort carrier would not be returning to port anytime soon. She soon joined with *Coral Sea* and *Corregidor* and, escorted by the destroyers *Franks* (DD-554), *Hoel* (DD-533), *Hughes* (DD-410), and *Morris* (DD-417), headed out to sea. Soon thereafter, *Liscome Bay*'s task group linked up with Carrier Task Force 52. This task force, which would become known as the Northern Attack Force in the impending operation, would eventually boast the battleships *New Mexico* (BB-40), *Mississippi* (BB-41), *Idaho* (BB-42), and *Pennsylvania* (BB-38), the three escort carriers of Carrier Division 24, four heavy cruisers, and fourteen destroyers. Five auxiliaries—*Neville* (APA-9), *Alycone* (AKA-7), *Pierce* (APA-50), *Leonard Wood* (APA-12), and *Calvert* (APA-32)—and *Belle Grove* (LSD-2) sheltered among them. They carried units of the army's 27th Infantry Division, a green unit that was eagerly—and perhaps naively—looking forward to its first combat operation. Task Force 52 was only one of three task forces at sea that day. Together, these three—comprising thirteen battleships, eight heavy cruisers, four light cruisers, four *Essex*-class carriers, four *Independence*-class small carriers, four escort carriers, seventy destroyers and destroyer escorts, over nine hundred aircraft, and nearly ninety transports and auxiliaries—represented the largest and most powerful U.S. naval force assembled in the Pacific up to that point in the war.[6]

Overall, this mighty armada, as part of the U.S. Navy's Fifth Fleet, fell under the command of Vice Admiral Raymond A. Spruance, USN. He was the officer who, along with Rear Admiral Frank J. Fletcher, had helped deliver victory at Midway. Although the Fifth Fleet as a whole fell under Spruance, Rear Admiral Richmond K. Turner, USN, commanding V Amphibious Corps, would be responsible for the amphibious stage of the impending naval operation. Once the troops went ashore they would be under the command of Major General Holland M. "Howling Mad" Smith, USMC.

For now, however, the invasion portion of the fleet came under Turner's purview. He made the battleship *Pennsylvania* his flagship. A 1908 graduate of the Naval Academy, Turner had logged time in destroyers, cruisers, and battleships in addition to earning his wings in Pensacola in 1927. The Japanese attack on Pearl Harbor had found him in Washington, D.C., where he was responsible for the navy's war plans. Gifted with an intellect capable of absorbing and retaining the smallest detail, pushed by a relentless drive, and expecting the same of his subordinates, Turner would later be described by *Time* magazine as "a mean son of a bitch."[7] His star had dimmed briefly when his war plans staff failed to accurately divine Japanese intentions leading up to Pearl Harbor. His army colleagues on the staff, to whom Turner was seldom capable of referring without the adjective "goddamned," were not sorry to see him go.

Despite Turner's forceful personality, the navy realized that he had much to offer the service, and in 1942 it placed him in charge of the amphibious portion of Operation Watchtower, the U.S. invasion of Guadalcanal. His experience with Watchtower, although marred by the disastrous Battle of Savo Island, made Turner one of the navy's leading authorities on amphibious assaults and operations. With *Pennsylvania* now flying his flag, it was clear that Turner had been entrusted with another operation—this one involving the mostly untried officers and sailors of *Liscome Bay*.

With Pearl Harbor receding in the distance, the destination of Turner's armada was the foremost thought on every officer's and sailor's mind. Many sailors predicted the Aleutians. Although the U.S. military had recently recaptured the Japanese-occupied Aleutian islands of Attu and Kiska, the sailors reasoned that they were being sent north to reinforce America's northernmost frontier from further attack.

Ensign Daily and the rest of the ship's supply department knew that such predictions were wishful thinking. They hadn't loaded any cold-weather gear at Pearl Harbor, which made operations off the Alaskan coast seem unlikely. One hour outside Pearl Harbor, Wiltsie's voice came over *Liscome Bay*'s loudspeakers and announced the invasion force's true destination: the Japanese-held Gilbert Islands, two thousand miles distant in the central Pacific. The skipper of the nearby *Corregidor* was even more dramatic. "We have just changed course to 270," he announced to his crew, "and that's not in the direction of Chicago!"[8]

Today, the Gilberts are part of the independent nation of Kiribati, but at the beginning of World War II they were a British colonial possession. Apart from the production of phosphate on the island of Banaba, the islands offered little other than their location. That particular attribute was enough for the Japanese, however, who were seeking to establish a perimeter of bases to block any advance on their homeland. Accordingly, in 1941, Japan's 51st Naval Garrison Unit occupied the Gilberts and began fortifying them.

The following year brought Japanese setbacks and defeats in the Battles of Coral Sea and Midway, coupled with American landings on Guadalcanal. By the middle of 1943 the tide seemed to be turning. The Allies had blocked Japanese advances in New Guinea, secured Guadalcanal in January 1943, and retaken the Aleutians. Now the United States and its allies were ready to begin the push toward Tokyo.

The Joint Chiefs of Staff, trying to balance the competing demands of army generals and navy admirals to support each group's pet offensive plans, compromised with a two-pronged approach. From New Guinea, soldiers under the command of General Douglas MacArthur would push northwestward, with their eyes on a return to the Philippines. Spruance, under the watchful eye of Admiral Chester W. Nimitz—the navy's commander in chief in the Pacific—bore responsibility for the second prong of the American strategic offensive, which would be directed south and westward from Hawaii and into the central Pacific. Nimitz wanted to strike directly and deeply into the Marshalls, but there were simply not enough trained troops or warships to support both MacArthur's operations and a strike by Spruance's forces so far into the perimeter belt of Japanese-held islands. Accordingly, the Joint Chiefs directed Spruance to first seize island bases in the Gilberts as the initial step in his advance eastward. They labeled the impending invasion of the Gilberts Operation Galvanic.

In the Gilberts, the Japanese had fortified a number of the islands, which were little more than low-lying coral atolls arranged in roughly circular patterns around interior lagoons. Mulling over aerial photographs and intelligence reports, the navy decided to target and seize the Tarawa and Makin Atolls. The men of the 2nd Marine Division would assault Tarawa. Approximately a hundred miles to the north, a regimental combat team of the army's 27th Infantry Division, built around the troops of the 165th Infantry Regiment, would attack Makin. The troops of the 165th were reinforced by a detachment from the 105th Infantry, two tank companies of the 193rd Armor Battalion, and three batteries of the 105th Field Artillery. In all, 6,470 army officers and men formed the Makin invasion force.[9] D-Day for them was set for November 20—ten days away. The navy labeled the Makin portion of Galvanic as Operation Kourbash.

Three of the naval task forces converged on the Gilberts in support of Operations Galvanic and Kourbash. Task Force 52, which contained *Liscome Bay,* bore responsibility for escorting the six ships of the 165th Regimental Combat Team and supporting their invasion of Makin. Once at sea, it sped toward its distant target. Although Tarawa, with its airfield facilities and heavier defenses, was the primary target, Turner elected to position himself with Task Force 52. He realized that Makin lay closer to the Japanese-held Marshall Islands and that U.S. forces in Makin's waters would likely be the first to suffer an enemy counterattack. Turner might have been a "mean son of a bitch," but he wasn't afraid to put himself in what would likely be the thick of the fighting if the Japanese retaliated against the American invaders.

Shortly after Captain Wiltsie announced the task force's military target to his ship, Admiral Turner, the task force commander, underscored the deadly business *Liscome Bay* and her fellow ships were now undertaking by conducting antiaircraft gunnery drills. Land-based planes from Hawaii towing targets behind them appeared in the skies over the task force. Gunnery officers barked orders over their bullhorns, and the antiaircraft crews blasted away at the banners with newfound concentration. For all they knew, the next time they fired their guns it would be at real targets.

With gunnery practice complete, Carrier Division 24, accompanied by one or two destroyers, began a routine that would last for the remainder of its time with the task force. Every two hours, the three escort carriers would leave the safe fold of the task force. Turning into whatever wind was available, they would launch and retrieve planes that were out flying combat air patrol for the task force. Blackshoe—that is, nonaviator—officers like Daily continued to marvel at the operations on *Liscome Bay*'s short flight deck. As he commented, takeoffs and landings aboard the escort carrier "were rarely routine."[10]

The launches of the heavy Avengers were especially exciting. The takeoff process would begin with airedales positioning the fully fueled and armed Avenger on the catapult and then scurrying out of the way as the pilot revved his powerful engine up to its launch rpm. Following a quick thumbs-up from the pilot, the Avenger would hurtle toward the end of the flight deck, mere dozens of feet away. Once clear of the deck, the heavily laden plane would disappear from sight, to all appearances plummeting toward the sea. At times it would be nearly ten seconds before the Avenger labored back up into sight off the end of the flight deck. This dangerous business took nerves of steel.

The launches from *Liscome Bay*'s deck were, in fact, more hair-raising than the ship's designers, or the navy, had intended. According to the specifications, she was supposed to be capable of making 20.5 knots under full speed. Captain Wiltsie and his chief engineer, Lieutenant Commander Richard W. MacAdams, E-V(G), USNR, had discovered, however, that the carrier was cursed with inadequate blowers attached to its exhaust system.[11] Any speed over 19 knots caused disturbing amounts of black smoke to billow from her stacks. Obviously, such telltale smoke—which would have been visible to an enemy aviator or submariner from miles away—was unacceptable. Consequently, Wiltsie kept his ship below 19 knots. In the often windless conditions of the Pacific, this made takeoffs for the ship's pilots particularly challenging if not outright dangerous. One aviator recalled that the fully loaded Avengers could not "be flown away safely with less than 30 knots of wind over the deck and should not be landed with less than 26 knots." Nevertheless, "it was necessary for the squadron to land part of the time with less than 20 knots."[12] This meant that the Avengers would arrive back on deck with a much higher relative speed than desired.

Faced with the speeding Avengers, the ship's arresting gear officer ordered that the cross-deck pendants be tightened in order to stretch the arresting gear cable more tautly across the deck. This was a controversial decision, and the wardroom banter among the pilots generally sided in favor of looser pendants. Their planes might get more banged up on a typical landing, but a too-tight arresting gear cable could trigger a catastrophic landing if the plane was traveling too fast. Nevertheless, the arresting gear officer kept the pendants tight, and the pilots continued to land with extra beads of sweat dotting their foreheads.

In addition to the regular launches and landings of the combat air patrol, *Liscome Bay* settled into a daily routine. Sailors stood their assigned watches, then caught whatever naps they could between the gunnery and fire-fighting drills. At least once a day they assembled for their "clean sweep down fore and aft" to ensure that the ship was free of debris that could damage a plane's propeller or serve as fuel for a fire at sea. Meanwhile, Blakley and his aerography staff kept a careful eye on the weather, Daily tended to his paymaster paperwork, and Dorie Miller and his fellow cooks kept the crew supplied with hot biscuits of such quality and quantity that the ship's veterans remembered them fondly years later. In the air plot, the staff planned the carrier's daily missions as

Mullinnix, Crommelin, and his staff kept their eyes on *Liscome Bay* and her sister ships.

During those days, Aviation Metalsmith Third Class Laurent S. Aden found a few spare moments to pen a quick letter to his parents back in Cincinnati. He knew that navy censors would cut out any references to his ship or his voyage, so he kept his letter short and general. "You may not hear from me for a long time," he concluded.[13]

On the second day at sea, Beebe led VC-39 aloft for a tactical exercise. Joining with the Wildcats and Avengers flying from *Corregidor* and *Coral Sea*, the aviators simulated an air attack on their task force. The exercise revealed a troubling deficiency among the aviators of Carrier Division 24—there had been little time to train together as a group. Owing to their unfamiliarity with each other's flying habits and skills and their dispersal on three different ships, most of their operational coordination had to take place by radio once they were in the air. In combat, radio discipline and, at times, radio silence would be critical. Officers like Mullinnix and Beebe likely wondered if their aviators would have enough time in the next few days to come together as an effective tactical team.

In fact, Beebe began to doubt whether all of his pilots were qualified for the difficult task of flying from the short escort carrier. Ensign Frederic C. Fairman, A-V(N), USNR, a young naval reserve officer from Rhode Island, had arrived as a replacement to fill an empty slot in VC-39's ranks just before *Liscome Bay* had left San Diego. Watching Fairman handle his Wildcat, Beebe wondered who had decided the young ensign was ready for combat operations.

Pulling Fairman aside one day, Beebe learned that the ensign had only eight carrier landings to his credit. He asked to look at Fairman's flight log, and as he spoke with the ensign Beebe eventually concluded that the aviator was simply not ready for the operational tempo of wartime flying. Privately, Beebe doubted that he was even ready for carrier operations at all. At the end of their conversation, Beebe squeezed behind a typewriter in a crowded office aboard the ship and banged out a quick memorandum in which he recommended that Fairman be restricted from flying duties until further shore-based training could be conducted. He passed his memorandum to Wiltsie, who concurred and passed the information on to Mullinnix. Mullinnix, however, needed every aviator he could get his hands on if Carrier Division 24 was going to be able to fulfill its mission in the hostile waters of the Gilberts. He sent his decision regarding Beebe's recommendation back down the chain—disapproved. Fairman kept flying.[14]

Beebe had a problem of a different sort with another one of his pilots. Nineteen-year-old Ensign Frank Sistrunk, A-V(N), USNR, had never passed his pilot swimming qualification tests. Obviously, this was a serious deficiency for a naval aviator. Before they sailed, Beebe had summoned the husky Louisiana native, whom he recalled as a "short, cocky lad," to explain his delinquency. "I just can't get the knack of it!" Sistrunk had exclaimed. "We never had a swimming pool in our town, not even a lake or a stream big enough for a swimming hole."[15]

Beebe had nodded. He knew that Sistrunk's failure wasn't for lack of trying. For weeks the ensign had risen each morning long before flight quarters and headed for the swimming pool to practice. Then, between flights, he would be back in the pool. He had managed to learn to swim with desperate, catlike strokes, but the remaining qualifications—the sprint swim, fire-on-the-water evasion tactics, the mile swim, and prolonged floating—were apparently well beyond his current aquatic abilities.

Beebe should have transferred Sistrunk to another squadron going to sea at a later date in order to give the ensign more time to pass the swimming tests. The fact of the matter, however, was that Sistrunk was a natural pilot. In addition, his gunnery skills placed him at the top of the squadron. Beebe needed all the good pilots he could get his hands on—swimmers or not—and so he had brought Sistrunk aboard. Consequently, Beebe and VC-39 were heading for Makin with a talented pilot who couldn't swim and a young aviator barely qualified for carrier operations. Beebe probably wondered what else he would learn about his aviators once the unbloodied squadron first encountered the Japanese.

On November 12, *Liscome Bay*'s 20- and 40-millimeter gun crews conducted further antiaircraft gunnery practice, this time shooting at balloons. That same day, while some of his aviators flew antisubmarine patrol, Beebe's squadron trained for attacks on enemy shipping. One of the task force's warships towed a target spar behind it, and the Wildcats and Avengers of VC-39 practiced strafing and glide-bombing attacks.

The following two days brought similar activities—combat air patrols, antisubmarine patrols, antiaircraft gunnery drills, and simulated air attacks by VC-39's aviators on the task force's ships. Meanwhile, the troops of the 165th Regimental Combat Team test-fired and cleaned their weapons as their officers pored over maps of Makin aboard their hot and crowded transports.

On November 15, disaster struck. Ensign Fairman climbed into his Wildcat, gave the catapult launch crew the thumbs-up signal, and roared off the end of the deck. The frightening sounds of an underpowered engine warned the flight deck crew of trouble. Seconds later, Fairman's Wildcat plummeted into the sea, six hundred feet off the carrier's starboard bow. The downed fighter came to rest on its belly. Aviation Machinist's Mate Tim Woodham had been standing on the flight deck as Fairman took off, tending to his Avenger. At the sight of Fairman's crash, he and other crewmen ran to the starboard side of the ship. As the carrier pulled alongside the ditched Wildcat, Woodham and his fellow sailors soon had front-row seats for an unfolding tragedy.

Below them, the young khaki-clad ensign struggled to pull himself out of the cockpit. He was obviously having trouble making what should have been a routine escape. By now, the carrier had drawn close enough for the crew to see the fear etched on the ensign's face. Apparently, his left foot was pinned in the cockpit beneath the rudder pedal. Despite his frantic tugs at his left knee, Fairman couldn't dislodge his foot. A few seconds later, the Wildcat's heavy engine pulled the nose down. For a moment, the aircraft's tail stuck above the waves like a makeshift cross. Then it followed the ditched fighter and its pilot in their plunge into the ocean's depths. Fairman, despite Beebe's and Wiltsie's best efforts, had become *Liscome Bay*'s first casualty in Operation Galvanic. His body was never recovered.[16]

Despite the loss of Fairman, on November 16 the crew entertained themselves with navy tradition when Task Force 52 crossed the equator. At that point, the carrier's young crew realized that there were two kinds of sailors: those who had crossed "the line" before, and those who had not. Men in the former group were known as "shellbacks"; the latter group contained the "pollywogs," and they made up about 90 percent of

Liscome Bay's crew. The pollywogs wouldn't graduate to shellback status until they withstood the ritual of the ship's Neptune party.

The festivities, if one could call them that, began with the pollywogs wandering around the ship, clad in bizarre uniforms as dictated by the ship's few shellbacks. Tradition spared no one, not even the officers, and Daily found himself snaking through the ship's passageways and across her decks clad only in his skivvies and electrical wire, chanting "Morning becomes Electra" and similar obscure doggerel.

After an ignominious half hour, the pollywogs assembled on the flight deck. Clustered in an expectant pack, they watched as King Neptune and his Court rose from the depths of the ship on the forward elevator. A fat chief petty officer, bare from the waist up, played the role of King Neptune. Painted in green and white, he wore a cotton mop for a wig.

King Neptune led his retinue grandly onto the flight deck, where more festivities ensued. The King pronounced that it was time for the pollywogs to be initiated into the "Solemn Mysteries of the Ancient Order of the Deep" and summoned the Court's Royal Barber forward. With a pair of aviation metal shears, the Royal Barber commenced shaving the eight hundred or so pollywog heads, which were then doused with a nasty mix of fuel oil and graphite. Blasts from a fire hose completed the bathing. Shellbacks grabbed pollywogs, blindfolded them, and dropped them down the flight deck elevator shaft, where they landed in a tank of water that had been placed on the partially elevated flight elevator.

From there, the shellback party degenerated even further into chaos. Woodham endured electric shocks and a terrible food concoction while watching other crewmen have red crosses painted on their heads. Daily remembered running through a gauntlet of paddle-wielding shellbacks, while Fireman James King recalled having to crawl through a parachute packed with garbage and then being dragged before King Neptune. The jolly King Neptune ordered King to kiss the rotund belly of his "baby," who was portrayed by one of the ship's cooks. King complied with as much good nature as he could muster.

Once the festivities ended and the flight deck was cleared of debris, the crew returned to business as usual. There were no flight operations that day, but the carrier refueled from a tanker. She also took on more aviation fuel for the aircraft of VC-39. The ship returned to its routine on November 17—combat air patrols, antisubmarine patrols, and gunnery practice.

During this time, Daily enjoyed a special treat for a naval officer. Fred Sheppard, his assistant in the disbursing office, invited the paymaster to dine one evening in the chief petty officers' mess. Typically, the officers and chiefs were careful to adhere to regulations and rigorously maintained the separation between the two groups. Consequently, it was a high compliment for Daily to garner an invitation to the chiefs' mess, and the highlight of the voyage for the young officer.

On November 18, Captain Wiltsie addressed the crew over the loudspeaker: "This is the captain. We are going to attack Makin Island. We are being depended upon for air support for the invasion. There is no question in my mind that every man will do his job and do it well. We are going to strike with everything we have and strike day and night until our job is done. That is all now. Good hunting."[17]

That day, the task force began to transition to its invasion tasks. Avengers from the escort carriers ranged out in front at a distance of 170 miles, scouring the seas and skies for signs of enemy activity. Despite the enemy's reverses at Guadalcanal, Coral Sea, and Midway, the Japanese still possessed a formidable fleet, and the invasion of the Gilberts meant that the Americans were operating on the front steps of occupied Japanese territory. The threat of sailing into an enemy trap was very real, and Admiral Turner, his reputation still singed by the disastrous Battle of Savo Island, was taking no chances.

Turner's caution proved justified. On November 18, Japanese planes stumbled across the sluggish flotilla of LSTs, sailing separately some distance away as Task Group 52.6. A running dogfight ensued, with Wildcat fighters eventually splashing a Mitsubishi G4M "Betty" twin-engine bomber. The next day, more Japanese planes made an appearance. The LSTs escaped damage once more, although this time their antiaircraft gunners claimed a Mitsubishi G3M "Nell" bomber.

The fliers on board *Liscome Bay* had yet to see their first Japanese plane. On the carrier, the most excitement for VC-39 came when Frank Sistrunk hesitantly reported to Lieutenant Commander Rowe, the ship's flight surgeon, that he was experiencing sharp stomach pains. Rowe quickly diagnosed acute appendicitis. He performed a successful emergency appendectomy on Sistrunk, but the ensign would be out of action for over a week. Unhappily, Sistrunk settled into a bunk in the sick bay.

On November 19 the first reports of unidentified aircraft within range of *Liscome Bay* came in, and VC-39 scrambled patrols of Wildcats that struggled to reach altitude in time to intercept the Japanese. In the end the reports turned out to be bogus. As the day progressed, the radar operators reported other groups of enemy aircraft, and further scrambles revealed these to be false alarms as well. *Liscome Bay*'s pilots accepted the faulty warnings philosophically. They knew that the next day—November 20, 1943—would dawn with the invasion of Makin. Soon there would be action for everyone.

5
Galvanic and Kourbash

The appearance of Turner's invasion flotilla came as a surprise to the Japanese commanders, whose limited intelligence on the movement had led them to believe the ships were bound for the Solomons or New Guinea. Capitalizing on that surprise, American aviators began striking at the Japanese forces. On November 13, heavy bombers from the army's 7th Air Force started pounding the Gilberts and also the Marshall Islands, which lay several hundred miles to the west. Then, as the carriers slipped within range of the islands, their aircraft joined these air attacks on November 19.

The next morning the ships of Task Force 52 crept within gunfire range of Makin, while Task Force 53, escorting the 2nd Marine Division, arrived off the coast of Tarawa. Task Force 50, which had been assigned the role of the covering task force, provided general support to the operation. Its aircraft struck at Makin as well as a number of outlying islands and worked to screen the invasion forces from enemy air or submarine attack. A Japanese naval infantryman, or *rikusentai*, dolefully noted the arrival of the overwhelming American invasion force. "The god of Death has come," he told his comrades on Tarawa.[1]

That evening the Japanese launched their first major counterattack. Sixteen torpedo planes, flying unsupported, streaked through the tropical dusk at *Essex* (CV-9), *Bunker Hill* (CV-17), and *Independence* (CVL-22). American antiaircraft guns chattered to life, splashing eight of the Japanese attackers. The remaining Japanese planes pressed home their attack, focusing on *Independence*. Soon five torpedoes dropped in the water and sped toward the American carrier. Four missed, but the fifth punched into *Independence*'s starboard side. The resulting explosion killed seventeen sailors and wounded forty-three. In a matter of minutes, the aft engine room, fireroom, and magazine flooded as damaged bottom plates strained to keep the rattled carrier intact. Converted from a former cruiser hull, *Independence* was made of stern stuff. She survived and began limping toward Funafuti for repairs.

Before *Independence* departed the area of operations, the task force parceled out some of her veteran pilots to other carriers. Among them was Lieutenant (jg) Foster J. "Crud" Blair, USNR, a veteran combat pilot who had served in *Saratoga* throughout 1942, fought at Guadalcanal, and then flew with VC-21 off the escort carrier *Nassau* during operations in the Aleutians. He had been with *Independence* since June. Following the Japanese attack on *Independence*, however, he transferred to *Liscome Bay*.[2]

On board *Liscome Bay*, the attack on *Independence* caused some rethinking of how the 20- and 40-millimeter antiaircraft guns ringing the carrier were manned. Captain Wiltsie realized that he needed his brawniest men topside to help quickly reload the antiaircraft guns if *Liscome Bay* faced a similar aerial attack. Accordingly, Seaman William Fisher received orders that his general quarters station had changed. Previously his station had been the aft engine steering room, several decks below the waterline in the rear of the ship, where he was prepared to take directions over his headset and steer the ship should the main steering room be knocked out in battle. Now he was assigned to a 20-millimeter gun crew on the carrier's port side. Another sailor, Seaman Second Class Arthur J. Morrow Jr. of Elma, Washington, took Fisher's place belowdecks.

As Fisher reported to his new battle station, *Liscome Bay*'s Wildcat and Avenger pilots focused squarely on Makin Atoll, a roughly triangular formation of islands and reefs that enclosed a large lagoon. Butaritari Island, a long, ribbon-shaped piece of land ending in a shallow curve on the western end, was its most dominant land feature. The army's terrain assessment described the island as "shaped like a crutch with the armrest facing generally west and the leg of the crutch pointing east and slightly north."[3] From lagoon side to ocean side, its average width was about eight-tenths of a mile. In places it was even narrower.

The Japanese had constructed a seaplane base on Makin, taking advantage of the atoll's sheltering lagoon. Approximately five hundred Japanese aviation personnel, ground crewmen, and Korean construction laborers serviced the base, which was home to a variety of Kawanishi H8K2 "Emily" reconnaissance seaplanes and Mitsubishi A6M2-N "Rufe" fighter seaplanes. To defend them, the Japanese stationed three hundred *rikusentai* on the atoll, mostly on Butaritari, and constructed a makeshift line of defenses that consisted primarily of two lines of tank barriers protecting the seaplane base itself. Shielding the western approach, one tank barrier line was approximately twelve feet wide and five feet deep and extended from the lagoon two-thirds of the way across Butaritari. A concrete pillbox, an antitank gun, six machine-gun nests, and fifty rifle pits overlooked the line. On the base's eastern side ran the other tank barrier line, fringed with a double apron of barbed wire. Fourteen feet wide and six feet deep, it ran from the lagoon for two-thirds of the distance to the other side of the island. Palm log barricades further blocked each end of this barrier, which was covered by an intricate system of gun emplacements and rifle pits dug into the atoll's sandy soil.

Overlooking the ocean approaches to Butaritari, the Japanese built a string of gun emplacements containing 8-inch coastal defense guns, three 37-millimeter antitank guns, and ten machine-gun nests. They scattered eighty-five rifle pits among the gun positions. Surveying his small island command, Lieutenant (jg) Seizo Ishikawa knew that his forces, without hope of reinforcement, stood little chance of repelling a determined American assault. Nevertheless, he and his men resolved to make an enemy assault as costly as possible for the attackers.

Ishikawa's forces on Makin were weak, but they would likely have been even weaker had it not been for an American raid on the atoll a year earlier. Back on August 17, 1942, some two hundred marines of the 2nd Raider Battalion, under the command of Colonel Evans F. Carlson, USMC, had disembarked from two submarines, paddled ashore in inflatable rafts, and engaged the four dozen surprised and outnumbered defenders in a day of sporadic fighting. Major James Roosevelt, USMC, one of FDR's four sons serving in the military during the war, saw action on Makin as the Raiders' second-in-command.

Although they annihilated the Japanese garrison, the Raiders soon came under increasing air attack from nearby bases. Struggling with the rough surf in their rubber rafts, the marines executed a confused withdrawal. American casualties for the Makin raid totaled twenty-one killed and nine captured. The Japanese later beheaded the captured marines.

At the time of Carlson's raid, the small garrison on Makin was the only Japanese force in the Gilberts. In response to the raid, the Japanese navy embarked immediately upon a steady buildup of its forces garrisoning the islands. Consequently, by the time the Americans returned to the Gilberts fifteen months later they faced a number of fortified island strongholds rather than a scattering of forgotten administrators and bored rear-echelon troops.

Regardless of the strength of Makin's garrison, the navy and the 165th Regimental Combat Team intended to seize the atoll. To do so they developed a relatively complicated plan for seizing the small island. Following air strikes and a short naval bombardment, the assault would begin with landings from the ocean on Red Beach and Red Beach 2, two beaches on the western side of Butaritari. The Americans hoped that this would draw the Japanese defenders out of their seaplane base citadel to counterattack the amphibious invaders. Then, once the counterattacking Japanese were in the open away from their prepared positions, a second wave would land on Yellow Beach, in the lagoon's atoll on Butaritari's northern side near King's Wharf and Chong's Wharf. Major General "Howling Mad" Smith had pushed for a simple landing and all-out assault on Yellow Beach but had eventually, and unhappily, deferred to the army planners on the staff of Major General Ralph Smith.

Liscome Bay steamed into sight of Makin at dawn on November 20. Commander Hall peered through the early-morning mists in his binoculars and calmly drawled, "There she is."[4] Within minutes, Wildcats and Avengers of *Liscome Bay*, *Corregidor*, and *Coral Sea* launched into the air and headed for the atoll. At 0610, the first Wildcats, their engines screaming, roared across Butaritari and laced the Japanese positions with machine-gun fire. Moments later, the Avenger pilots slanted in toward the narrow island for their bombing runs.

For the next half hour, the carrier pilots lashed at Butaritari's defenders, leaving mangled Japanese seaplanes and burning buildings in their wake. The air attack, however, was only a taste of what awaited Ishikawa's men. At 0640 the battleships *Mississippi* and *New Mexico,* sailing in front of *Liscome Bay,* commenced firing. Lieutenant Gardner Smith, the ship's communications officer, had been a radio announcer in New York before the war. Now, from his vantage point on the bridge beside the executive officer, he observed the scene unfolding before him with eyes seasoned to look for descriptive detail. "Salvo after salvo screamed over the island, stabbing the early morning mist with sheets of flame," he later wrote. "The island seemed to be twisting in a frenzy under the terrific pounding."[5] Huge eruptions of sandy soil and shattered palm trees marked the shells' impacts on the battered island, and soon columns of greasy black smoke were billowing into the tropical sky. An accidental turret explosion aboard *Mississippi* marred the bombardment, killing forty-three sailors and wounding nineteen.

As the remaining naval guns continued to fire, the first wave of assault troops clambered down rope cargo nets from *Leonard Wood, Neville, Alcyone,* and *Pierce.* Weighed down by combat gear, weapons, and ammunition, the troops of the 1st and 3rd Battalions of the 27th Infantry Division's 165th Regimental Combat Team dropped awkwardly into their waiting thirty-six-foot-long LCVPs (landing craft, vehicle and personnel). Somewhere between the top of his helmet and the soles of his combat boots, the typical soldier carried a .30-caliber M1 Garand semiautomatic rifle, enough K rations for two days, pouches of grenades, a long trench knife, and an extra bandolier of ammunition. It all made for a difficult climb down the cargo nets into the LCVPs, but the troops were eager for action. Their regiment traced its lineage back to the famed "Fighting 69th" of World War I fame, but the division's lack of a combat record at this point in the war had caused some wags to label it the "non-fighting 69th." The men piling into the LCVPs were eager to erase that nickname.[6]

As the LCVPs were slowly loaded, two LSTs opened their bows and disgorged eight amphibious tractors, also known as "amtracs" or "alligators." The amtracs and LCVPs began circling impatiently offshore, waiting for the signal to make their run for Red Beach and Red Beach 2.

At 0750, with smoke still rising from battered Butaritari, the landing force's amtracs moved for the line of departure. Crossing it at 0813, they churned noisily toward the two beaches. As rocket fire whooshed overhead, the gunners on the amtracs opened fire with their .30- and .50-caliber machine guns, hammering at unseen enemy positions in the palms and scrub beyond the landing beaches. Ominously, the Japanese defenders, if there were any on this part of Butaritari, didn't return fire.

At 0831 the amtracs crawled onto the beaches, and the GIs, accompanied by the shouts of their officers and sergeants, scrambled over the sides and into the soft sand, ready for their first taste of combat. "I jumped down from my boat and stood straight for two or three minutes, waiting for somebody to shoot me," remembered Major Edward Bradt. "Nobody shot," he added.[7]

Moments later, the LCVPs bringing the rest of the Red Beach and Red Beach 2 landing force headed toward the shore. In all, the Americans planned to put 460 men and eight tanks ashore at the two beaches within a matter of minutes. Their plans quickly went awry. A rising tide lifted several of the LCVPs over the island's reef, after which they were able to make it to the waiting beach, but the majority either ran aground on the reef or, faced with such an obstacle, simply turned around and retired back to sea. That may have been for the best, as both Red Beach and Red Beach 2 were almost hopelessly inadequate for landing. Red Beach was covered in large coral boulders, while Red Beach 2 was only wide enough to allow three landing craft to unload at once. "Just plain stinko profoundo," Admiral Turner would snarl later.[8]

The LCVPs on the reef unloaded their unhappy passengers, and soon the heavily laden infantrymen were slogging through high swells toward the distant beaches, joined in the high surf by equally unhappy tankers nursing their wet vehicles ashore. The 27th Infantry Division had been a New York National Guard unit before the war. No doubt a litany of Brooklyn- and Long Island–accented curses filled the air that morning in the waters off Butaritari. On their way in, the troops passed the amtracs, heading back out to sea to ferry in their fellow soldiers on the other LCVPs.

By the time the last group of assault troops hit Red Beach and Red Beach 2, the invasion was already an hour behind schedule. The 1st Battalion, under the command of Lieutenant Colonel Gerard Kelley, began to push inland from Red Beach. Japanese resistance was minimal, but thick, tangled vegetation, pockmarked with deep, water-filled craters created by the air and naval bombardment, slowed their progress. The 3rd Battalion, under the command of Lieutenant Colonel Joseph Hart, also struggled through the vegetation and debris of the preliminary bombardment as it advanced inland from Red Beach 2. Pushing back a squad of Japanese soldiers, and killing five of them, the two battalions linked up at 1055.

Two hours after the first LVTs (landing vehicle, tracked) headed ashore at Red Beach, the transport *Neville*, accompanied by two LSTs, moved into Makin's lagoon. Containing the regimental combat team's 2nd Battalion, commanded by Lieutenant Colonel John McDonough and accompanied by Company A of the 193rd Tank Battalion and Z Detachment from the 105th Infantry Regiment, these troops were destined for Yellow Beach. At 0830 the first LST opened its bow doors and sent its amtracs beachward. A collection of LCVPs and tank-carrying LCMs (landing craft, motorized) followed. Some of the army troops sang as they headed for the enemy beach, which was still being bombarded by naval gunfire. Others simply munched on cold sandwiches or slept in the LCVPs rocked by the Pacific swells.

When the lead amtracs were six hundred yards off the lagoon's shore, the navy ships lifted their gunfire. Seconds later, carrier aircraft once again appeared in the skies above Butaritari and laced the Japanese positions with several strafing runs. Fuel dumps and ammunition depots exploded with massive roars under the American aerial attack. The mushrooming fireball of one exploding ammunition dump caught one of *Coral Sea*'s Avengers. The pilot pulled up from his bombing run too late, sending the bomber slamming into the island among the coconut trees. Faced with such a spectacle, the amtrac drivers slowed their approach, nervous about coming under fire from the zooming and diving naval aircraft. This marked the first delay at Yellow Beach.

When the LVTs pulled within five hundred yards of the lagoon's beach, the Japanese opened fire at the approaching amtracs. In the chaos of the air attacks, it was impossible to tell exactly where the Japanese were firing from. Nevertheless, the amtracs returned fire as best they could, blasting at the shoreline with .50-caliber machine guns and boat-mounted rockets as their passengers hunkered below their gunwales. The enemy fire seemed to be coming from hidden positions located on two rusted and half-sunk ships in the lagoon as well as from troops stationed on the two cargo wharves stretching into the lagoon. The American LVTs concentrated their return fire on the wharves and hulks as they passed through the enemy crossfire.

At 1041 the first amtracs splashed ashore Yellow Beach. The GIs quickly secured King's Wharf, but they encountered more resistance at Chong's Wharf. After some sharp fighting, the American troops captured the wharf and bagged thirty-five Korean laborers as their confused prisoners. In the meantime, the follow-on waves, transported in LCVPs and LCMs, hit the barrier of the lagoon's reef. Like the landing craft at Red Beach and Red Beach 2, these had to disgorge their troops and tanks far from the shore. Soldiers and tankers struggled and splashed through 250 yards of knee-deep water, dodging heavy gunfire from the two hulks that splashed in the water around them. Fortunately, the Japanese gunfire was inaccurate, and naval gunfire and air strikes against the hulks soon silenced their defenders. The remaining Japanese defenders quickly withdrew inland.

As McDonough's 2nd Battalion completed its landing at Yellow Beach, its lead elements, supported by Lee medium tanks and Stuart light tanks, advanced deeper into Butaritari. By noon they had secured their beachhead and settled in to await the linkup with their sister battalions from Red Beach and Red Beach 2.

On board *Liscome Bay*, the air operations continued at a frantic pace. As the carrier cut a wide circle around the atoll, she launched Wildcats and Avengers to fly combat air patrol, patrol for enemy submarines, or strike at the Japanese ashore Makin. The atoll lay in sight beneath a pall of greasy smoke, with scars of war laid bare for the carrier's sailors to see. "The trees were all just torn down," Seaman Maxsy Homec recalled. "All you could see were the stumps."[9]

In the midst of this activity, Aviation Machinist's Mate Tim Woodham, serving as a TBM Avenger plane captain, continued a mechanical struggle that had plagued him for days. His Avenger's engine had recently undergone its scheduled overhaul, and Woodham, with ears attuned to aircraft engines from his time working with Al Blackburn at the Monrovia Airport, knew that the bearings were too tight. Nevertheless, the flight deck crew positioned Woodham's Avenger for takeoff that afternoon from *Liscome Bay*'s short flight deck. Five times Ensign Willard H. Youtz, A-V(N), USNR, revved up the Avenger's engine, and each time Woodham ran over to the flight officer to warn him that the Avenger still sounded questionable. What might have grounded a plane in peacetime was not going to ground an aircraft needed to protect the ship or to assist army troops ashore in the midst of a combat operation.

"Get the hell out of here," the officer yelled over the roar of the aircraft engines, "or I'll put you on report."[10] Reluctantly, Woodham returned to his post and watched tensely as Youtz confidently gave the thumbs-up signal and rocketed off the end of the flight deck. Like all the heavily laden Avengers, his aircraft plummeted from sight as it cleared the end of the ship, but this time the Avenger didn't pop back into view. Instead, with its engine failing, it slammed into the ocean with a massive crash of spray. For a moment it settled flat atop the ocean swells. Youtz and his top turret gunner managed to scramble out, but Aviation Radioman Third Class Norman Bersin wasn't so fortunate. The Avenger soon sank, taking Bersin with it. A nearby destroyer steamed to the site of the crash, rescued the survivors, and returned them to *Liscome Bay*. In return, *Liscome Bay* sent over to the smaller destroyer the typical reward paid to rescuers of downed airmen—a few gallons of ice cream.

On Butaritari, the 1st and 3rd Battalions advanced eastward along a narrow road that wound through splintered coconut plantations. Their progress, however, soon slowed in the face of Japanese snipers lurking among the palm fronds atop the coconut trees. Confusion about the proper chain of command for the U.S. tanks further stymied progress. Then, the attacking column of tanks and infantry encountered a massive shell crater that blocked the road and bogged down the lead tank. Now the attack stalled altogether. An obstinate Japanese machine-gun nest, skillfully covered by snipers in the surrounding trees, halted the advance on the battalions' left flank. Colonel Gardner Conroy, the regimental commander, trotted to the front to get his troops moving once again. A sniper's bullet hit him between the eyes, killing him instantly and slowing the assault even further.

Eventually, the U.S. soldiers simply contained and bypassed the Japanese strongpoint and continued their advance. In the meantime, the three batteries of the 105th Field Artillery landed at Red Beach and began firing their howitzers in support of the infantry. Major General Ralph Smith, commander of the 27th Infantry Division, arrived onshore and set up his command post. He ordered the 165th's units to halt their advance and dig in for the night. As they did, they tallied their casualties for the first day of fighting as twenty-five killed and sixty-two wounded. Enemy losses amounted to fifty dead and forty-one wounded.

A sleepless night followed for the green American troops. Japanese sniper fire harassed their positions, while other enemy soldiers set off firecrackers and taunted them with garbled English curses. The nervous GIs blasted away into the tropical darkness, wasting ammunition and drawing Japanese fire at their positions. Even after daybreak, a false alarm along the lagoon resulted in dozens of U.S. troops blasting indiscriminately into the tree line.

Meanwhile, on board *Liscome Bay*, the tired but excited pilots of VC-39 made it back to their bunks to catch a few hours of sleep. Gardner Smith found Ensign David P. Barrett, A-V(N), USNR, an Avenger pilot, sitting on his bunk. Barrett, a native of Baltimore, had graduated from Princeton in 1941. He had enlisted the following February, completed flight training in Atlanta and Jacksonville, and joined VC-39 back in April. Barrett had two brothers in the service—one was a naval aviator who had survived the sinking of *Hornet*, and the other was a marine lieutenant.

"What was it like?" Smith asked the twenty-four-year-old pilot.

"We caught them square," Barrett answered. "The Japs threw up a lot of ack-ack. My first bomb was short, but the next two went home."[11] With that said, he rolled over to go to sleep. He had a busy day ahead of him.

On the second day of Operation Kourbash, November 21, the 165th Regimental Combat Team renewed its efforts to complete the capture of Butaritari. Officers ashore called in air strikes on the troublesome half-sunken ships in the lagoon, and VC-39 responded, sending Wildcats and Avengers in over the lagoon to repeatedly strafe and bomb the hulks. By the end of the attacks they had expended more than five thousand rounds of .50-caliber machine-gun ammunition. Army troops moved up and secured the hulks, thereby allowing landing craft to continue to land more troops on Yellow Beach without fear of sniper fire from hidden enemy soldiers.

Meanwhile, other troops of 1st Battalion moved against the pocket that had delayed their advance the previous day. With four Stuart light tanks operating in support and raking the Japanese positions and treetops with machine-gun and 37-millimeter canister shell fire, the Americans were making progress when a navy dive-bomber arrived overhead. Misjudging his location, the pilot dropped a bomb near the tank platoon. Three tankers were killed, including the platoon leader, and several others wounded. By the time the smoke and dust cleared, the Japanese had withdrawn.

Despite such mishaps, the 165th had secured the western side of the island by midday and turned its full attention to the eastern portion of Butaritari. E and G Companies of the 2nd Battalion, a unit of marines from V Amphibious Corps' reconnaissance company, the 105th Infantry's Z Detachment, and ten Lee medium tanks moved into position as the carrier aircraft resumed their ground-attack missions against the island's Japanese defenders.

Once again, Carrier Division 24 sent its Wildcats and Avengers aloft to support the imminent attack. Ripping low across the atoll, they strafed and blasted the eastern side of Butaritari. Despite their best efforts, the ground attacks failed to even begin to approach the level of sophisticated air-ground coordination that would become a staple of American combat operations later in the war. In this particular amphibious operation, "poor communications, poor coordination, and poor training all combined to reduce the effectiveness of the support missions."[12]

The last Wildcat had scarcely flown back out to sea when the Lee tanks and ground troops began to advance eastward, struggling through machine-gun nests, barbed wire, and bunkers reinforced with coconut logs. All the while, snipers sent rifle bullets zipping through the tangled jungle undergrowth around their heads. The narrowness of this part of the island—at places no more than three hundred yards—meant that the GIs couldn't simply maneuver around the stubborn defenders. They had to slug it out toe-to-toe with the enemy, earning every yard of their advance, capturing enemy positions one bunker and pillbox at a time. By the end of the day they had worked their way a thousand yards east and were facing the island's eastern tank barrier.

In addition to contending with the Japanese, Major General Ralph Smith faced another challenge—the arrival of "Howling Mad" Smith. Smith was commander of V Amphibious Corps, which included both the 27th Infantry Division and the 2nd Marine Division that had assaulted Tarawa the day before. Infuriated with what he perceived to be the slow progress of the 27th Division's troops ashore Makin—especially in the face of the bloody and bitter combat the marines were facing on more heavily defended Tarawa—Smith toured the Butaritari landing beaches and pointedly suggested that the 3rd Battalion be sent to Tarawa to assist the marines fighting there. Ralph Smith and Admiral Turner, focused on accomplishing the seizure of Makin per the original battle plan, declined to release the battalion and instead kept it on Makin, where it advanced to relieve the 2nd Battalion for the assault on the eastern tank barrier line. "Howling Mad" received their decision with ill humor, which was likely further exacerbated by a night spent in the army command post on Makin. Errant bullets from nervous American sentries thwacked into the command post's sandbags all night, making for restless hours of darkness for the visiting general.

On the morning of November 22—the third day of the invasion—the troops of the 3rd Battalion, supported by tanks, advanced on the tank barrier. As they did, the guns of the 105th Artillery pounded the Japanese positions, dropping almost nine hundred shells within two hours. As the American assault commenced, the lack of return fire indicated to the advancing GIs that the defenders—if there were any—had withdrawn even further eastward. They discovered only a few Japanese bodies among the shattered fighting positions. Now, only the stifling heat and thick vegetation slowed the 3rd Battalion's advance. Pushing twelve hundred yards further down Butaritari, they halted at 1645 to dig in for the night.

As the troops of the 3rd Battalion pushed forward, *Liscome Bay*'s aviators continued to fly combat air patrols and antisubmarine patrols. On

November 22 the carrier suffered another operational loss. Ensign Barrett, piloting his Avenger, returned to the carrier from his antisubmarine patrol only to discover that he couldn't lower the tail hook of his bomber. Without a tail hook extended to catch the flight deck's arresting cable, there was no hope of landing on the carrier. Wiltsie ordered Barrett to crash-land in the waters of Makin's lagoon.

As Barrett peeled away from *Liscome Bay* and headed for Makin, the smoke from the fighting on Butaritari's eastern side still hung thick in the air. Flying in over the lagoon—and hoping there wasn't a Japanese soldier hiding among the coconut trees waiting to take a shot at him—Barrett smacked his Avenger down on the lagoon's placid waters. He and his enlisted crewmen clambered out of the sinking TBM and inflated their life raft. Within moments, an amtrac churned out from the lagoon's beach and hauled them aboard. The amtrac then turned and headed back to shore, where Barrett and his crew awaited recovery to *Liscome Bay*.

Barrett soon discovered that the army's decision to dig in for the night had been a wise one. Shortly after dark, many of the island's remaining defenders began a series of violent but uncoordinated small-unit attacks, while others attempted to infiltrate the three-hundred-yard-long American line of foxholes and improvised palm log barricades. The GIs' machine guns and Browning automatic rifles chattered throughout the night, warding off each attack. When morning dawned on November 23, the tired Americans counted fifty-one dead Japanese troops in front of their positions. Behind the lines, Barrett longed to return to the "Listing Lizzie."

At 0715 the Americans ashore on Makin resumed their push eastward. Following a spearhead of twenty-one tanks, three companies of the 3rd Battalion quickly mopped up the few remaining Japanese still at large on the eastern end of Butaritari. By 1030 the companies reached the eastern tip of Butaritari. With "Howling Mad" Smith's criticism still ringing in his ears, a satisfied Ralph Smith sent Admiral Turner a succinct message. "Makin taken," he signaled the commander of Task Force 52. The capture of Makin had cost 66 American lives, with another 152 wounded.

The conquest of the atoll came not a moment too soon for the officers and men of *Liscome Bay*. As the GIs ground their way slowly forward across Makin, the men of Carrier Division 24 had a growing sense that their mission was complete. The U.S. fleet had stolen a surprise march on the Japanese navy with its quick thrust into the Gilberts and had successfully put an overwhelming force ashore on Makin. Now it was time to head back out to sea, where a defense against any enemy counterattacks could be more readily mounted.

Rather than slip away to safer waters, however, *Liscome Bay* was tied down with the rest of the task force waiting for the GIs of the 27th Infantry Division to finish mopping up the last pockets of Japanese defenders on Butaritari. The predictable maneuverings of the carriers and their task force back and forth off Makin were inviting trouble. The Japanese knew they were there. Every evening at sunset, a Japanese Betty would fly high overhead, too high to be reached by an interception of Wildcat fighters or a volley of antiaircraft fire. Its nightly presence drove tensions even higher on *Liscome Bay*. "We're going to get hit," an upset Mullinnix reportedly announced one evening in the wardroom.[13]

Despite the tension and the fighting on nearby Makin, life went on for the sailors aboard the jeep carrier in a deceptively routine manner. Seaman Beasley recalled of these days that "for the most part, the operation was routine aboard ship—general quarters, flight quarters, planes taking off and landing to take on fuel and ammunition. We seemed to be far removed from the actual battle. We did hear talk of the difficulties the Marines were having with the invasion at Tarawa. During the more critical times we spent four hours on watch and four off."[14] During some of those off hours during the morning of November 23, Beasley and his good friend Seaman Third Class Chester R. "Chuck" Williams went topside to sit on the catwalk alongside the ship's signal flag bags. As Beasley read *Moby Dick*, Williams fell into a deep sleep. Later, with the approach of noon, Beasley shook his friend awake.

"We'd better go below and get ready for chow," Beasley told Williams.

Williams sleepily opened his eyes with a dreamy smile.

"Sam, I sure wish you would have let me sleep and finish my dream," Williams drawled, using Beasley's shipboard nickname. "I was having the most wonderful dream. The war was over and I was back home in Alabama. It was springtime—the most beautiful spring I had ever seen. The grass was green, the flowers were in bloom, the weather was nice, and it was the most wonderful day of my life. I was with my girlfriend and back on the farm. Both of us were very happy. We had decided to get married. But, before we were to marry, we decided to have a party and invite all our friends."

Beasley nodded. Williams spoke often of his girlfriend—a pretty redhead back in Williams's hometown of Holtamville, a tiny crossroads hamlet in Clarke County, Alabama. "All of our friends and relatives came to the wedding," Williams told Beasley, "and I had invited the entire signal gang from the *Liscome Bay*. Everyone was having a great time." But then, as Williams told his story, a look of concern crossed his face.

"Sam, you were not there. I was very anxious to find you, for two reasons. I wanted you to meet my girlfriend and I wanted to repay the $20.00 I borrowed from you [the day before]. Not being able to find you caused a lot of anxiety. Then, while looking for you I discovered that four other signalmen were missing from the party—Chief Warner Duff, Wally Andrews, Gerald Goss, and Pete Unbehagen. This was very upsetting, because I especially wanted you to attend the party."[15]

The two signalmen talked about the dream for a few minutes and then, with the universal optimism of young Americans, laughed it off. Rising to their feet, they hurried belowdecks to grab lunch at the mess hall.

Despite Williams's foreboding, optimism prevailed on board the ship. Following the army's capture of Makin, it finally seemed time for *Liscome Bay* to depart the area of operations. Two new operational units were formed from Task Force 52 for the withdrawal. *Liscome Bay* and her sister ships *Coral Sea* and *Corregidor* became Task Group 52.3. They were encompassed within the larger Task Group 52.13, which also included the battleships *Mississippi* and *New Mexico,* the cruiser *Baltimore* (CA-68), and seven destroyers—*Morris* (DD-417), *Maury* (DD-401), *Gridley* (DD-380), *Hughes* (DD-410), *Hull* (DD-350), *Franks* (DD-554), and *Hoel* (DD-533).

As the task groups stood ready to receive the coveted orders for their withdrawal back to Pearl Harbor and points east, air operations continued on *Liscome Bay*. The knowledge that the Japanese fleet could be lurking anywhere over the horizon hung heavy over the crew. Each day they remained off Makin only compounded their anxiety. Late on the afternoon of November 23, their worries bore fruit. *Liscome Bay*'s radar operators called out an ominous warning. They had spotted a collection of suspicious blips on their screens to the northwest of the task force. "Bogies inbound," they reported to Lieutenant Ries, the flight operations officer. Grabbing his telephone, Ries scrambled the carrier's ready fighters.

At 1600, Lieutenant "Crud" Blair took off in his Wildcat to intercept, accompanied by Lieutenant (jg) George W. McFedries, A-V(N), USNR, Ensign Richard D. Cowger, A-V(N), USNR, and ensigns named Bagby and Wells in four other fighters.[16] With the dusk rapidly approaching, Beebe watched their departure with trepidation. Finding the carriers in the dark at the end of their patrol would be difficult, and executing night landings would be equally demanding. Adding to Beebe's concern, Blakley's aerography shop warned of electrical storms in the area. Even if Blair and the others encountered no enemy planes, they still faced a difficult flight. To aid its pilot's navigation efforts, the Wildcat's cockpit contained only a compass and a plotting board. Coupled with radio communication with the ship and whatever information could be gleaned from the aerography staff, it was all a Wildcat pilot could do to support his efforts to dodge bad weather and find his way back to the carrier.

A decade later, author James Michener imagined the thoughts that must race through a carrier's commander's mind at a moment like that, as the droning engines of Blair's patrol faded into the darkening sky. "Why is America lucky enough to have such men? They leave this tiny ship and fly against the enemy. Then they must seek the ship, lost somewhere on the sea. And when they find it, they have to land upon its pitching deck. Where do we get such men?"[17]

In the small cockpits of the Wildcats there was little room for such lofty thoughts. Blair and his patrol were focused on their mission, and the five Wildcats soon fell into formation and sped northward. For forty miles, *Liscome Bay* tracked their progress toward the bogies. About fifteen minutes after their departure, the planes disappeared from the carrier's radar. In their place, a steady buildup of massive thunderclouds appeared on the radarscopes. *Liscome Bay* made repeated but fruitless radio calls to her missing fliers. Even calls from other ships in the task force failed to locate the five Wildcats. By now, the situation seemed dire—the five planes were missing. Each carried only a few hours of fuel, and with each passing hour Beebe's concern for their safety grew.

The rest of the carrier's officers shared Beebe's anxiety. They went to dinner with heavy hearts, wolfed down a quick meal, and began congregating in the muggy passageway outside the ship's radio room. By 1930 they began drifting glumly away. By their reckoning, if Blair's patrol was still out there, they would have heard from it by now.[18] Beebe refused to give up so quickly. At 2140 he returned to the radar room, where the radar operator peered intently at his radarscope. The scope's ghostly green light in the dark room illuminated the beads of sweat on the operator's forehead. Beebe glanced over his shoulder, hoping for the best. He saw no blips.

Easing out of the radar room, Beebe decided to go up onto the flight deck. He stepped out onto the catwalk that ran the length of the ship and climbed up the three-step ladder that led to the flight deck. A light rain drizzled on his worried face as the squadron commander stood in the darkness. He scanned the dark skies from bow to stern and then from stern to bow, hoping to see the running lights of the approaching patrol. Beebe saw only darkness, and the only sound on the flight deck was the wind blowing through the ship's rigging.

Disappointed, Beebe looked to his wrist. The luminescent glow of his watch showed the time to be 2155. The patrol had been gone for nearly six hours. There was no hope that the planes would make it back to the carrier. Beebe only hoped that they had executed a safe ditching in the water and that Blair had managed to get all of his planes down in the same general area. With any luck, they were all in their life rafts, tied together and floating on the gentle ocean swells awaiting rescue during the daylight hours. Blair was an experienced pilot. Perhaps he could pull it off.

Beebe knew that the pilots of VC-39 were congregating in the squadron's ready room, awaiting word of the lost patrol. For them, he decided, having the evening continue with no news would be worse than hearing bad news. He headed back below. A hush fell over the room as Beebe entered. Looking out over his assembled pilots, he explained the situation. "No word has been received from any other ships, and you know as well as I do that they had to land by this time," he said. That was all he had to offer them, and he turned to leave.

"Oh, what the hell," responded Ensign Jake Marvin, the aviator whom Beebe had reprimanded earlier regarding his profanity. "We'll send out a search in the morning. We'll damn sure find them all."[19]

Marvin's comment broke the somber mood of the ready room, and the pilots quickly began talking among themselves. Stepping up to the area charts, they made quick calculations and even began to argue about where the downed aviators would likely be found. Ensign Dutch Polman, Beebe's stout and steady wingman, even hazarded a theory that they might have found carriers from one of the other task forces. Polman was not prone to undue optimism, and his thoughts encouraged the young pilots even further. In groups of twos and threes, they trickled away from the ready room. Missing patrol or not, another day of combat operations loomed, and in six short hours they would have to be on board their own planes. It was time to grab some sleep.

Events proved Polman's guess to be correct. Blair's patrol had discovered that an approaching squall line had caused the suspicious radar blip. With darkness rapidly approaching, they turned and sped back. Instead of *Liscome Bay*, however, Blair's errant Wildcats found the big carriers of Task Force 50, operating some sixty miles south of *Liscome Bay*'s task force. By now it was dark, and the Wildcats were eager for any port in a storm. *Yorktown* (CV-10) signaled she could recover them, and the first three Wildcats touched down gratefully on her accommodating deck.

Now it was Blair's turn to land. Coming in fast and hard, his Wildcat hit the flight deck, bounced out of control, and smashed into a collection of planes parked on the flight deck near *Yorktown*'s bow. Frantically unfastening himself from his safety harness, Blair scrambled out of his cockpit, bounced off the wing, and dashed for safety. Seconds later, his aircraft's belly tank exploded. Five of *Yorktown*'s deck crewmen died in the resulting conflagration, and only quick work by her fire-fighting crews prevented further disaster.[20]

As flames licked skyward off her flight deck, *Yorktown* unhappily radioed the remaining Wildcat, piloted by Ensign Wells, to land on the nearby *Lexington*. With a steady hand, Wells executed a safe landing. *Lexington*'s crew quickly nestled Wells's relatively small Wildcat among its larger Grumman F6F Hellcat cousins and made sure Wells found a hot meal and a clean bunk.[21]

As Blair, Wells, and the other pilots enjoyed the hospitality of *Yorktown* and *Lexington*, they no doubt counted themselves fortunate that they had found any American carriers at all in the dark expanse of the Pacific. Little did they know just how fortunate they were.

6
Three Task Forces, Three Brothers

On board *Liscome Bay*, Captain Crommelin, Mullinnix's chief of staff for Carrier Division 24, remained unaware of Blair's patrol's landings on *Yorktown* and *Lexington*. Like Beebe, he feared the worst. The prospect saddened him. Crommelin was well aware of the fears and anxieties that wracked families back home. His own family was bearing a remarkable burden in that regard, especially with respect to Operations Galvanic and Kourbash.

In an unusual coincidence, Crommelin's younger brother Charles was also participating in the invasion as the commander of *Yorktown*'s Air Group 5. *Yorktown* was steaming as part of Task Force 50. In addition to John and Charles, a third Crommelin brother, Henry, served in the area of operations as a destroyer division commander. Operating with Task Force 53, his destroyers would support the Tarawa landings. Even more unusual, two other Crommelin brothers, Richard and Quentin, were also navy officers back in the States. When the youngest, Quentin, had graduated from the Naval Academy in February 1941, it marked the first—and only—time five brothers had attended and graduated from the academy.

The Crommelins' naval legacy began in 1919 when John Crommelin, after a brief, rambunctious stint at the University of Virginia, entered the Naval Academy at Annapolis when a slot for him couldn't be secured at West Point. "My mother felt that Southern boys needed discipline," John commented laconically.[1] The academy's yearbook had a kinder assessment of John: "Here he is, folks, the typical Southern gentleman, fond of dogs, little children, and pretty women."[2] John had a tough streak, though, as evidenced by his success on the school's intercollegiate boxing squad.

Back home in Wetumpka, Alabama, on the family's plantation called Harrogate Springs, John's mother possessed a string of sons that also apparently needed discipline. As John entered his third year at the academy, younger brother Henry arrived at Annapolis in 1921. Henry graduated in 1925 and took to sea in the battleship *Tennessee* (BB-43). At the time, John was serving as the communications officer aboard the transport ship *Chaumont* (AP-5).

John had higher aspirations than the radio shack of a transport ship, and in 1926 he managed to wrangle a flight physical on board *Langley* (CV-1). It was a fitting place for John to begin his naval aviation career. In 1922 the navy had commissioned *Langley* as its first aircraft carrier after converting her from the collier *Jupiter* (AC-3). After passing the physical, John headed for Pensacola and navy flight training, earning his wings in 1927. Henry's poorer eyesight prevented such a career change, and 1927 found him serving in the destroyer *Bruce* (DD-329) as its chief engineering officer.

That same year, a third Crommelin brother entered the Naval Academy when middle brother Charles matriculated on June 21, 1927. Not surprisingly, most of his experiences at the tradition-bound academy were similar to those of his older brothers. There was at least one striking difference, though. By 1927, the navy, in recognition of the increasing importance of naval aviation, had added three months of special ground and flight instruction to the midshipmen's curriculum, in addition to a course titled "Seamanship and Flight Tactics." Capitalizing on this training, Charles attended elimination flight training upon his graduation in 1931, served six months in the battleship *Arizona* (BB-39), and then earned his wings at Pensacola in 1933. Meanwhile, John was earning accolades as a top naval aviator. He flew with the "Three T'Gallants'ls," a navy stunt flying team (a precursor to today's Blue Angels), chalked up victories in the military's air races, and garnered commendations from his superiors for his gunnery skills. John Arbes, one of his wingmen, commented that "John Crommelin was the only aviator in our squadron with both an 'E' in gunnery and in bombing—no mean accomplishment since the SB2U [Vindicator] was not particularly suited for either. He was one smooth flier."[3]

A year after Charles graduated from flight school at Pensacola, a fourth Crommelin brother, Richard, left "the piney hills on the banks of the Alabama to get his first taste of salt from Maryland's mighty Severn."[4] Richard entered Annapolis in the summer of 1934 while older brother Henry was back at the academy serving as a discipline officer. Three years later, the fifth and final brother, Quentin, followed his four older brothers to the Naval Academy and completed the family dynasty. As the Navy Department commented, "The only reason there aren't any more Crommelin brothers in the Navy is because the Crommelins are out of boys."[5] According to family legend, a field hand back on the Crommelin plantation had a simpler explanation. "They've had another one," he announced at the local general store upon Quentin's birth in 1918, "but this looks like it. They're calling him Quittin'."[6]

In 1938, Richard graduated from the academy and headed for the battleship *Pennsylvania* (BB-38). In February 1941, with war clouds looming on the horizon, the navy graduated Quentin's class early and sent the young ensign to the Pacific to serve as an antiaircraft gunnery officer on the carrier *Saratoga*. There he impatiently awaited orders for flight school at Pensacola.

In the months following the United States' entry into World War II, the Crommelin brothers were stretched across the navy. John escaped a job as a staff officer with the Bureau of Aeronautics in Washington and took to sea as the air officer for the carrier *Enterprise* (CV-6). Henry took command of the destroyer *Fitch* (DD-462), operating in the tense, submarine-stalked waters of the Atlantic. Charles remained in Washington, serving as a test pilot at NAS Anacostia. Richard sailed for the Pacific as a Wildcat pilot aboard the first carrier to bear the name *Yorktown* (CV-5). Quentin, still waiting for a chance to go to flight school, bided his time as a gunnery officer aboard *Saratoga*.

Before long, the Crommelin brothers found themselves in the thick of the action. Henry's destroyer escorted Atlantic convoys and took part in the invasion of North Africa. *Enterprise*, with John directing its air operations, battled the Japanese among the Solomons in support of the invasion of Guadalcanal. His aggressive leadership earned him the nickname "Bomb-Run John." Richard, flying off of *Yorktown*, took part in the early air raids on the New Guinea ports of Lae and Salamaua, shot down two Japanese Zeros during the Battle of the Coral Sea, and fought a month later in the Battle of Midway. He earned the Navy Cross for his flying at Coral Sea, and added a Gold Star in lieu of a second Navy Cross for his disruption of an eighteen-plane enemy attack at Midway. In the meantime, young Quentin survived two torpedo attacks on *Saratoga* before finally receiving his orders for flight school. Charles was scarcely any safer back home in the States during this time. Still serving as a naval test pilot at Anacostia, he barely survived the crash of one of his test flights.

By the time of Operation Galvanic and the invasion of the Gilberts, Henry was commanding Destroyer Division 50 from the bridge of the destroyer *Ringgold* (DD-500). *Dashiell* (DD-659) and two other destroyers rounded out his command. Destroyer Division 50 formed part of Task Force 53, tasked with the seizure of Tarawa. Charles, recovered from his test flight crash and now aboard the new *Yorktown* (the previous one had been lost at Midway), commanded the "Fighting Lady's" Air Group 5. *Yorktown* sailed as part of Task Force 50, which was assigned to provide a screen to the north to shield the Gilbert Islands invasion force from Japanese attack and to attack enemy air bases on Wake Island, Mille Atoll, and Marcus Island. As the chief of staff for Carrier Division 24 aboard *Liscome Bay*, eldest brother John watched the campaign unfold. He had a nervous vantage point from which to keep an eye on the developing battle and the role of his two brothers in it.

Henry commenced the three brothers' participation in Galvanic on November 19 when *Ringgold* surged ahead of the invasion force and attempted to secure a good radar fix on Tarawa to guide the oncoming American ships. As *Ringgold*'s radar operators worked to establish the radar fix, her lookouts kept a sharp eye out for enemy submarines in the dark waters off Tarawa. Their vigilance was rewarded at 2200 when they spotted a submarine caught in shallow water, trying to slip out of one smaller coral atoll's lagoons. *Ringgold* opened fire, peppering her adversary with salvos of shells. One punched through the sub's conning tower.

It failed to explode but still did significant damage to the submarine's piping and valves. The furtive submarine managed to limp away and submerge in deeper water. Satisfied with her first clash with the "Japanese," *Ringgold* returned to the task force. Only later did the destroyer learn that she had been firing not on a Japanese submarine but instead on *Nautilus* (SS-168), which was conducting a pre-invasion reconnaissance of the islands. The submarine survived, however, and her officers later took great delight in displaying *Ringgold's* dud shell behind the bar at the Pearl Harbor submarine base's officers club.

The next day, *Ringgold* had an opportunity to redeem herself. As the U.S. fleet heralded the arrival of morning on November 20 with a massive naval bombardment, and as five thousand men of the 2nd Marine Division clambered down cargo nets into their waiting landing craft, *Ringgold* and *Dashiell* steamed into position outside Tarawa's large lagoon. Then, following in the wake of a minesweeper, *Ringgold* surged through the narrow opening in the coral reef into the lagoon. The entry into the lagoon was tricky, and even the presence of a former resident of the atoll on the bridge with Henry and the destroyer's skipper couldn't save *Ringgold* from running aground on the reef. With a muffled crunch of metal on coral, *Ringgold* shuddered to a halt. Frantic maneuvering extricated the destroyer from the reef, but she left her hull-mounted sonar equipment behind.

Just as Henry's ship pulled clear of the reef, the Japanese batteries on Betio opened fire. A 140-millimeter shell smashed into *Ringgold*, piercing her hull below the waterline. Fortunately, the shell was a dud and failed to explode, but the impact nevertheless damaged the ship's electrical and power systems. Power failed, and seawater began blasting through the gaping hole. Lieutenant Wayne Parker leaped into action and plugged the hole with the only item readily available—his own rump—until sailors could secure bedding from nearby bunks to provide a more conventional patch. Later, the navy reportedly awarded Parker a "rather uniquely worded Navy Cross" for his actions.[7]

Floating free of the reef but still struggling to regain power, *Ringgold* was a sitting duck for further Japanese fire. A second 140-millimeter shell—also a dud—smashed into the destroyer amidships, plunged through a 40-millimeter gun magazine, ricocheted off a live torpedo mount, ripped through the sick bay's medical supply storage area, and punched through the radio shack before disappearing over the side.

In the meantime, the marines' landing craft churned toward the charred and smoking island of Betio, Tarawa's main island. An outlying barrier reef blocked the landing craft, however, and the marines were forced to slog through up to a kilometer of surf to reach Betio's shore. As expected, they encountered much stronger resistance on Betio than the army troops had met at Makin. The Japanese had concentrated their defensive forces at Tarawa. Three thousand naval infantry, sheltered in thick concrete blockhouses connected by a clever trench system, hit the marines struggling in the surf with devastating blasts of machine-gun and mortar fire.

As the fighting ashore progressed, *Ringgold*, joined by *Dashiell* in the lagoon, traded fire with the Japanese shore batteries. Enemy shells continued to burst over the two ships, but the destroyers remained on position to provide close fire support to the marines struggling ashore into the carnage of Red Beach 3. "That anyone made it to Red-3," it was later written, "can be attributed in large part to *Ringgold* and *Dashiell*" remaining on station and blanketing the beach with "pinpoint fire."[8]

By the end of the first day's fighting, more than fifteen hundred marines lay dead or wounded in Tarawa's surf or among the devastated bunkers and foxholes of its bloodied beaches. As the rest of the American fleet withdrew further offshore to guard against air or submarine attack, *Ringgold* remained in the lagoon. There, despite a twenty-six-degree list caused by the hole in her side, she served as a floating artillery battery for the marines clinging to their tiny beachhead. So valuable was her service that, rather than pull *Ringgold* out to resupply, the navy ferried more ammunition to her in smaller boats.

Ringgold stayed there for two more days, pummeling the Japanese positions with her guns, as the marines slowly wrested control of the island from its fanatical defenders. Events proved the decision to leave *Ringgold* in the lagoon a wise one. When Rear Admiral Keiji Shibasaki, the overall commander of Japanese forces on the atoll, tried to relocate his command post, shore-based forward observers spotted the movement and radioed back to *Ringgold*, which quickly showered the area with airburst shells. Shibasaki was among the casualties, and his death left the Japanese defense of the atoll fragmented and uncoordinated. Some historians consider his death one of the pivotal moments in the marines' capture of the island.[9] Furthermore, as the nearest "secure" American location, *Ringgold* took on the role of a floating hospital, albeit a combative one. Soon her decks, covered with wounded marines and the canvas-shrouded bodies of their comrades, were literally awash in blood.

On November 22, Henry withdrew his weary destroyers from the lagoon and rejoined the task force at sea. Ashore, the marines remained locked in deadly struggle with Tarawa's Japanese defenders, but at least the beachhead was secured. The navy awarded Henry the Silver Star for his work in Tarawa's lagoon. "In bold defiance of heavy shore-based artillery fire," the citation read, "Commander Crommelin entered the perilous and uncharted waters of Tarawa lagoon in the first assault wave to this important Japanese stronghold. Operating in the treacherous, coral-studded lagoon, he valiantly directed his command in the vigorous bombardment of shore installations and contributed to the success of his division in silencing several enemy batteries."[10]

Before Henry had even begun his fierce battle with the Japanese from Tarawa lagoon, and as John was still supervising the initial staff combat operations of Carrier Division 24 off the coast of Makin, middle brother Charles took to the air in his F6F Hellcat from the deck of *Yorktown*. On November 19, Charles began what would eventually be a series of five air strikes led by him on Mille, Makin, and Jaluit Atolls. The Hellcats of Charles's Air Group 5 played a key role in keeping the Japanese aircraft pinned down and ineffective for the duration of Operation Galvanic. The first four strikes gave Charles no problem. The fifth, however, was almost his last.

The fateful fifth mission took Charles on a reconnaissance flight over Mille Atoll on November 21. Spotting two Japanese aircraft on the atoll's airfield, Charles rolled in for an attack. Ignoring the enemy antiaircraft fire streaking through the air around him, he roared back and forth over the airfield, strafing the first of the two aircraft with his .50-caliber machine guns until it burst into flames. Peeling back around, he started back in for a pass at the second aircraft. By then, every Japanese gun on the airfield was blasting at the aggressive pilot tormenting their airfield. As Charles lined up for another strafing run, an enemy 40-millimeter shell exploded in his cockpit. A contemporary chronicler compared the effect to "a Mack truck" breaking "into a china shop at sixty miles an hour and com[ing] to rest."[11] The shell punched through the Hellcat's windshield, demolished the instrument panel, and left Charles's body peppered with shrapnel. The shatterproof windshield had held, but it was laced with hundreds of cracks that reduced visibility to nearly zero.

Badly wounded, Charles strained to pull up from his attack run and headed back out to open sea, trying desperately to make it back to his waiting carrier. It would be an agonizing journey. He had no vision in his left eye, and little in his right. His right wrist was fractured, and his punctured uniform was red with blood from the dozens of wounds to his mouth and chest. All the while, wind rushing through holes in his mangled canopy pummeled his torn body.

Charles's fellow Hellcat pilots soon joined up with their wounded leader in a loose formation and began to shepherd him home. It was a long and painful journey for Charles—over 120 miles back to the waiting *Yorktown*. About thirty minutes later, however, the ragged formation pulled into sight of their carrier. As his fellow pilots and shipmates watched fearfully, Charles guided his battered Hellcat for *Yorktown*'s flight deck. Landing a warplane on an aircraft carrier's deck was never an easy task, even under the best of conditions. Charles's odds seemed marginal at best, and nervous crash crews prepared for the worst.

But Charles was up to the challenge. Ignoring his painful wounds, he lined his mangled fighter up on the narrow deck as he squinted through bloody eyes to make out the landing signal officer's paddles. Somehow, he maintained a textbook approach angle in to the waiting carrier and was rewarded the unmistakable "cut" signal. Unhesitatingly, Charles slapped his Hellcat down on the deck in a landing that fellow pilots later agreed was good enough to have been included in a training film. Then, in a remarkable gesture of sangfroid, Charles taxied his plane out of the carrier's arresting gear, shut down its engine, crawled out of the cockpit, and lowered himself to the flight deck. Only when he started walking for the sick bay did he succumb to his wounds and collapse to the deck.

Charles's heroic return to *Yorktown* quickly became the stuff of legend in naval aviation circles, although the severity of his wounds dictated a quick return to shore hospitals in Hawaii and in the States. The recuperating pilot's further antics only fueled his fellow aviators' admiration. After being returned to Pearl Harbor for medical treatment, Charles directed his enlisted ambulance driver to stop off at the Ford Island officers club. Pushing aside his attending corpsman, the heavily bandaged Charles grabbed a cane and hobbled into the club. Ignoring the amazed stares from his fellow officers, he calmly ordered a shot of bourbon, downed it in one gulp, and headed back out to the waiting ambulance.

"Are you crazy?" asked an angry doctor at the hospital when he learned of Charles's unauthorized detour.

"Hell," Charles answered. "I just wanted to show those boys that it wasn't too bad getting shot up."[12]

Charles had already earned the Distinguished Flying Cross, and the navy awarded him a Gold Star in lieu of a second Flying Cross for his actions over Mille that day. "Commander Crommelin's superb airmanship, indomitable fighting spirit, and valiant devotion to duty throughout this extremely hazardous mission," the citation read, "were in keeping with the highest traditions of the United States Naval Service."[13]

Charles, however, continued to make light of his wounds. Back in the States, he attended a showing of the war documentary *The Fighting Lady*. One of the movie's scenes featured his dramatic return to *Yorktown*. After the movie ended, Charles fell in step behind a couple of WAVES.

As they walked, the two women chatted excitedly about the heroics of the Hellcat pilot who had returned his crippled plane to *Yorktown*. Charles simply couldn't resist. He reached forward and tapped one of them on the shoulder.

"How do I look now?" he asked.

According to one of Charles's companions, "The poor girl looked bug-eyed, her mouth went wide open, and she almost collapsed."[14]

John, sitting in the air plot of *Liscome Bay* on the evening of November 23 awaiting word of Blair's flight, didn't know of the extent of his brothers' heroics, or even if they were alive or dead. Even if he had, there was nothing he could do about it. At this point, every officer's focus was on his duty and on the men counting on him to perform it. There was little time to worry about his brothers, whether they were equally close to the fighting or far away from it.

Looking around the air plot, John realized that four days of continuous combat operations had taken their toll on him and the rest of the Carrier Division 24 staff. Bloodshot eyes, rumpled uniforms, and stubbled chins bespoke the never-ending cycle of staff work during a combat operation. There was only so much the scalding hot and tar-black coffee could do to keep exhausted heads from nodding and heavy eyelids from flapping shut.

John knew he probably looked the worst of the bunch and decided he'd better catch a few hours of sleep. Wearily, he headed for his cube-like quarters on the gallery deck. Outside, thick clouds plastered much of the heavens. The occasional sprinkle of rain splattered across the flight deck. And somewhere on the dark, gently rolling seas off Makin, a Japanese submarine searched for target. Within a few short hours, she would find one.

7
"The God of Death Has Come"

Caught by surprise in the Gilberts, Japanese Admiral Mineichi Koga scoured his forces desperately for anything to hurl at the massive U.S. fleet menacing Makin and Tarawa. His first gambit, the aerial attack that had damaged *Independence*, proved ineffective. The frantic maneuvers of the Imperial Navy's surface ships, which amounted to little more than scurrying sorties between various islands in preparation of the Americans' next blow, were even less productive. Koga would have to find something else to throw at the Americans. In desperation, he turned to his submarine fleet.

Hurried orders recalled four Japanese submarines from their patrol southwest of Hawaii and directed them to head for the Gilberts at best possible speed. Five others sortied from Truk and Rabaul. In all, nine submarines converged on the American fleet centered on the Gilberts. They hoped to find a battleship, cruiser, or aircraft carrier shackled to supporting one of the amphibious assaults on Makin or Tarawa. Unable to maneuver to fullest advantage, such a ship would be an easy victim and a worthy target to a predatory sub.

During World War II, the Imperial Navy boasted essentially two classes of submarines. The RO class contained the older, prewar models. Originally designed for coastal security duties, the submarines of this class were limited to missions involving shorter patrols. The larger, faster I-class boats, with an operating range long enough to cross the Pacific and the capability to remain at sea for sixty days, represented the greatest threat to the U.S. Navy.

Japan's design of the I-class series of submarines underscored its prewar naval strategy. War planners had envisioned that one great, decisive fleet battle—similar to the clash of British and German dreadnoughts at Jutland during World War I—would decide the anticipated conflict with the U.S. Navy in the Pacific. As a component of that strategy, Japan designed its newest submarines to be offensive weapons. Their long range, ability to stay at sea for long periods of time, and fast surface speeds all contributed to their offensive punch.

One of the finest features of the I-class submarines were the Type 95 21-inch-diameter torpedoes they carried. These torpedoes were far superior to the American torpedoes at this stage in the war. Naval historian Samuel Eliot Morison went so far as to proclaim them one of the "outstanding technical achievement[s] of the Japanese Navy" in World War II.[1] Powered by a pure oxygen mix and capable of being fired at considerable depth, they left much less of a wake than their American steam-powered counterparts. Consequently, they were harder to spot from the decks of their targets and thus that much more difficult to evade. Japanese submariners were also well versed in how to use their torpedoes. Coupling the lethal torpedoes with highly trained crews resulted in a deadly threat to American ships.

Japan's submarine captains, however, labored under several serious limitations. The heavy emphasis on the boats as an offensive weapon resulted in numerous design flaws. Notably, Japan had paid less attention to enabling its subs to counter enemy antisubmarine warfare operations than had the navies of other nations. Japanese submarines were noisier than their American counterparts, submerged more slowly, lacked sufficient diving depth, and were relatively unwieldy when maneuvering while submerged. Tactical deficiencies exacerbated these design flaws. High-speed ascents, dives, and maneuvering, while thought to be necessary to avoid visual detection, made detection that much easier for American sonar operators. Other limitations compounded these difficulties. Unlike their American counterparts, the Japanese submarines at this stage in the war were not equipped with radar—a distinct disadvantage when operating on dark nights. Their radio equipment was also inferior, making it difficult to communicate with their home bases and with one another. Consequently, coordinated operations were always difficult.

Despite these limitations, Japan's submariners were among the most determined and motivated men in the Imperial Navy. Both officers and men were volunteers selected from pools of young, highly rated individuals. Officers received their initial submarine education in one of several courses at the submarine school at Kure, while enlisted sailors took a six-month training course. Their actual training came on the job. Picked from among the finest officers and sailors the Japanese had to offer, and infused with the Bushido warrior spirit, the Japanese skippers believed that they and their crews could easily best their American opponents.

Bushido or not, the operational and technical shortcomings of the Japanese submarines likely contributed to the initial disastrous setbacks in the Imperial Navy's counteroffensive into the Gilberts. Its submarines generally proved a poor match for the prowling American destroyers and aircraft supporting Operation Galvanic. Four boats, upon receiving their orders to strike at the Americans, sailed for the Gilberts and were simply never heard from again.[2]

The *I-35* was more fortunate—at least at first. She managed to make it to the Gilberts by November 22, but by 1530 that day she was in trouble. The destroyer *Meade* (DD-602) detected *I-35* with a sonar contact and quickly closed in. Joined by fellow destroyer *Frazier* (DD-607), *Meade* pummeled the submerged Japanese vessel with a series of five depth-charge attacks over the course of two hours. The attacks damaged *I-35* and forced her to surface.

Once the battered I-boat broke the surface, the deck crews of the two destroyers peppered her with gunfire for five minutes. Then *Frazier*'s skipper, determined to finish off *I-35*, rammed his destroyer into her and smashed into the port side of the boat abaft her conning tower. Caught in a close battle, shaken Japanese sailors ran to man their 5.5-inch deck gun. Up above them, lining the rails of *Frazier*, American officers and sailors blasted at them with pistol fire. Their volleys succeeded in keeping *I-35*'s sailors away from the deck gun and cowering back at the sub's conning tower or in the hatches leading to her deck. Throwing her screws in reverse, *Frazier* backed off from the mortally wounded submarine with a metal screech. Seawater rushed through the gash in the sub's hull behind the conning tower, and in a matter of moments *I-35* sank stern-first beneath the waves, leaving four wounded survivors splashing desperately in the water.

With the enemy vessel dispatched, the destroyers dutifully launched whaleboats to rescue the survivors. As a boat approached the first Japanese sailor, the submariner opened fire with a handgun at his would-be rescuers. The Americans returned fire, killing him with a fusillade of bullets. Electing not to follow the dead sailor's example, the other survivors surrendered and were pulled from the water.

The action was not yet over for *Meade*'s boat crew. As they returned with one of the wounded prisoners, a dive-bomber operating from the escort carrier *Suwannee* spotted it. Mistaking the whaleboat for the conning tower of an enemy submarine, *Suwannee*'s pilot dropped a six-hundred-pound delayed-fuse bomb at the boat of terrified sailors. It plunged into the ocean a mere three feet away from the boat. Seconds later, the ensuing underwater explosion lifted the whaleboat clean out of the water. Although it was holed by the force of the explosion, the boat managed to make it back to *Meade* without any casualties. For her part, *Meade*, unaware that the attacking plane was "friendly," peppered the Avenger with antiaircraft fire. Fortunately, the pilot avoided injury and had only minor damage to his aircraft.

Lieutenant Commander Sunao (sometimes translated as Naoshi) Tabata, skipper of the Japanese submarine *I-175*, guided his boat into the Gilberts's waters a day after the arrival of the *I-35*. A 1931 graduate of the naval academy at Eta Jima, Tabata had served as the commanding officer of *I-7*, a submarine squadron flagship, earlier in the war. Now, however, he was on the attack.

His ship and crew, unlike the young men in *Liscome Bay*, had logged months of combat operations. In fact, *I-175* scored one of the Imperial Navy's first submarine successes of the war when she torpedoed an American freighter off the Hawaiian island of Kauai on December 17.[3] At the time, she was designated *I-75* (the Japanese renumbered their submarines in May 1942). Other combat operations had included patrols in the Solomons in 1942 and participation in the daring evacuation of troops from the Aleutian island of Kiska in May 1943.

This time, however, Tabata's mission was one of destruction, not evacuation. As night fell on November 23, thick stratocumulus clouds scudded overhead at five thousand feet, pushed by winds out of the southwest at 10 knots. Tabata noted the night sky with grim satisfaction. His charts told him that moonrise wouldn't occur until 0357, and the sun wouldn't rise until 0613. There was plenty of time to hunt American ships under the cover of darkness. The lieutenant commander ordered his helmsman to take up a course to place their boat south of Makin. As the evening stretched into the dark early-morning hours of November 24, the diesel engines of *I-175* pulled her across the smooth surface of the black ocean, eager to find unsuspecting prey.

Unaware of Tabata's approach, Rear Admiral Robert M. Griffin, USN, sailing on board *New Mexico*, shepherded Task Group 52.13 through the dark night south of Makin. At any moment, Griffin expected to receive word to turn for the northwest and head for Hawaii. For him, those orders could not come soon enough. Tied down to supporting the invasion, the ships of Task Force 52 and its various task groups had, to a large extent, surrendered the initiative. Every passing hour gave the enemy more time to assemble an attack force and strike back. For the past three days, radar had reported unidentified aircraft, and intelligence reports contained ominous warnings of enemy air and submarine activity. Nevertheless, Griffin remained hopeful. Makin was secure, and the orders to return to Pearl Harbor would arrive at any moment. In the meantime, though, Task Group 52.13 was ordered to maintain position south of Makin and remain prepared to provide air support to the remainder of Turner's task force some twenty miles to the east.

Griffin's experience seemed to mark him as a good choice for command in the dangerous waters of the Gilberts. The son of an admiral, he had attended prep school in Washington, D.C., before entering the Naval Academy. He graduated in 1911, ranked sixth in his class. In World War I, he had served aboard the destroyer *Cushing* (DD-55), escorting American ships in the face of prowling German submarines. By the end of the war he was assigned to the antisubmarine division of

Admiral William S. Sims, USN, the commander of U.S. naval forces operating in European waters. Sims recognized Griffin's role in developing antisubmarine tactics by successfully recommending him for the Navy Cross. In later years, Griffin commanded a squadron of subchasers, served as the acting naval aide at the White House, and commanded the battleship *New York* (BB-34).

Griffin began World War II in the Fleet Training Division, Office of the Chief of Naval Operations. By March 1943 he was commanding Battleship Division 3 from on board *New Mexico*. He led Battleship Division 3 in the Aleutians campaign, helping to drive the Japanese out of the occupied Aleutian islands of Attu and Kiska. Under his guidance, *New Mexico* and *Mississippi* had spent the last few days providing fire support to the army troops ashore Makin.

From *New Mexico*, Griffin called for Cruising Disposition 73, putting the group into a circular formation that placed the thin-skinned escort carriers in the middle of the task group. *Liscome Bay* assumed the role of guide for the task group. As such, she sailed in the dead center of the formation—what should have been the safest position in the formation. Several thousand yards ahead of her steamed the cruiser *Baltimore*. *Corregidor* and *Coral Sea* steamed off *Liscome Bay*'s starboard beam and starboard quarter sides, respectively, matched on the port side by battleships *New Mexico* and *Mississippi*. The two battleships, the cruiser, and the pair of escort carriers completed the first circle of protection around *Liscome Bay*. Beyond that circle steamed a screen of seven destroyers. *Gridley* sailed in the vanguard, and completing the screen clockwise were *Franks*, *Hull*, *Morris*, *Hughes*, *Maury*, and *Hoel*. The combined task group sailed a westerly course, bearing 295 degrees, holding a steady pace of 15 knots. Makin lay approximately fifteen miles to the north, but it was out of sight on this dark night. Some vessels in the task group recalled visibility of four thousand yards; others reported it being as far as ten thousand. Regardless of the actual distance, all agreed it was limited. Rather than zigzagging, the blacked-out ships maintained a steady course through the darkness. Despite the intelligence warnings, collisions, rather than an enemy submarine attack, seemed to pose the greatest threat.

At 0245, *Mississippi* called out a warning of unidentified aircraft thirty-five miles to the south. Then silence dulled the airwaves until 0339 when *New Mexico*'s radar operators called out two contacts fifteen miles, sailing in the darkness to the northwest of the task group. They were directly in the path of *Gridley*, but Griffin established that they were two friendly destroyers, *Mustin* (DD-413) and *Burns* (DD-588). The two destroyers quickly scurried north and out of the way of the approaching task group. At this time, Seaman Beasley was already awake and in the signal shack, sipping on a cup of coffee and being briefed by the signalman from the previous watch. All seemed routine, and at 0400 he relieved the sailor and settled in for the morning watch on the bridge.

Meanwhile, a crescent moon began to rise in the night sky. On board *Liscome Bay*, a sailor shook Lieutenant Commander Beebe awake in the converted linen closet that served as his quarters. Beebe reached for the uniform he had stacked neatly beside his bunk and quickly slipped into it. Inquiring among the officers who had stood the evening watch, Beebe learned that, as far as *Liscome Bay*'s air operations staff knew, Blair's patrol was still missing. Pouring himself a cup of coffee and conferring with the watch officers, Beebe decided that once the combat flights had been launched they would send out a search patrol at 0800 if Blair was still missing.

Just as Beebe was awaking, Rear Admiral Griffin dispatched the destroyer *Hull* to Makin to retrieve a downed aircrew ashore at Butaritari. The *Liscome Bay* aviators who had splashed down in Makin's lagoon—Barrett and his crew—had been picked up previously by the destroyer *Dale* (DD-353) from their overnight accommodations on Makin and were already at sea. *Hull*'s departure left an ominous hole in the screen off *Liscome Bay*'s starboard side as the task group continued to sail along its westerly course.

Twenty minutes later, Mullinnix radioed Griffin: "Request following be passed to Carrier Task Force 52. Five Wildcats which departed November 23 from *Liscome Bay* [at 1745] did not arrive at *Liscome Bay*. All ships and stations be on the lookout for planes or pilots."[4] Griffin forwarded the message to Task Force 52.

At 0430 reveille sounded, waking most of *Liscome Bay*'s crew. Some officers who had previously stood watch, such as Ensign William Davis, simply rolled over in their cramped bunks and tried to catch some more sleep. Along with Davis, there were six to ten other officers still sleeping down in the wardroom on the ship's first platform deck—just below the waterline. Elsewhere on the ship, sleepy sailors pulled themselves out of their bunks and headed for their battle stations.

At the same time, tensions were rising in *New Mexico*'s flag plot. *Baltimore* alerted the battleship of two separate groups of unidentified aircraft closing in from the southwest. As the cruiser signaled her warnings, the destroyer *Franks* called in to Griffin.

"Chestnut, *Franks*," radioed *Franks*'s skipper, using Task Group 52.13's call sign. "We have just spotted a very dim flashing light bearing 050 true. Over."

"This is Chestnut. Investigate and report. Over."

"Wilco."[5]

Franks's helmsman swung his wheel to the right, and at 0434 the destroyer headed off to investigate the mysterious flashing light. Her departure left an even bigger gap in the protective screen shielding the task group to the northeast.

Two minutes later, the radar operators on *New Mexico* warned Griffin's staff of a surface contact to the north approximately five miles away. Before it could be investigated further, however, the blip disappeared. *New Mexico* chalked it up to a false reading—not an unusual occurrence in those early days of shipboard radar, especially with low-lying rain clouds in the area. The battleship didn't realize that the radar signal had actually shown Tabata's *I-175* sliding into position. The disappearance of the blip signaled the submarine's dive to prepare for an attack on the task group.

Flight quarters sounded on *Liscome Bay* at approximately 0450, sending the pilots and aircrew to their aircraft. Thirteen planes, fueled and armed, awaited them on the flight deck. One, a Wildcat, was placed on the catapult to prepare for dawn launch. Down below on the hangar deck, seven others sat armed but not yet fueled. At this point, despite several days of combat operations, the carrier still had more than 200,000 pounds of bombs and ammunition. In addition to this arsenal, she carried thousands of gallons of aviation fuel for her thirsty brood.

Aviation Machinist's Mate Tim Woodham, now a plane captain without a plane after Ensign Youtz's crash, lacked a battle station now that his Avenger lay on the ocean floor. When he awoke, he headed for the showers. Captain Crommelin made a similar decision and also elected to take a shower. Beebe, having missed his nightly shave the previous evening due to the ongoing watch for Blair's lost patrol, took a razor to his stubble. With Blair still missing, Beebe had pulled himself from the early-morning flight schedule in order to assist in coordinating further searches and, if necessary, recovery operations.

As Beebe's tired pilots headed for their cockpits, still wondering about the fate of Blair and his companions, *Liscome Bay*'s helmsman executed another course change. Now the formation was heading on a course of 355 degrees—almost due north. At approximately the same time, Griffin radioed *Franks*'s skipper to rejoin the task group.

"Wilco," came the terse response.[6]

Meanwhile, at 0500, a messenger from the bridge woke Captain Wiltsie. Quickly slipping on his khaki uniform, Wiltsie headed for the bridge.

At 0505 the carrier sounded her routine general quarters, sending *Liscome Bay*'s sailors to their battle stations. Dawn general quarters was customary for a ship at war. Common military wisdom held that the transition between night and day was the most likely time for an enemy sneak attack. Accordingly, military units at war, whether manning a line of foxholes or crewing an escort carrier, would always stand ready at that time. Dorie Miller, for example, responded to general quarters by heading to his 20-millimeter gun position midship on the carrier's port side. Fireman Robert Haynes reported to the shipfitters' shop by the forward elevator, while Seaman Raymond Bergquist slipped into a starboard 40-millimeter gun position forward of the carrier's island. Seaman James Honold reported for duty in the parachute storage room next to the pilot's ready room and prepared to hand out parachutes to the men flying that morning. Meanwhile, the executive officer, "Fee" Hall, stepped into radar plot and joined the small group of men there.

On the bridge, Ensign Bill Woodward stood duty as the officer of the deck. The ship's navigation officer was also on the bridge with him, along with *Liscome Bay*'s gunnery officer, Lieutenant Commander John Bodler. Wiltsie joined them moments later. Outside, it was a balmy eighty-two degrees.

At that point, Beasley left the bridge momentarily to go below to make sure that all the signalmen were awake. Sleeping through general quarters was a serious offense, and Beasley wanted to make sure none of his comrades were committing it. He exited the bridge by climbing through an escape hatch and ladder that Wiltsie, with great foresight, had ordered the shipfitters to construct to enable easier access to the flight deck. Once there, Beasley met his friend Wally Andrews coming up from the crew quarters.

"Are all the signalmen up?" Beasley asked.

"Yes, Sam," Andrews answered. "I just came up from the quarters." With that said, Beasley and Andrews climbed up to the bridge. There they found Lieutenant Glenn Hunt, the ship's signal officer, and Chief Signalman Warner J. Duff.[7]

Daily reported to the decoding room, his battle station, for general quarters. With ten officers and men crowded into the compartment there weren't enough seats to go around, so Daily simply took a seat on the deck, his back against the bulkhead, to sit out what he assumed would be another uneventful alert. As he reported in, Fireman James King arrived at his battle station in the degaussing room and was joined there by Seaman Edward Jonas, the ship's tailor.

Aviation Machinist's Mate John Beymer, who had joined *Liscome Bay* in Hawaii following the rough Pacific crossing in an LST, wasn't assigned for flying duty that morning. Accordingly, he occupied a battle station as an assistant gunner on a 40-millimeter antiaircraft gun just forward of the bridge, on the starboard side. Nearby, Seaman First Class Carl J. Jelsema slipped into position behind a 20-millimeter gun in front of the bridge, while Fire Controlman Second Class John E. Jenkins Jr. took his place in the 40-millimeter gun director and slipped on his phone headset.

The Homec brothers and their friend Johnny Cristando also picked their way through the carrier's shadows to their battle stations. The previous night all three had been stationed on the ship's starboard side, but tonight Maxsy was assigned as one of the loaders on a three-man 20-millimeter gun crew on the port side.

Belowdecks, Seaman Leonard Bohm had just completed the night watch in the mess hall. Since he was coming off watch, he was excused from routine general quarters and instead slipped gratefully into his bunk. Further belowdecks, just before general quarters sounded, Fireman Phelan Allee left his watch station in the aft engine room to take his battle station in the forward engine room. He had to double-time it through the ship's passages to cover the distance.

At the same time, Yeoman First Class Robert J. Charters, wearing his dungarees and a set of comfortable marine shoes he had bought in San Diego, reported to his battle station in the office of Lieutenant Commander Buzz Carroll, the ship's first lieutenant. During battle, Carroll served as the ship's damage control officer, directing the damage control parties through his post in his small office. Charters, a six-year veteran of the navy, served as a talker for the station, sitting at a switchboard and manning a headset. They shared this battle station with a lieutenant (jg) and Seaman Second Class Milton A. Galliano, who manned the headset connected to the bridge circuit.

Despite the early hour, and despite the fact that he had only been able to snatch five hours of sleep the previous night, Charters couldn't help but smile when he arrived at the compartment and saw Carroll still thumbing through a copy of *The Virginian*. The lieutenant commander enjoyed the book so much that he was rationing its pages, reading them only during the daily morning general quarters. Carroll was almost finished with the book and was likely wondering which of his shipmates had a novel he could swap it for. In such a way books passed dozens of times around a ship like *Liscome Bay*. Charters wasn't particularly interested in books these days. He had intended to marry his girlfriend in San Diego before they left port, but in the hectic days before the ship's final departure for Pearl Harbor the couple hadn't been able to find a moment to tie the proverbial knot. These days his spare moments were fixed on the girl he had left behind him.

In the sick bay, Ensign Frank Sistrunk stirred at the sounding of general quarters. It had been only days since his appendectomy, and he was still recovering. He had company in the sick bay—Yeoman First Class Robert J. Schroeder, who had also developed appendicitis and had been transferred from his ship to *Liscome Bay* for surgery. Dr. Rowe had operated on Schroeder as well, since smaller vessels often carried no more medical staff than a couple of pharmacist's mates. Rowe was also in the sick bay at the time, along with four of his medical staff and one guest—Storekeeper Clovis Roach.

The sick bay occupied an excellent location for Roach—astride the only passageway leading to the issue room two decks below. During general quarters, Roach was supposed to be in the issue room, prepared to hand out emergency issues of flight and engine gear as needed during battle. Unhappy with a battle station deep in the bowels of the thinly skinned carrier, he had opted to position himself in the sick bay in what he considered a happy compromise. Perched there, he could spot men heading down to the issue room, follow them down, and issue the necessary equipment. It was a practical arrangement for Roach, if not a strictly military one. When questioned about his self-initiated adaptation of his duty station, he had a ready explanation: "As long as it's necessary to stay below, I'll stay there, but if it's not necessary, I won't."[8]

Trying to stay out of sight of Rowe and other officers, Roach sat in one of the sick bay's treatment rooms. He sat on the treatment table while a pharmacist's mate plopped down in a chair. The two men were soon shooting the breeze, discussing the recently concluded operation against Makin and the marines' reported struggles further south on Tarawa. The pharmacist's mate complained about the boredom of yesterday's operations and expressed fear of similar monotony today.

"I've seen it calm like this before," Roach warned ominously. "Something will happen. It always does when it's calm."[9]

Outside it was still dark, but by now *Liscome Bay*'s antiaircraft guns ringing the ship were fully manned, as was the carrier's island. Aerographer's Mate Bob Pinder slipped into the air plot, prepared to brief the operations officer and the captain on the day's weather. Aerographer Lyle Blakley and his assistant, Perry Bruce, were on the catwalk chatting near the thermoscreen and enjoying the fresh morning air, while Jack Mahood stood watch in the aerology office. Donald Cruse, the fifth member of the aerology team, had stood the previous watch and was still asleep in his makeshift bunk in the weather balloon inflation room.

Belowdecks, Chaplain Carley roamed through the ship, checking on sailors in the various battle stations. Without an assigned station, he typically tried to use general quarters as an opportunity to visit with the men. One compartment he knew not to visit, however, was the pilots' bunkroom in "officers' country." There, pilots like Gene Tornquist who were not scheduled to fly until later that day were catching a few extra hours of sleep.

By now Mullinnix was in the carrier's flag plot, keeping a watchful eye on the charting of the division's course for the upcoming day. The admiral had been up for days, catching rare snatches of sleep, and was bone-tired. "He was a terrifically hard worker and the most conscientious man I ever saw," his chief of staff later wrote.[10] Mullinnix's flag quartermaster, P. W. Rairden, joined the admiral in the plot. The admiral had become known among the ship's sailors by then as a "kind, friendly man," and the two men shared a few moments of quiet conversation as the ship around them slowly came to life.[11]

On the flight deck, crews scurried as they continued to prepare for the dawn launch of the combat air patrol, thirty minutes away. They pulled gasoline lines across the deck and began fueling the waiting aircraft. For safety's sake, the planes were defueled each evening and then refueled immediately before the morning launch. Pilots circled their aircraft, making a final preflight check and stretching their legs before climbing into the cramped cockpits for a long morning's flight. Mechanics tinkered with engines, wiped the sea salt from cockpit canopies, and double-checked the ammunition belts feeding the wing-mounted machine guns. Meanwhile, on the outer perimeter of the task group, the remaining five destroyer skippers were still struggling to fill in the gaps in the screen left by the departure of *Hull* and *Franks*.

In flag plot, Mullinnix drained the last drops of coffee from his mug and sent Rairden for a fresh pot. With a quick nod, Rairden headed for the nearest galley. Meanwhile, on the bridge, Lieutenant Gardner Smith paced back and forth along its starboard side, occasionally looking out to sea whenever the veil of clouds slipped off the moon's face. Nearby, the signal officer, Lieutenant Hunt, chatted casually with Chief Duff and Ensign Beasley.

Just as general quarters was sounding on board *Liscome Bay* at 0505, the destroyer *Franks*—turning to go back to the task group—called back in to Rear Admiral Griffin.

"Chestnut, *Franks*. This white light that I am investigating looks like a flashlight from a raft. Do you wish me to rejoin or investigate? I can see it distinctly. Over."

"*Franks*, Chestnut. Continue investigation and keep me informed. Over."

"Say again your last message, please."

"Continue investigation, expedite, and keep me informed. Over."

Silence.

"*Franks*, Chestnut. Acknowledge. Over."

"I received your last message very faintly. Please repeat again. Over."

"*Mississippi*, Chestnut. Please relay my message to *Franks*. Over."

"This is *Mississippi*. Wilco. *Franks, Mississippi*. Following received from Chestnut. 'Continue investigation. Expedite and keep me informed.' Over."

"*Mississippi, Franks*. Please advise Chestnut."

"Wilco. Out."

"Chestnut, *Mississippi*. *Franks* has received your message."

"This is Chestnut. Roger. We can hear *Franks*. Out."[12]

Moments later, *Franks* discovered the light to be a signal beacon dropped from a Japanese plane—likely the Betty that had been flying over the American ships each evening. Later, a theory would emerge that the signal beacon had been dropped as a signal to draw off escort vessels such as *Franks* in order to leave a hole in the screen to be exploited by a waiting Japanese submarine. Samuel Eliot Morison noted, however, that the complete lack of communication and coordination between Japanese aircraft and submarines made the validity of that theory unlikely. Rather, he surmised, the signal was intended for other Japanese planes, such as the ones that had assaulted *Independence* four days earlier.[13]

As *Franks* was discovering the signal beacon's true nature, and as *Baltimore* reported another unidentified aircraft sixteen miles to the northwest, Griffin's ships executed another sixty-degree turn, moving toward a heading of 055. Now the formation was heading to the northeast, sixteen miles south of Makin.

There was still, however, a hole in the screen on the starboard side of the task group's formation. Griffin radioed the commander of Destroyer Squadron 47, who was in charge of the task group's screen of protection:

"All destroyers from Africa [the destroyer squadron's call sign], Chestnut. Orient towards hole in the screen. Out."[14]

As the destroyers worked to close the gap, the task group's last turn had brought *Liscome Bay* on an almost perpendicular course to Tabata's submarine. No one knows what exactly transpired at that moment aboard *I-175*, but circumstantial evidence and Japanese naval doctrine indicate that Tabata likely elected for a *zembotzu hassha*, or submerged firing. Using his submarine's sound bearing equipment, Tabata drew a bead on the distant formation while staying concealed beneath the waves from American surface radar. Remaining outside the loose screen of destroyers, he fired a spread of at least three torpedoes at the American ships and hoped for the best. Once his bow torpedo tubes spit out their deadly fish, Tabata quickly ordered his submarine to dive even further for safety.

On board *Liscome Bay*, as Tabata's submarine sank deeper into the nautical gloom and rigged for the inevitable depth-charge attack, Ensign Thomas D. Yuill, D-V(G), was standing at his battle station, a 40-millimeter gun fire director on the galley walkway in the aft starboard quarter of the carrier. Peering out to sea, Yuill's keen eyes spotted a white bubbling wake in the dark water at approximately 0510. Grabbing for his station's telephone, he shouted into its mouthpiece: "Christ, here comes a torpedo!"[15] Seconds later, the streaking torpedo punched into *Liscome Bay* at the worst possible location: the aft starboard quarter—precisely where the carrier's aircraft bomb magazine was located. *Liscome Bay* hadn't quite completed her turn to the new heading of 055; according to Woodward's memory, she was steaming on a northerly course of approximately 025.

Tabata's torpedo exploded into the side of the escort carrier with a thunderous boom. A split second later, a blast of almost unimaginable size followed as fragments from the torpedo ripped through the thin walls shielding the carrier's bomb magazine and detonated its contents. A pillar of orange flame, speckled and dotted with burning pieces of white-hot metal, shot into the air a thousand feet. As it did, a massive blast wave roared through the open hangar deck and across the flight deck, scything through luckless sailors. The life of nearly every officer and sailor standing watch aft of the auxiliary machinery spaces—in other words, anyone positioned in the ship's after third—was extinguished immediately by the explosion. Ironically, had the ship not been at general quarters at the time, much of that section would have been unmanned.

Below, in the forward machinery spaces, the forward engine room, and the boiler room, the shock of the blast ripped away steam lines, compressed-air piping, and oil and water piping, rendering the main and auxiliary machinery in these spaces useless. In that same instant, the ship's electrical lighting snuffed out. Few of the emergency hand lanterns flicked on in response, leaving the interior of the ship in stygian darkness. The burning hiss of escaping steam from the ruptured piping added to the hellish environment.

On *New Mexico*, the bridge crew had been keeping a careful eye on *Liscome Bay*, tracking her as she led the formation onto the new course. From fifteen hundred yards away, they now had a front-row seat for viewing the initial deadly results of Tabata's torpedo attack. "There was a great explosive flare of streaked, yellowish-whitish flame which appeared to burst up from the water, fanning up higher than the superstructure of the *Liscome Bay* and spreading out so that the *Liscome Bay* was blotted from sight," recalled the battleship's skipper, Captain E. M. Zacharias. Moments later, "a second explosion which appeared to come from inside the *Liscome Bay* burst upward, hurling fragments and clearly discernable planes two hundred feet or more in the air. The entire ship seemed to explode and almost at the same instant the interior of the ship except for the extreme bow and stern sections glowed with flame like a furnace."[16]

New Mexico's sister ship, *Mississippi*, was sailing two thousand yards off to the side of *Liscome Bay*. Her captain, J. L. Hunter, also witnessed the terrible series of detonations:

> The first indication of the hit was a bright quick flash of fire on the bearing of the carrier, followed within two or three seconds by a great explosion and towering mass of fire which seemed to engulf the ship and brilliantly illuminated the surrounding area. This column of fire rose to a height of several hundred feet carrying with it burning wreckage and fragments which showered down into the sea for several minutes on all sides. A second heavy explosion was

> seen and heard about twenty seconds after the first. . . . A large mass of flaming wreckage was thrown clear of the ship by the initial eruption and fell into the sea to leeward where it drifted slowly away burning strongly. When the cloud of fire lifted from the ship she was seen to be a blazing wreck with fires raging throughout her structure.[17]

On *Liscome Bay*'s bridge, Beasley, who just happened to be looking aft when the torpedo struck, viewed the blast from a terrifying perspective: "The most violent explosion I had ever seen, heard, or could imagine seemed to open the entire after part of the flight deck. For a moment, it looked as if I could see the entire bowels of the *Liscome Bay*. We were thrown backwards very violently. I picked myself up and again looked down where the flight deck had been. It was a blazing inferno. There are no words to describe the scene."[18]

As the reality began to settle in, a rush of transmissions crowded the radio airwaves:

"Chestnut, *Franks*. Did you see that explosion? Over."

"This is Chestnut. Roger."

"All destroyers with Africa, this is Africa. Shift to the right and left. Move and cover advance. Out."

"Chestnut, *Franks*. I am rejoining. Over."

"This is Chestnut. Roger. Task group, emergency tackline four turn. Out."

"Chestnut, *Mississippi*. Say again your last transmission."

"I say again my last transmission. Four turn. I say again emergency tackline four turn. Out."[19]

Ensign Barrett, having been retrieved along with his Avenger crew from ashore Makin, witnessed the detonation from the deck of the destroyer *Dale*. "Although I didn't know it at the time[,] it was my carrier," he recounted later. "I saw the orange blossom which shot up on the horizon. It seemed to tower 3,000 feet. Thirty seconds later there was another explosion and then a red glow on the horizon."[20]

The blast tossed the planes in the hangar deck into a mangled jumble in the forward section of the deck and splattered oil from this maintenance area up onto the flight deck, where it ignited immediately. The massive jolt triggered the carrier's catapult, flinging the Wildcat sitting on it like a flaming arrow off into the darkness. Another aircraft fell overboard, where it floated, burning, along the ship's starboard side. A third plane, knocked into one of the forward gun galleries, caught fire as well.

On the carrier's island, the ship's radar antenna plummeted with a screech to the deck. So did the mighty bullhorn apparatus. Both toppled and fell onto the flight control platform, barely missing Beasley, who had been knocked to the deck by the series of explosions. A boatswain's mate and the ship's bugler, however, were not so lucky. The twisted mass of metal pinned them both to the deck just feet from Beasley's face. He could see that the boatswain was still alive; the bugler, however, seemed dead.

On board one of *Liscome Bay*'s sister ships, Baker First Class James Calfee witnessed a scene he later described to the *Los Angeles Times:* "The huge forward elevator hurled skyward one thousand feet. Planes on deck became burning meteors, shooting off hundreds of yards into the ocean. Then the gasoline-coated water about the ship caught fire. Smoke and flame so enveloped the area I couldn't see the abandoning crew struggling in the water."[21] Even sailors on the battleship *Pennsylvania,* operating sixteen miles away, saw the pillar of fire on the horizon. At closer range, Captain Zacharias, from his vantage point on *New Mexico,* witnessed the scene in horrific detail: "Oil particles and burning and extinguished fragments, deck splinters up to three feet in length, metal fragments in great numbers—mostly small but as large as one pound in weight—molten drops of metal, bits of clothing, dungarees, overshoes . . . and several pieces of human flesh" showered down on the stunned spectators on *New Mexico*'s decks.[22] Sailors on the destroyer *Maury,* five thousand feet astern of *Liscome Bay,* suffered the gruesome rain, while a sailor aboard *Coral Sea* was struck with one of *Liscome Bay*'s fire extinguishers falling from the sky.

At their distance, despite the light provided by the burning curtain of oil and gasoline that was already encircling the carrier, the sailors on the other ships couldn't see the most horrifying piece of handiwork rendered by the blast. The rear one-third of the ship was obliterated. It was as if a massive circular saw had arisen from the depths and simply cut away the after section of *Liscome Bay*. With her flight and hangar decks quickly becoming roaring conflagrations and tons of seawater pouring into the exposed sections of the ship, one fact was inescapable: the carrier was doomed. The only question was how quickly her final moment would arrive.

Ensign Francis X. Daily,
Liscome Bay's disbursing officer.
(Courtesy Francis Daily)

Irving D. Wiltsie, photographed here as a commander, ashore with his son Ronald.
(Courtesy Ronald Wiltsie)

Lieutenant Commander Oliver Ames. (Courtesy Borderland Archives, North Easton, Massachusetts)

Mess Attendant Second Class Doris Miller, after being presented the Navy Cross, May 27, 1942, at Pearl Harbor. (U.S. Navy photo, courtesy National Archives)

USS *Liscome Bay* (CVE-56). (U.S. Navy photo, courtesy National Archives)

Liscome Bay off the coast of California during September 1943. (U.S. Navy photo, courtesy National Archives)

Henry M. Mullinnix, shown here as a captain. (U.S. Navy photo, courtesy Naval Historical Center)

A Grumman F4F Wildcat, circa early 1942, of Fighter Squadron 41. (U.S. Navy photo, courtesy National Archives)

Tim E. Woodham, shown here circa 1944 with the chevrons of an aviation machinist's mate second class. (Courtesy Tim Woodham)

Commander John G. Crommelin. (Courtesy Southern Museum of Flight, Birmingham, Alabama)

Liscome Bay explodes, as photographed from *Mississippi* (U.S. Navy photo, courtesy National Archives)

Survivors gather on board *Leonard Wood* (APA-12) to witness the burial of two of their comrades, November 25, 1943. (U.S. Coast Guard photo, courtesy National Archives)

Stained-glass window commemorating *Liscome Bay* at the Valley Forge Military Academy's chapel. (Photo by David J. Jackson, Valley Forge Military Academy and College)

8
Twenty-Three Minutes and Counting

The blast from the secondary explosions had rolled through *Liscome Bay*'s lower decks with devastating effect, blowing out hatches, collapsing bulkheads, uprooting boilers, and wrenching pipes loose from the bulkheads. It punched into Buzz Carroll's office, tearing off Charters's life jacket, dungarees, headset, and shoes. Dazed and bewildered in the sudden darkness, Charters found himself sprawled on the deck wearing only his socks. The ship's lights failed, and the force of the explosion had knocked most of the emergency lanterns out of their relay sockets.

"Are you all right?" asked the lieutenant sharing the office with Charters. Squinting in the darkness, Charters replied that he was. Flames from somewhere overhead provided a small amount of light. The lieutenant turned to Carroll's dark shape.

"Are you all right, sir?" he asked Carroll.

No answer came.

"Sir, are you all right?" the lieutenant asked again.

"I'm all right," Carroll finally answered.

"I'm okay," Seaman Galliano volunteered, not waiting to be asked.

Carroll stood up and felt for the doorway to the passage outside. "We've got to get up pressure to fight the fires," he told his men.

Charters and the others followed Carroll into the passageway and struggled with the various valves lining the bulkheads that controlled water pressure for the ship's fire hoses. Despite their best efforts, the pressure gauges continued to register zero.

Charters sidled up next to Carroll.

"There's an awful gassy smell down here."

Carroll ignored him and continued to struggle with the valves, desperately trying to achieve some water pressure for the hoses.

"This is no place for us," Charters persisted. The stench of gasoline hung heavy in the thick air. "We better get out."[1]

Without saying a word, Carroll turned from the useless valves and followed Charters and the others as they headed forward into the ship, unsure of what else they would discover.

Further forward of the damage control office, in the sick bay, the blast had blown the bulkhead behind Storekeeper Roach inward. It struck him on the back and knocked him ten feet through the air and out the treatment room's door. The veteran of the naval battle off Guadalcanal stood back up long enough to shout, "There may be another one!" and then hit the deck again.

He was right. Another explosion followed almost immediately, and once the dust settled, Roach and the others struggled to their feet, calling to one another in the darkness. Some of the sick bay's emergency hand lanterns still functioned, and Roach's group soon established that they were all still alive. Roach picked his way back into the treatment room, found his life jacket, and rejoined the group.

Roach found Dr. Rowe and the other sick bay personnel examining the passageways leading from the sick bay. One was on the port side, the other to starboard, but flame and debris from the hangar deck blocked both passages. Even the passage down to Roach's issue room was blocked. The men paused for a moment, contemplating their predicament. They were out of communication with the rest of the ship, and the sick bay was beginning to fill with smoke. Diesel fuel dripped down from a ruptured line somewhere above. Just as ominously, the carrier began to list to starboard. Roach realized that there was no future in staying in their current location.

"I'm going to try working my way forward along the port-side passageway to the first-division compartment," he said. "Anyone want to come?"[2] Not waiting for an answer, he entered the port-side passageway and started forward. He could hear others following behind him.

The wiry Roach and the other sailors struggled to make it past blown-in bulkheads that blocked their progress. At one point the passageway was so tight that Roach lost one of his shoes. Ignoring it, he squirmed forward. He eventually made it to the first-division compartment. With satisfaction, Roach noted that it was empty. That must mean the sailors in this compartment had found a way out, he reasoned. If they had done so, he told himself, so could he.

Roach turned around and saw that only one other man had joined him from the sick bay. They picked up a trail of fresh air, clambered up a pair of ladders, and emerged on the ship's starboard side, heaving with relief at being above decks. Their joy, however, was short-lived. Flames licked and curled up over the flight deck on the starboard side, fed by the burning oil in the water below. Escape in that direction was blocked. They had escaped the frying pan. Now they had to face the fire.

Other men were still struggling to make their way out from below-decks. The initial explosions had sent Parachute Rigger Gibbons bouncing off the bulkheads of the second deck. Bruised and shaken, he felt his way through the pitch-black darkness back to the growing inferno of the hangar deck. Above him, he could hear men screaming and yelling. One sailor shouted that the port ladder to the flight deck was blocked by wreckage. Heeding his warning, Gibbons quickly moved for the starboard ladder and clambered up it to the flight deck.

Lieutenant Ries, the ship's flight operations officer, was lying in his bunk when the explosions rolled through the ship. He found himself lying on the deck of his stateroom, pinned in the dark beneath a bulkhead. After pushing it off, he stood up and groped his way to the door. Stepping out into the passageway, he saw men running forward from the after part of the ship. Flames blocked that escape route. Naked and barefoot, Ries thought he'd better find something to put on his feet. Ducking back into his cabin, he fumbled unsuccessfully in the darkness for his shoes. Giving up, he emerged into the passageway once more. Men were still retreating from the after section of the ship and clawing their way up the ladder to the deck above. Flames were already licking at that ladder, however, and Ries decided to try once more to find his shoes. Once again, he had no luck.

As he felt around in the darkness, Ries noticed that he couldn't hear any more men down in his section of the ship. Apparently, they had all headed topside. He was the only one left down there. It was an unpleasant feeling, and Ries decided that he had better get moving himself, "clothing and shoes be damned."[3] Taking off at a run, he clambered up the ladder. Tongues of flame licked at his bare feet and legs, but he made it up to the next level little the worse for wear.

Now Ries was in a passageway running athwartship underneath the flight deck. This passageway was also pitch black, and he had to feel his way along it as he searched for a way out. Fortunately, his grasping hands clutched a door handle. Pushing the door open, he tumbled out onto the catwalk. The sight that confronted Ries was "a good presentation of Hell," he told a hometown newspaper reporter later. "There was fire all over. Men were running around as they waited to get on the gun galleys or to the ropes to go over the side. Guns were going off automatically because of the heat. Bombs on planes in the hangars were going off as the planes burned. It was a terrific sight."[4]

The torpedo blast and exploding ammunition had knocked Aerographer's Mate Cruse out of his slumber in the balloon inflation room. He clutched desperately at his bunk as the ship shuddered, trying to avoid a fall onto the jumbled mess of helium bottles that the blast had knocked loose from their brackets. Gaining a secure grip, Cruse lowered himself to the deck and struggled among the piles of bottles to find his shoes. It took a few moments to locate them and work them to the top of the pile, but Cruse was patient. As he struggled to pull out his shoes, he breathed in a battery of smells that was all too familiar to him—a heady mix of diesel fuel, oil, gunpowder, electrical fires, and thick smoke. He recognized the odors from his experience during the sinking of *Wasp* and knew that they did not bode well for his latest carrier.

Wearing shoes and skivvies, Cruse stuck his head out of the balloon inflation room door and looked outside his ship. Off the bow he could see the burning wreckage of the Wildcat fighter that had been jolted into a premature and disastrous catapult launch. He climbed out of the balloon inflation room and up to the flight deck, wondering about the fate of his fellow aerographers. Unbeknownst to Cruse, Pinder was one of the few survivors from the carrier's air plot. He had linked up with Mahood in the aerology office, and the two men had made good their escape topside. Blakley and Bruce, standing on the catwalk near the thermo-screen at the time of the torpedo strike, had been catapulted off of the catwalk back into the balloon inflation room. After struggling sorely to their feet, they had also headed topside. "The vessel," Bruce recalled later, "reacts as if taken up in giant hands, shaken and twisted in an unimaginable way. There are no words to describe the feelings that engulf those serving on the ship that is first listing and then sinking from underneath them. Every person aboard begins to grab for their life jacket—if they can find it."[5]

Like Cruse, Ensign Davis was also knocked from his bunk by the blasts. Unlike Cruse, however, Davis was four decks deep within the bowels of *Liscome Bay*. Nevertheless, he could still hear ammunition exploding up above him. Davis desperately pulled on whatever clothes he could lay his hands on. In the darkness around him, about a half dozen other men did the same, struggling in the jumbled maze of tumbled furniture and collapsed partitions.

Within a matter of moments, dense, acrid smoke began rolling into Davis's wardroom. The officers hurried out of the compartment, looking for a path topside. The port-side ladder was crumpled and blocked with debris, but the starboard ladder remained clear. Coughing and choking, the officers clambered up the ladder onto the ship's second deck, where they encountered Rowe and the majority of the sick bay party, slowly picking their way through the warped passageways among the wreckage and bodies. With the viscous smoke and failed electrical lighting, visibility was reduced to practically zero.

As Davis struggled through the darkness, a shuffling figure lurched past him. It was Sistrunk, fresh from the sick bay. The ensign might not be a good swimmer, but he wasn't about to go down with the ship—appendectomy or not. The odds didn't look good for an able-bodied individual aboard the darkened carrier, much less for a marginal swimmer whose stomach was being held closed by a line of sutures, but Sistrunk was a fighter. Taking him by the arm, Davis helped the groggy young pilot find a ladder leading up to the hangar deck. As he started to climb up the ladder, Davis noticed that the ship had started listing to starboard. As the thought of being trapped belowdecks on a capsized ship flashed across his mind, he frantically pushed Sistrunk up the ladder to the hangar deck.

Davis and Sistrunk found the hangar deck an inferno of mutilated aircraft, torn and blackened bodies, and roaring pools of burning oil. The force of the blasts had swept most of the wreckage to the forward portion of the hangar deck. Glancing around, Davis spied a hole blasted in the side of the ship on the port side and helped Sistrunk shuffle over to it. Leaning on the jagged edges of the hole and looking out over the water, Davis and Sistrunk gratefully gulped in mouthfuls of fresh air.

Meanwhile, the sailors assigned to the auxiliary machinery spaces below the second deck on the first platform were also fighting their way out of *Liscome Bay*'s depths. They didn't realize it, but those ten sailors, stationed in the ship's gyro room, generator room, machine shop (in the lowest level of the second deck), and electrical workshop, were the ship's aftmost survivors.[6] The blast had knocked most of them to their knees, but they wasted no time getting to their feet and looking for a way topside. Below *Liscome Bay*'s waterline was obviously no place to be.

The five sailors from the machine shop clambered up the port ladder and joined the other survivors from the auxiliary machinery spaces. Under the guidance of the section's chief petty officer, they squeezed their way across the ship through the athwartship passage. Normally the passageway was three feet wide, but the force of the blast had warped it so badly that now there was barely twelve inches to squeeze through.

Reaching the starboard ladder, the ten men started up toward the second deck, only to find the hatch covered with debris. Desperate moments passed as the lead sailors atop the ladder clawed at the debris, pushing and pulling it to try to clear a passage through. Beneath them, oily water was already lapping at the feet of their comrades. Finally, they managed to dig a hole large enough to pull themselves through. The last man to climb up the ladder left a foot of water steadily rising on the deck below him.

Once on the second deck, the sailors discovered more collapsed bulkheads, partitions, and decking in the area of the wardroom and the chief petty officers' mess. Picking their way aft, they stepped down onto the now-exposed tops of the ship's water tanks and crossed over to the ship's starboard side. Now, they were looking out onto open water as they peered out through the ripped stern of the carrier. Seven of the men exited the ship at the waterline from this point. They didn't need an officer to tell them that the ship was doomed. Three others grabbed a tangle of hanging cables and pulled themselves up to the ship's gallery deck.

Chief Shipfitter Lewis A. Ashley's battle station for general quarters was in the shipfitters' workshop. Edward Jonas, the ship's tailor, was also stationed in the shop as part of the ship's repair party. So were Fireman Robert Haynes and Electrician's Mate First Class Harry Greenbaum. Just as Ashley finished taking the station's muster roll call, and as Greenbaum stepped out in the passage to check the nearby forward elevator, the first massive explosion ripped through the ship, blowing the elevator totally out of its shaft. The explosion's blast blew off every stitch of Ashley's clothes, including his shoes and rubber life jacket. Ashley was left naked, standing in the dark, without communications with the rest of the ship, but still in charge of a group of frightened men.

Seconds later, Greenbaum stumbled back into the compartment. One arm hung limply at his side. The other had been blown off.

"What happened?" Haynes asked from the floor. Blown against a work table, his leg was broken in two places.

"We've been torpedoed," Greenbaum replied before slumping to the floor.[7]

One of the other survivors in the workshop, although wounded himself, managed to open a side hatch to the port exterior. As the sound of roaring flames echoed through the ship, he leaped out. It seemed to be a better option than remaining belowdecks. Haynes thought so as well. He crawled over to the hatch and dropped twelve feet into the water.

The other men in the shipfitters' shop turned to Ashley. "What do we do now, Chief?" one of them asked. On the hangar deck and in the elevator well, a devilish conflagration roared. Looking through an open hatch, Jonas saw that the hangar deck was a raging inferno.

"Let's make a run for it through the flames and try to get water on the fire!" Ashley shouted in response.[8]

Working their way past the burning elevator well, Ashley, Jonas, and the repair party found their path topside blocked by the flaming hangar deck. Abandoning that route, they struggled up twisted ladders through more wreckage. Eventually they made it onto the flight deck and began to break out the ship's fire hoses.

At the time of the initial blasts, the forward engine and boiler room had been fully manned.[9] The explosions knocked out the lighting, unseated boilers, and ruptured steam and air lines. Fireman Phelan Allee, who had arrived in the forward engine room only seconds earlier, felt the force of the blast rip his watch off his wrist. In the dark chaos filled with the shrieking hisses of escaping steam, Allee and the other engine and boiler room survivors pulled themselves off the deck and searched for a way out. They were on the tank top level—the lowest level of the ship. With four decks separating them from the fresh air of the flight deck, it was with considerable haste that one group stumbled toward the ladder leading up to the first platform deck.

The ladder, however, was blocked with debris and fallen piping. Abandoning that route, they headed for the escape trunk and used it to climb toward the second deck. They found the hatch leading to the second deck "dogged"—that is, tightly shut with a "dog" wrench inserted in the hatch's wheel to provide the necessary leverage for spinning it open. Desperate curses echoed up and down the escape trunk as the lead sailor struggled with the hatch. The few sailors with flashlights tried to give him what illumination they could. After a considerable amount of difficulty, he swung it open and the other sailors quickly followed him onto the second deck by Chaplain Carley's office.

Struggling over piles of debris and crumpled partitions, the band of sailors picked their way over to the starboard ladder leading to the hangar deck. That ladder, however, was damaged and, at any rate, only led into the maw of the raging fire on the hangar deck above them. The worried sailors headed back toward the escape trunk, exchanging nervous suggestions regarding any remaining routes to safety. Most of them decided to try to work their way aft.

Before they did, one sailor heard a frantic banging on the hatch leading out of the engine room. He and his fellow sailors gathered around the hatch, which had been warped in the devastating blasts that had rocked the ship. Three refugees from the engine room were behind it, struggling to get out of the smoky darkness. Water was already pooling at their feet, and the ship's increasing list underscored their peril.

Heaving, tugging, and shoving, the sailors managed to work the hatch until a space twelve inches wide opened. The stubborn hatch wouldn't budge any further. The first two sailors, twisting and squirming, slipped through the opening, but the third man was simply too big to make it through the hatch. After a couple of tries, it became obvious that he would never be able to slip out. With heavy hearts, his shipmates left him to his fate.

The sailors snaked through the damaged wardroom, following the route of the refugees from the auxiliary machinery spaces. Like them, they crossed along the tops of the water tanks and eventually emerged at the massive gash aft. By now the waterline was nearly at the second level of the sinking ship. This group also slipped into the water and started swimming away.

Allee had attempted an escape by a different route. When he saw that the regular exit topside from the forward engine room was blocked, he slipped down to the lower level one deck below. The carrier's drive shaft ran through that space. Allee noticed that the force of the explosions had bent the shaft. There was little time to ponder *Liscome Bay*'s mechanical difficulties. Scalding steam from the ruptured boilers made breathing difficult, and Allee quickly wet his handkerchief at a water fountain, covered his face, and began searching for a way out. Locating an escape hatch, he squirmed through its mangled and warped interior up to the hangar deck. Reaching that deck, he kept scrambling higher, desperate to avoid the hangar deck's exploding ordnance and burning fuel. In his haste, he cut his hand on a jagged piece of metal. Ignoring the pain and the bullets from exploding ammunition whizzing past his head, Allee continued to search for a way up onto the flight deck.

Before he could make it, another explosion ripped through the hangar deck and tossed Allee like a rag doll onto a pile of scrap metal, where he lay unconscious for an unknown length of time. When he awoke, he found himself sprawled across the bleeding body of one of the ship's officers. As he pulled himself off the unconscious officer, other sailors joined him. Allee held a portable light on the mangled man as the other sailors worked to pull him from the scrap metal. While they did, Allee took the opportunity to pull his uninflated life vest from a pouch he had attached to his belt and slip it on. Once they pulled the officer free of the scrap pile, the sailors could see the extent of his injuries for the first time. Fractured bones protruded from his arms and legs. It seemed doubtful the man would survive much longer.

If he did, Allee never found out. Nor did Allee even feel the explosive blast moments later that blew him out an opening in the hangar deck and into the sea. Struggling back to consciousness for a second time in a matter of minutes, he struggled to blow air into his leaking life vest. Another sailor blown overboard by the blast treaded water near Allee and asked him if he had an extra vest or preserver. He did not.

Chaplain Carley had been washing his face in the head when the double blasts rocked the ship. The force of the explosions hurled him to the deck. Picking himself up off the deck, he sifted through the jagged, jumbled rubble of broken sinks, toilets, and urinals to try to find his life jacket and personal kit. It was a hopeless search in the dusty darkness, and he abandoned his equipment somewhere beneath the shattered porcelain and broken pipes.

Stepping out into the passageway, Carley encountered the refugees from the sick bay, collected into an ad hoc party by the ever-attentive Dr. Rowe. Thick, gray smoke began to inundate the compartment. Clearly, their position was untenable. Ignoring a leg wound, Rowe gathered up whatever medical gear he could carry, organized the men into makeshift litter parties to transport the wounded, and began guiding them forward through the starboard passage. Feeling their way through dense smoke, they continued forward, looking for an avenue of escape. There were four options—two ladders leading up to the hangar deck, and two hatches leading further forward into the ship.

Rowe, Carley, and their band of walking wounded found both ladders blocked with wreckage and burning debris. Abandoning that route, they moved toward the port-side hatch, feeling their way carefully through the thickening smoke. Reaching the hatch, they discovered it hopelessly jammed from the force of the explosion. By now, even Carley felt a sense of fear creeping into his mind. "This is it," he thought. "We'll go down trapped."[10] They headed for the starboard hatch. It was also closed, but with a quick tug it swung open. The men quickly tumbled through it, advancing further toward the bow of the ship.

In the smoky darkness, Rowe and Carley's group intercepted Carroll's small band from the damage control office. Together, they picked their way carefully through the darkness, stumbling over torn metal and debris and guided only by the feel of fresh air on their faces. They eventually arrived in the aerology office.

By that time the aerology office was empty. After trying to bring some order to the office's chaos following the initial blasts, Aerographer Mahood had given up and headed topside. Passing through the vacant office, Carley tripped. In the darkness, the chaplain tripped over an object that felt like a life jacket. When he reached down he was happy to discover it was indeed a life jacket. He slipped it on. The delay separated him from Carroll, Rowe, and the others, though, and he made his own way up onto the carrier's high side walkway.

Meanwhile, Carroll's group reached the base of the ship's elevator shaft. The shaft, like much of the hangar and flight decks, was on fire, but Carroll and Charters found Boatswain Roy W. Hunt fighting the blaze. He had a portable CO^2 fire extinguisher in his hands. With sure, quick blasts of white foam, Hunt was trying to beat back the flames. Three empty extinguishers lay at his feet, evidence of the losing battle he had been waging.

"Come on, Boats," Carroll said to Hunt. "Get the hell outta here."[11]

Hunt ignored his superior officer and kept blasting at the flames. The other men in the party glanced nervously at Carroll, curious to see how the lieutenant commander would react to this insubordination. For the first time, with the light of the burning shaft providing illumination, Charters and the others noticed that Carroll was covered in blood. The initial blasts had peppered him with shrapnel, and he was bleeding heavily from wounds to his face and chest. Rowe asked Carroll if he wanted him to dress his wounds, but Carroll waved the doctor off. Instead, he led the group of men topside, coming out on the walkway around the flight deck.

Elsewhere aboard the mangled carrier, other men struggled to find ways topside and out of the smoky interior. Seaman Second Class Lester E. Bush, one of the ship's firemen, scaled a superheated steam pipe rather than wait to force his way up an overcrowded ladder. The scalding pipe seared both of his hands, but, ignoring the pain, he made it up to the flight deck. Seaman James Honold, having just finished handing out the morning's parachutes, had just laid his head down on a spare chute's pack to catch a quick catnap when the torpedo hit. The ensuing explosion knocked him unconscious.

Fireman James King had been at his general quarters station in the degaussing room at the time of Tabata's attack. At that station, he would sit, headphones in place, awaiting a call to flip the switches that would change the ship's polarity from positive to negative. In theory, such a switch would foil any magnetic mines the carrier might stumble across. The torpedo blast and secondary explosions knocked King to the floor, and the degaussing equipment tumbled down on top of him. He extricated himself from the jumble of equipment and staggered out into the passageway. It was clear to him that the degaussing station had suddenly become irrelevant. He started moving forward through the ship, passing through the main galley. As he did so, King had to pick his way over dozens of frozen turkeys which the cooks had taken out of the freezers to thaw for the next day's Thanksgiving meal. King could only hope that there was another such meal in his future.

He soon joined several other sailors moving through the carrier as they searched for a way topside. The group came to a closed and tightly dogged hatch blocking their way further through the passageway. The hatch's dog pipe was missing, though, and the sailors came to a halt, simply staring at the closed hatch in numb frustration. King wasn't going to accept defeat so readily, well aware that thousands of gallons of aviation fuel rested mere feet below them. He pushed his way to the hatch, grasped it with both hands, and, with a surge of adrenaline, spun the wheel. The hatch swung open, and King led the group onward. Moments later, they emerged on the flight deck.

Seaman Leonard Bohm was in his bunk when the torpedo struck. Although the blasts plunged his compartment into darkness, Bohm was berthed well forward of the hangar deck, away from the initial detonation. He quickly scrambled out of his compartment, up a ladder, and onto the catwalk surrounding the flight deck.

Others had tougher escapes. Woodham had just returned to his bunk from the showers when the torpedo hit. The explosions hurled him to the deck, causing him to rap his head on his locker. Struggling to his feet, Woodham immediately began to search for a way topside through the mangled passageways. The issue of clothes didn't cross Woodham's mind. He just knew he had to get above deck. Naked, he began to search for a way out of the ship's dark interior.

Woodham first tried to exit through the chiefs' quarters, located near the hangar deck, but a furnace of roaring flames blocked his path aft. Chastened, he turned and worked his way forward through the ship. Joining with five or six other survivors, Woodham wiggled past and under warped bulkheads, helping the others in the group drag a wounded man with them. All around them, the sound of stressing metal and further explosions told them they had little time to find their way off their carrier. Eventually, the little group found a familiar sight in the dark—the room that housed the ship's catapult machinery. A ladder led upward from the room, and Woodham and his companions clambered up it and onto the ship's catwalk above deck. They were safe—for the moment.

Beebe had been on an early-morning schedule similar to Woodham's. Freshly shaven and with a towel draped over his arm, he had just stepped into the head when he felt a tremendous rumble shake the ship. A second later, a massive explosion snapped him off the deck. By the time he fell back to the deck, the head's lights were knocked out. Rising slowly, Beebe stepped gingerly through the darkness to the head's entry door. His fumbling hands found no opening, though, and he thought he must be disoriented. Backing off, he felt all the way around the head, blindly palming the washbasins, the passage to the shower stalls, the shower stalls, and then back to the end of the room. He was right—the one door out of the head was blocked.

For a moment, Beebe was gripped by fear. He recalled a grim tale of two sailors trapped in compartments below the waterline of a sunken ship at Pearl Harbor. At least they reportedly had a deck of cards with which to calmly spend their final hours. All Beebe had was a damp towel. He wondered how soon he would feel the seawater lapping at his ankles, and if he would go to his death with the same savoir faire as the sailors at Pearl.

As Beebe considered his predicament, a series of smaller explosions wracked the ship. As *Liscome Bay* settled once again, Beebe noticed that the blackness in front of him was beginning to fade to gray. Slowly, his eyes were able to make out the outline of the head. But where was the light coming from? Squinting his eyes and peering hard, Beebe realized that flames on the hangar deck were illuminating the head. A set of two bulkheads separated the head from the hangar deck, but the explosive blast had apparently blown the bulkheads down from the overhead. The separation between the top of the bulkheads and the deck above them was allowing the light of the hangar deck's flames to flicker into the head. Looking forward, Beebe saw that the forward bulkheads had been breached as well. He scrambled over the bulkhead, dropped down into the bunkroom on the other side, popped out into the passageway beside it, and headed topside.

Beebe had just missed sharing his experience with Captain Crommelin in the shower room. Crommelin was running slightly ahead of the squadron commander that morning and had already returned to his cabin following a shower. It had been a quick one—random suds still clung to the chief of staff's back and shoulders. Seconds after he stepped back into his quarters, the first detonation rocked *Liscome Bay*, followed by the violent secondary explosions.

Crommelin didn't know what had happened to the carrier, but he knew it couldn't be good. Still naked, he stepped out of his quarters. Another explosion hurled debris down the passageway, and a steel fragment smacked him in the head. Ignoring the pain flashing through his skull, Crommelin picked his way down the passageway. He stepped carefully over a pair of dead bodies, trying to block out the smell of burned flesh. Reaching a hatch at the end of the passageway, he pulled it open. It proved an almost fatal mistake.

Flames instantly burst through the opening, burning hungrily in the fresh air, scorching Crommelin's right side and burning his face, shoulders, legs, and arms. He stumbled back in shock and severe pain. For a brief moment, Crommelin thought he was finished. He had a wife and three-year-old daughter back in Coronado, California. Would he see them again? The flames advanced no further, however, and he stumbled back to relative safety. Abandoning his initial route, Crommelin made his way through the dark passageways to the catapult room that Woodham and his group had discovered. Ignoring the pain coursing through his burned arms and hands, he pulled himself up a ladder and onto the chaotic flight deck.

Lieutenant Smith had been walking aft of the starboard side of the bridge when the torpedo and bomb magazine detonated. The first blast hurled him fifteen feet through the air. He landed facedown with a heavy thud and had only just pulled himself to his knees when a second blast tossed him into the air once again. Crumpled on the deck, the dazed lieutenant felt a rain of oil smattering down on him. All around, a steady roar of crackling flames grew ever louder. Trying to clear his battered head, Smith saw that the deck abaft the island was a furnace-like mass of flames, the metal on the bridge "hot enough to sear the flesh of a man's hand to the bone."[12] Waves of intense heat pounded him and the other survivors as they stared at the amazing conflagration. Smith wondered if his lungs would sear from the heat. Doubtful of the ship's chances, he pulled a life jacket from a storage bin and slipped it on.

Daily, sitting on the floor in the ship's communications office when the torpedo smashed into *Liscome Bay*, was unhurt by the blasts that rocked the carrier. As he struggled to his feet in the sudden darkness, his first thought concerned the flight deck gasoline line that ran up the port side just outside the office. If it had ignited, the ten officers and men in the communications office and the three officers in the decoding room next door would be doomed. Trying to ignore that possibility, Daily reached for his kapok life jacket. He had thrown it against a forward bulkhead when he had arrived in the office. Now, however, a snapped girder blocked his access to the life jacket. He would have to do without it. Fortunately, he still had his survival belt around his waist. It contained a folded blow-up life belt, a payroll list containing the names and amounts of all officers and men who still had money "riding the books" from the previous payday, a fishhook with thirty feet of nylon line, and some matches in a waterproof wrap. All told, he was in far better shape than many of his shipmates for a disaster at sea.

Nevertheless, the survival belt around his waist was little consolation to Daily at the time. *Liscome Bay*'s outlook appeared grim. Dozens of small fires had sprung to life around him, providing flickering illumination to the communications office. In the decoding room, all three of the officers were slumped over their typewriters. Electricity crinkled and flashed all over the room. At this point, heading for the flight deck looked like Daily's best bet. As he moved for the compartment's door, Ensign Harry W. Taylor, C-V(S), USNR, stepped in front of him. Falling in behind Taylor, Daily passed the nearby radio shack. Fireman Second Class Russell K. Van Buren and about six other sailors stepped out of the shack and joined the two officers. Linking his hand in the back of Daily's belt, Van Buren followed the ensign as the procession snaked through the jumbled passageways.

Taylor soon reached an athwartship passageway. Turning left, they reached the ship's port side and the executive officer's cabin. Hall's cabin contained a light lock leading to the exterior of the ship, and Taylor quickly threw it open. A raging wall of flame, fed by the oil on the water off the carrier's port side, confronted the two ensigns. Behind them came the train of nervous enlisted men, and Daily briefly imagined himself being pushed into the blazing furnace ahead.

"About face!" he shouted.[13]

Navy discipline paid off. Van Buren and the sailors obeyed instantly, and Taylor and Daily were able to step back from the fire. Before they could even breathe a sigh of relief, though, a nearby antiaircraft ammunition locker exploded. The blast hurled Daily and Taylor into the executive officer's cabin, where they landed on a pile of burning metal scrap. Van Buren and the radiomen were blasted back out into the passageway.

Scrambling off the flaming rubble, the two ensigns discovered that the force of the blast had snuffed out the fire in their immediate vicinity. Calling for the radiomen to join them, they clambered up a ladder onto the port-side catwalk just off a gun platform on the ship's exterior. From this position they were shoulder high to the flight deck and directly opposite the bridge. Scanning the flaming deck, they could see no sign of life through the thick clouds of black smoke and walls of fire.

An unspoken thought crossed both ensigns' minds. The list of casualties from this attack was going to be high. The life of virtually every crewman aft of the torpedo strike had been snuffed out by the blast of the bomb magazine. This group included the men manning the various antiaircraft gun positions ringing the ship, which likely included Doris Miller. Most of the officers, pilots, aircrewmen, and sailors on the flight deck and hangar deck had also been cut down by the massive blasts. For the moment, Daily and Taylor were among the survivors. Whether they would remain so was still in doubt.

9
Abandon Ship!

Climbing off the high walkway and onto the flight deck, Chaplain Carley stepped into a scene as nightmarish as any description of hell he had ever read during his seminary days. A roaring conflagration blocked his view of the after part of the ship. Forward, blackened and mangled aircraft lay crumpled and burning on the flight deck. Thick clouds of inky smoke billowed in the sea breeze, stinging Carley's eyes and scorching his throat. Flames rose from belowdecks and from the burning patches of oil in the water, licking greedily over the side of the carrier. Along the edge of the flight deck, rounds of 20- and 40-millimeter ammunition exploded in the heat, spitting deadly projectiles through the air in all directions. Occasionally, star shells would also ignite, sending flares popping into the dark sky and sea. "No fire extinguishers, no communication system, no lifeboats," Carley observed. "All was chaos."[1]

Nevertheless, Carley counted himself lucky to have simply reached the flight deck. He looked around and saw that Dr. Rowe, Lieutenant Commander Carroll, and naked Captain Crommelin were working to bring some semblance of order to the forward part of the ship. Carroll in particular seemed to be all over the ship, trying to organize repair parties and put fire hoses into action.

In radar plot, broken and bleeding men lay sprawled in the dark amid shattered equipment. Commander Hall quickly organized the survivors and pushed them aft and up onto the flight deck. Rather than join them, however, he turned back belowdecks to search the ship for more wounded. He would not be seen again.

Up on the flight deck, Rowe tended to the numerous wounded as best he could. One sailor writhed in pain, his hands gripping a broken leg. He was too badly injured to move across the burning flight deck, so Rowe administered a shot of morphine and then, with the aid of another sailor, gently lowered the man into the water by the starboard side and allowed him to float clear of the vessel. There were few other options, and Rowe moved on to other men. In later days, his comrades would recall his "splendid conduct" among the carnage of the flight deck.[2]

As Rowe ministered to the wounded, other sailors continued to battle the blazing fire and assist the injured. Seaman Richard Abbot, like Boatswain Hunt belowdecks, provided a conspicuous example to his shipmates. Blown to the deck by the initial series of blasts, he had struggled to his feet and grimly assessed the situation. The stern of the ship—what was left of it—was a mass of roaring flames. Abbott stumbled over to one of the fire-fighting station's water valves. He could see that two other men had already unwound a fire hose and were ready to go into action. Abbott twirled the valve open—with no effect. Apparently, the main line had been blown. Elsewhere, other frustrated sailors were making the same discovery.

Ensign Woodward, the officer of the deck, had been standing on the bridge near Wiltsie at the time of the torpedo strike. The first blast threw both men to the deck. Neither was injured, though, and they quickly pulled themselves to their feet. From his vantage point on the bridge, Woodward watched in amazement as flames engulfed *Liscome Bay* within thirty seconds. Gaping holes dotted the flight deck—a deck that now ended just aft of the ship's forward funnel.

Beset by rolling waves of intense heat, Woodward and the others huddled for a moment behind a raised rim of steel that ran around the bridge. To Woodward, "it was clear . . . that the ship was untenable."[3] Wiltsie apparently reached a similar conclusion. The bridge crew moved to abandon their perch, only to find all escape routes down the island's ladders and passageways blocked. Unflustered, Woodward and Wiltsie broke out an escape line and dropped it over the coaming to the flight deck some twenty feet below. Hand over hand, the officers and the other members of the bridge crew lowered themselves to the flight deck, approximately four minutes after the first explosion.

Fire Controlman Jenkins had heard Ensign Yuill's cry of "Torpedo!"

over his headset seconds before the initial blast—a blast that knocked one of *Liscome Bay*'s Avengers off the flight deck onto the fully manned starboard forward 40-millimeter gun platform. Almost instantly, the torpedo bomber exploded and began burning, incinerating the gun's crew. Seconds later, the gun station's ammunition started popping off amid the flames.

A rapidly growing oil fire also threatened Jenkins's fire director station and the gun crews on the ship's starboard side. Leaving their positions, Jenkins and the surviving gun crews climbed up to the flight deck. They found themselves in the unenviable position of standing above tanks containing thousands of gallons of aviation fuel while an uncontrolled fire spread over their ship. "We decided it was time to go," Jenkins wrote years later.[4] He and his men took off their shoes and lined them up neatly along the edge of the deck as they prepared to abandon ship from the port-side bow.

Aviation Machinist's Mate John Beymer was one of the men assigned to those forward starboard 40-millimeter guns. The first blast had thrown him and his fellow gun crew members into the air, and Beymer hit the deck bleeding from multiple shrapnel wounds in his right arm and leg. Rolling over, he saw the decapitated torso of the lead gunner lying nearby. A second, more powerful blast exploded aft of the bridge and rocked the entire ship. With a sick feeling, Beymer realized that he had friends from VC-39 who were—or had been—mustering for flights in the vicinity of the second blast. He couldn't imagine how any of them would have survived.

After struggling to their feet, Beymer and the other survivors stumbled onto the flight deck. They witnessed a confused scene, with men milling about the flight deck, some pulling out hoses, others throwing ammunition boxes and clips over the side. Secondary explosions sent debris hurtling through the air. A boatswain's mate stepped up to Beymer. Beymer knew him only as Jack.

"Captain Wiltsie has gone aft to assess the damage," Jack explained, yelling to be heard over the thunderous flames. "The word is being passed—abandon ship."

It was a word Beymer welcomed. Despite his wounds, he and others helped the more badly injured sailors move to the side of the ship where lifelines had been dropped into the water. With careful hands, they helped those men negotiate the lines off the deck and down toward the water. Then, when there appeared to be no more he could do, Beymer followed suit. Meanwhile, Jenkins and his gun crew were apparently satisfied with the military precision with which they had lined up their shoes and began jumping off the port side, taking the long plunge into the dark water below.

On the starboard side, Seaman Bergquist, who had been manning a 40-millimeter gun, struggled to consciousness. The initial explosion had blown off his life jacket and knocked him out. As he came to his senses, he found himself alone, sitting propped up against a bulkhead. With blood dripping from his nose and ears, Bergquist stirred painfully. His shoulder was broken, an ugly gash sliced from his underarm to his shoulder, and his hands and face were burned. Once on his feet, Bergquist struggled to make it to the flight deck.

By now, Woodham had emerged on the flight deck. He came across one of his fellow airedales, a captain for a Wildcat, lying on the flight deck. The man had been standing in front of his fighter, which had been positioned on the catapult, when the torpedo had smashed into *Liscome Bay*. The force of the explosion had triggered the catapult and launched the pilotless aircraft. As it rocketed off the catapult, the Wildcat's wing had clipped the airedale, breaking both of his shoulders and injuring his back but somehow still leaving his eyeglasses perched on his nose.

"I can't move," he told Woodham. "Can you find me a life jacket?"

Limping on a wounded left foot, Woodham found a life jacket hanging on the back of one of the 20-millimeter gun platforms. He brought it over to the injured man and gently slipped it on him.

"Carry me over to the side, and drop me over," the man asked.

Woodham carefully hoisted the wounded sailor and dragged him to the port side of the flight deck. It seemed to be listing even more sharply to starboard than before. Woodham reasoned the sailor was right—his chances were much better in the water.

As they approached the edge of the deck, however, Woodham's wounded shipmate yelled out, "Put me down!"

Woodham hesitated. He knew that the sooner he could get him off the ship, the better. With every passing moment, the distance between the edge of the port deck and the waterline below was growing greater. Nevertheless, he put the sailor on the deck.

"Take my glasses off," the wounded man told Woodham. "Toss them over the side."

With a quick snatch, a puzzled Woodham did as requested.

"Now throw me over," he added. Apparently, he had no desire to see what was about to happen.

Woodham pulled him to the edge and let him go. He fell awkwardly into the water, landing with what Woodham reckoned to be a painful splash. At least he was off the ship, Woodham reasoned. He turned to see what else could be done aboard ship.[5]

Aviation Machinist's Mate Jack Wells also made his way onto the flight deck, though he wasn't sure exactly how he had managed to reach it. Shaking off his dazed state, he helped inflate several life rafts and tossed them over the side. Then Wells noticed several crewmen attacking one of the many outbreaks of fire on the oily deck. He joined them in their battle and, moments later, staggered from another explosive blast. The area where he had been standing seconds ago had erupted in a violent detonation.

The fires were clearly out of control, and ammunition in the antiaircraft gun positions around Wells began to cook off, firing rounds past his ears. He tried to inflate his life belt but found that he could not. It was an unhappy discovery. The ship was burning more furiously than ever, and even the water surrounding it was on fire. Clearly, the time had come to abandon ship. Running to the edge of the flight deck, Wells made a flying leap, smashed into the water, skirted patches of burning oil, and reached a life raft.

By now, Gibbons was also on the flight deck. He stumbled across a crewman who had two broken shoulders. Ignoring the man's cries of pain, Gibbons slipped a life jacket on him and lowered him off the deck into the ocean. Turning back from the side of the ship, the parachute rigger spied another sailor dragging himself across the deck with a broken leg. He also lacked a life jacket. Gibbons didn't have one either, but he managed to find one for his wounded shipmate, slipped it on him, and lowered him into the water. Then, convinced that the ship was sinking,

Gibbons dove overboard. Having already survived the sinking of the carrier *Lexington*, he had no intention of ending his lucky streak with *Liscome Bay*.

Seaman Lloyd Whalen, who had at one time thought he wanted to be a radio operator on one of VC-39's Avengers, also seemed to be on a lucky streak, though he may not have realized it at the time. Having decided not to pursue his radio operator rating, the Texan had spent most of *Liscome Bay*'s voyage as a cook in the officers' mess. His general quarters station was an antiaircraft gun position on the starboard side of the carrier, near the bridge. Consequently, when the torpedo hit he was standing on the starboard catwalk, not down in the killing zone of the hangar deck with so many other VC-39 crewmen.

Whalen did not, however, escape without injury. During general quarters, antiaircraft crews were required to wear helmets, gloves, socks, dungarees, and shirts with the sleeves rolled down in order to protect their skin from the flash burns associated with exploding aviation fuel. In the balmy central Pacific, though, enforcement of that rule had become lax, and Whalen was standing between the magazine loader and the gunner's mate with no gloves and his sleeves rolled up.

The explosion triggered by *I-175*'s deadly torpedo had instantaneously sent a blast of flame along the catwalk. It left Whalen and his fellow crewmen with bright red flash burns on their exposed arms, legs, necks, and faces. Fortunately, the pain wouldn't set in until later, and Whalen was able to start inflating his life belt. As he blew into the valve, one of the secondary explosions rocked the carrier. The force of the explosion caused Whalen to chip a tooth on the valve—a minor injury considering what was transpiring around him.

"We better get out of here," one of Whalen's companions on the gun crew announced. "This thing is going down."[6]

On the other side of the ship, Seaman Bill Fisher reached the same conclusion. He had also been serving as a 20-millimeter antiaircraft gun team's loader, but he was fortunate enough to be on the relatively protected port catwalks. Fisher didn't think of it at the time, but he was far more fortunate than his replacement, Art Morrow, down in the aft engine steering room—it was a battle station that no longer existed. More immediately, the blasts that had rocked *Liscome Bay* convinced Fisher that the time to abandon ship had come. With a strong leap he jumped overboard, splashed into the dark water forty feet below, and started swimming for safety.

Lieutenant Smith, ignoring the searing heat, stepped carefully into the smoking remains of the open bridge, hoping to find Captain Wiltsie. The bridge was a complete shambles. Smith didn't find Wiltsie, but he did find Beasley. Beasley's helmet had been blown off, his shirt and pants were torn to shreds, his left shoe was sliced open and oozing blood, and each breath brought sharp pain to his lower ribcage. Ignoring the pain, he was struggling to free the ship's bugler and a boatswain's mate from underneath the bridge's fallen bullhorn and radar antennas. The falling apparatus had missed Beasley by scant feet. Beneath it, the bugler did not move, but the boatswain's mate appeared alive. The crumpled mass of wreckage was so tightly wedged against the platform that Beasley couldn't pull them out.

Smith and another survivor moved to assist Beasley. Together, they strained at the bullhorn as the choking smoke rolled over them. The metal of the bullhorn, decks, and railings grew hotter by the moment as they struggled to pull the sailors out of the wreckage. With one final effort, they managed to extract the two men and drag them free. The mate was in severe pain; the bugler's body still appeared lifeless.

Pausing from the exertions, Beasley realized that he did not have a life jacket. He had left it in the signal shack, located directly behind him. Beasley turned to open its hatch—only to find it jammed.

"Open the door!" someone screamed from inside.[7]

Looking around, Beasley spied a two-foot-long metal rod lying on the deck. Taking it in hand, he hammered open the latches on the hatch. The door swung open, and Beasley's friend and fellow signalman Seaman Second Class Donald L. Schlegel stumbled out, followed by Chief Signalman Lloyd A. Luzzani. Both men were already wearing their life jackets.

As soon as the two men cleared the hatch, Beasley stepped into the signal shack, grabbed his life jacket, and slipped it on. He then hurried around to the area of the bridge where Wiltsie usually stood. The captain wasn't there, nor was he in the steering or chart rooms. Beasley found both rooms in a state of confusion as their occupants struggled to find a way down onto the flight deck. As they were discovering, fire, smoke, and debris blocked every passageway off the bridge.

In a nearby unlit compartment, almost completely choked with smoke, Beasley barely made out a man slumped over a desk. Entering the compartment, the signalman called out to the man. His calls elicited no response. Drawing closer, he reached the desk, lifted the man's arm, and let go. It fell back onto the desk. Beasley left the body where he found it, later learning that Admiral Mullinnix had last been seen in that area. In the poor visibility, Beasley had been unable to establish the man's identity.[8]

As Beasley was searching the dark compartments on the bridge, Lieutenant Smith had encountered Lieutenant Commander Bodler, the ship's gunnery officer, amid the chaos.

"Can the ship be saved?" he asked Bodler.

"Not a chance, Smitty. We have to get off at once," Bodler responded.[9] There seemed to be no point in arguing, and Smith began to look for the safest route into the uncertain water below.

Beasley also ran into Bodler.

"Sir, you seem to be the senior officer on the bridge. What should we do?" Beasley asked.

"Abandon ship, and get off as quickly as possible," Bodler answered immediately.

"Yes, sir!" Beasley said.[10]

Beasley turned to execute Bodler's suggestion and saw that Lieutenant Hunt, the ship's signal officer, and Luzzani had been standing behind him. They had also heard Bodler's order.

"Do you know a way off the bridge?" Hunt asked Beasley.

"Yes, sir," Beasley replied. "Follow me."[11]

Beasley led the two men to the escape hatch that, only days earlier, Wiltsie and Carroll had ordered the shipfitters to construct. He opened it, allowing Hunt to slip past him, through the hatch, and down the ladder. Beasley followed him, trailed by Luzzani. Seconds later they reached the flight deck, only to find themselves surrounded by lapping flames, scorching heat, and billowing, inky smoke. The ship was listing heavily to starboard. The three men, with Hunt in the lead, started working their way aft.

A few steps later, Hunt stopped and turned to Beasley. "It's impossible to go further," he said. "Do you know a way we might get off the ship?"

"Yes, sir," Beasley said. "There are some lines just aft of the superstructure in the catwalk—let's try them." The group turned around and headed for the catwalk. The lines were just where Beasley had remembered them on the ship's starboard side, and he wasted no time removing them from their containers and throwing their unsecured ends over the side. One was knotted; the other was not.

Luzzani grabbed the knotted line and started down.

"How is it, Chief?" Beasley called after him.

"Fine, come on down," Luzzani yelled back.[12]

Beasley grabbed the same line and swung over the side, but before he could begin to lower himself down the rope his descent stopped with a sudden jolt. Try as he might, he couldn't lower himself any further. In fact, he was now dangling forty feet above the dark water below. Looking around frantically, Beasley realized that the top fastener on his life jacket had gotten fouled in some metal that jutted out from the ship's side. Despite his struggles, Beasley couldn't free himself. He realized that he would have to cut himself loose, and reached for the knife he kept on his belt.

Before he could do so, Hunt apparently decided that he could wait no longer. Grabbing the very same line on which Beasley was trapped, he clambered frantically down the line and over Beasley. He even used Beasley's shoulders as footsteps on the way down.

"Damn it, Lieutenant Hunt, what are you doing?"

"Sorry, Beasley," Hunt said sheepishly as he climbed past. It was the last time Beasley saw Hunt or Luzzani. Despite wearing a fully inflated life vest, neither man was rescued.[13]

Beasley continued to struggle with the life jacket and eventually managed to work his way free. He continued down the line toward the choppy water. At the end of the line, however, he encountered another sailor. Apparently, the man had been struggling in the water and had come across the line dropped by Beasley.

"I can't swim," he screamed at Beasley as the signalman lowered himself into the water beside him. Beasley saw that the panicked sailor did not have a life jacket.

"I can swim," Beasley told him. "I'll share my life jacket with you."

The sailor calmed down somewhat, and Beasley allowed him to grasp his life jacket. It was a nervous moment for Beasley—in the light of the numerous oil fires, he could see that *Liscome Bay* was listing ominously toward him. Gobs of fiery oil dripped off the deck, splattering on him and burning his head and hair. Taking the frightened sailor in tow, Beasley began kicking and stroking awkwardly away from the flaming carrier.

By now, Beebe had emerged on the starboard side of the flight deck, bracing his legs against the ship's ten-degree starboard list. His eyes beheld a scene of fiery disaster. All electrical power was gone. The after part of the carrier—what was left of it—was ablaze, and a skirt of flaming oil encircled *Liscome Bay* off her bow. The flight deck itself was awash in oil, making his footing extremely slippery. Taking care to stay on his feet on the slick deck, Beebe began the uphill climb to the port side. Along the way he encountered a wounded sailor sprawled amid the oil. Picking the man up, Beebe carried him "like a mother cat carrying a kitten" across the treacherous deck.[14] On the other side he found Ashley's group of shipfitters and other sailors spooling out fire hoses as they tried to fight the hungry flames consuming the carrier.

"Hit the water," the sailors called to their comrades manning the hose valves. In response, they spun the valves open. The hose men tensed and braced themselves for the imminent blast of water.

A second passed, then two, then three.

"Water," they called again.

The men by the valves called back in frustration: "The valves are full open." But as Abbott had discovered, there was no water pressure. Aerographer Blakley, who had also organized a fire hose party on the flight deck, made an identical discovery at about the same time. As he and his men slipped on the oily deck and tripped over tangles of wire with the useless fire hose, they cursed in frustration. By now, Aerographer's Mate Donald Cruse was also on the deck, struggling with fire hoses rendered useless by the lack of water pressure.

Observing this scene, the naked and burned Captain Crommelin stepped forward to confer with Beebe. First, however, the two officers placed the wounded sailor whom Beebe had been carrying near the ship's bow. He was too badly hurt to drop in the water, and they had little choice but to hope that he would wash free when the ship sank. With the sailor back on the deck, Crommelin and Beebe turned to one another. They had to lean forward and yell to make themselves heard over the roaring flames and blasts of aircraft and 40-millimeter gun ammunition.

"There's nothing to do but abandon ship," Crommelin shouted.

Beebe cast a quick look around, his eyes taking in the useless fire hoses, wounded sailors, burning oil, and clouds of smoke billowing forward from the remaining sections of the ship.

"There doesn't seem to be any choice," Beebe agreed, his statement punctuated by further blasts of exploding ammunition. But abandoning the ship was easier said than done. The water off the ship's bow was aflame, and the aft section of the ship was also on fire. That left precious little room to squeeze through in order to make it off the doomed carrier.

"Move aft," Beebe and Crommelin told the sailors around them. "Find a safe place and go over the side." Calmly, the sailors obeyed. As they did, Crommelin and Beebe began to move further aft, looking for a safe place to enter the water.[15]

As Crommelin and Beebe headed aft, Cruse climbed down into the forward 40-millimeter gun tub and began to work his way aft as well. As he walked, he realized he was having trouble using his right leg. His right Achilles tendon had been severed. Cruse's examination of his leg, however, was cut short by another roll of the listing ship to its starboard side. Tendon or not, he had to keep moving. Finding a kapok life jacket, he pulled it on and, when he reached the end of the catwalk amidships, eased himself off the catwalk and onto the side of the ship. Given her list, Cruse was able to simply slide down the port side and into the water below.

Ensign Woodward, having escaped the bridge, moved across the flight deck to where the flag bags were stored on the starboard side. With a bold leap, he jumped into the darkness and down to the water below. As he rose back to the surface, he began swimming away from the ship, only to be blocked by a burning patch of oil. Changing course, he worked his way around *Liscome Bay*'s bow. Looking up at the ship, he could see that the "whole after end of the ship was gone, from the after funnel on back, and the rest of the ship was solid flame except for a small portion of the forecastle and forward edge of the flight deck."[16]

Abbott, still standing on the flight deck, heard the word to abandon ship. He jumped from the flight deck down to the catwalk encircling it ten feet below. There he discovered the ammunition shed for the anti-aircraft guns burning brightly. The sight hit him like a punch in the stomach. He knew that if the ammunition cooked off in the shed, it would send bullets spraying up and down the carrier's decks and into the water where survivors were already swimming. There was nothing he could do about the shed, but Abbott saw a nearby 40-millimeter gun loaded with ammunition. Flames were licking at it as well, but that didn't stop him from ripping the shells from the gun and throwing them overboard. The hot metal and flames seared his hands, but he scarcely noticed it at the time.

With the gun emptied, Abbott stepped back down the catwalk, only to stumble into a sailor lying with a broken leg and no life belt. Slipping off his own life belt, Abbott fastened it carefully around the wounded sailor in the hope that he would be able to float clear of the ship once it sank. But now it was time for Abbott to look out for himself. He found a line tied off to the catwalk's railing, climbed over, and began slipping down it toward the water below. He had lowered himself twenty feet when he looked up and saw five other sailors crowding the line above him. Abbott doubted that the line could hold that many men, so he let go and dropped into the sea, hitting the water like a load of bricks. Gasping for air, he began swimming away from the sinking carrier through the thick globs of oil.

Around this time, Carley also headed aft, wondering if other sailors were left in what remained of the stern. Through the smoke, he spotted three men huddled motionless around an antiaircraft machine gun. Reaching for their necks and wrists, he checked each for a pulse. All were dead. Grimly, he looked around for other crewmen. Further aft, he saw another group of three men around a similar gun position. Their sluggish movements at least indicated that they were still alive. Carley moved to join them.

Although they were still dazed from the explosion, the gun crew showed no sign of abandoning their weapon. Their steadfastness was even more remarkable to Carley when a puff of wind blew back the smoke and enabled him to see further aft. It was an amazing sight. He realized, for the first time, that the entire after half of *Liscome Bay* had been blown off. Only the front half of the carrier still floated in the gentle swells among the smoke and flaming oil. Carley ripped his eyes from the astounding vision and turned to the gun crew.

"It's time to abandon ship," he told the men.

Obeying the chaplain's order, the three sailors moved to a knotted rope hanging over a life rail and lowered themselves into the water one by one. Carley took a final look around and then followed them down. Reaching the end of it, he found the last of the three sailors still clinging desperately to the rope, afraid to let go and swim away into the dark water. Carley pried the man's fingers out of their death grip, pushed him away from the doomed ship, and followed immediately behind. Once in the water, the chaplain realized that one of the men lacked a life jacket. Carley and a fellow sailor grabbed him and kept his head above water until they could find a floating plank to which he could clutch.

Back on deck, the three sailors in Maxsy Homec's 20-millimeter gun crew had also been stunned by the blasts rocking *Liscome Bay*. Tottering to his feet, Homec struggled across the flight deck, trying to make it to the starboard side where his brother Frank and Johnny Cristando were stationed, but a wall of flames blocked his path and he rejoined his gun crew. Still dazed, they stood by their gun and awaited orders. All around them, fires roared more fiercely by the second.

A boatswain materialized out of the smoke. Grabbing life jackets, he stuffed them over the young sailors' heads.

"Get off this ship," he yelled over the flames.

The three men quickly jumped over the side. "If it wasn't for him," Homec recalled years later, "we wouldn't have made it. We were too inexperienced to understand what was going on."[17]

Meanwhile, Lieutenant Ries emerged on the flight deck and considered his predicament. The burning deck was no place to be caught barefoot and without a stitch of clothing. Abandoning ship certainly seemed like the right call. Ries dashed across the deck, flames searing his legs and feet. To his left and right, guns and flares on the burning remnants of the aircraft on the flight deck popped off. Smaller explosions ripped across the deck, sending splinters whistling through the air. Ries survived the gauntlet and reached the line of men crowding the gun galleries and the life rails. One sailor offered to let Ries stand on his shoe-clad feet. Ries gratefully accepted.

Leaning over the railing, Ries saw that sailors were lowering themselves down lines into the water. Occasional blasts of flame would scorch the men on the lines, however, causing them to let go and plummet awkwardly into the water. Ries decided that he would just as soon take his chances jumping from a gun gallery and moved toward the nearest one.

A seaman in a life jacket stood in that gallery, looking speculatively at the sea below him and the burning ship behind him. The courage to make the forty-foot plunge into the sea below seemed to be lacking.

"Let's go, sailor," Ries said.[18]

The sailor held his ground, still looking at the dark water beneath him.

Ries had no time for niceties. With a quick shove, he sent the sailor over the side. He landed with a heavy splash in a clear patch of water and began swimming away. Ries vaulted over the side after him. Once in the water, he started swimming through the oily mess, pushing his way through litter and past several bodies.

Lieutenant Smith also decided to simply jump into the ocean from the flight deck. It was a frightening leap that dropped him into a thick patch of gooey oil. Struggling to the surface, he discovered that he had landed next to a sailor. Together, the two men started swimming for safety.

Standing on the flight deck, Aerographer Lyle Blakley listened to the ship heaving and emitting metallic groans. He thought she was breaking up. Looking down into the hangar deck, he saw a scene as bright as day—despite the failure of the electrical lighting, burning planes, fuel, oil, and decking provided plenty of illumination. It was little better on the flight deck. Blakley saw that the ship's railings had been torn off in the initial blasts. There didn't seem to be any life rafts left. With oil everywhere, some of it already on fire, and ammunition exploding at every quarter, it was a grim situation.

Further forward, the wounded Carroll took in the same grim sights. Bracing on the listing deck, he recognized that *Liscome Bay* was beyond salvage. By remaining aboard he would only risk being burned alive, or struck by an exploding piece of ammunition, or sucked down with the ship when it eventually sank. As he assessed the situation, he encountered King, who was now on the flight deck following his escape from the degaussing room. King asked him what he could do.

"Just get the hell off the ship," Carroll replied.

It seemed like a good idea to King. He moved over to the side of the carrier and contemplated how best to accomplish Carroll's order. Another sailor joined him.

"What are you going to do?" he asked King.

"I'm going to jump into that damn water," King snapped.

"What if we don't sink?" the sailor responded.[19]

King decided that was a question that didn't warrant answering, and with a quick jump he leaped over the side into a bare patch of water that was still free of flames. He surfaced next to the carrier's side and pushed off with his legs as he started his swim for safety. In the dark water without a life jacket, King knew the odds were not in his favor.

Carroll was now ordering other sailors, including Charters, to abandon the carrier. They needed no encouragement. Eager to get away from the bursting ammunition shells, Charters unhesitatingly made the jump into the oily seas below. The others in his group followed him. After pulling a few strong strokes, Charters turned to look back at the ship. To his surprise, he saw that Carroll was still on board. The bloodied first lieutenant was walking up and down the flight deck, shouting at some sailors to abandon ship while helping others over the side.

Seaman Carl Jelsema, who had formerly manned a 20-millimeter gun near the bridge, didn't need to hear the word to abandon ship. He and a fellow sailor knew the time had come to leave their burning, listing vessel. They cut loose a life raft near the bow and lowered it by a line into the water. Jelsema slid down that same rope toward the water, burning his bare hands on its coarse fibers. Joined by his companion, he cut the raft away from the rope. The two men kicked the raft away from the burning ship, trying to open as large a gap as possible between themselves and *Liscome Bay*. In a matter of moments, other survivors joined them.

Down on the hangar deck, Ensigns Davis and Sistrunk looked through the hole in the hull to the water below. They wanted to find a place to leap from that was clear of the encroaching flames. Sistrunk contemplated the dark water doubtfully, the recent surgical cut in his abdomen still aching painfully from his appendectomy.

"Come on. Let's go!" Davis said.

"I can't swim," Sistrunk admitted dolefully.

"The hell you can't. Get in that water," Davis retorted. To him, entering the water below, even with its thick patches of burning oil, was a far more inviting prospect than staying aboard the sinking carrier. The two men leaped into the sea. Once in the water, Davis helped Sistrunk find a floating piece of debris, and the two men clung to their makeshift life raft as they tried to lengthen the distance between themselves and the carrier.[20]

By this time, Boatswain Hunt had finally abandoned his futile fight against the fire in the elevator shaft and climbed topside. Once on the flight deck, he again encountered Carroll. Hunt moved to intercept the officer, urging him to join the others in the water.

"Come on," Hunt said. "Let's go."

"No," Carroll insisted. "You go. I'm going to stay."

"I'm not going without you. I'll get you a life preserver."

"No," Carroll said again. "Go home to your wife and kids."

"If you're not going, I'm not," Hunt retorted. Turning from Carroll, he began walking across the flight deck, trying to ignore the ammunition exploding around him as he searched for a life preserver or jacket for the wounded officer.

"Come on back!" Carroll shouted at the stubborn boatswain. "Don't go back there—I'll jump with you."[21]

Hunt returned to Carroll's side, and they moved to the edge of the flight deck, where they were joined by Dr. Rowe. Positioning Carroll between them, the three men jumped, hitting the water below with a heavy splash.

Quartermaster Rairden had just stepped out of the flag plot on his coffee errand for the admiral when the first blast slammed the hatch into his shoulder, knocking him to the deck unconscious. Quartermaster Third Class Dale A. Wilker pulled Rairden to his feet as he slowly regained his senses. Together, they moved aft on the catwalk, where they encountered Wiltsie.

"Go over the side," Wiltsie ordered. Without a public address system, he seemed determined to pass the word to abandon ship by word of mouth. Not waiting for an answer, he headed further aft to search for other survivors.[22]

Now, however, Rairden remembered the admiral back in the flag plot. Leaving Wilker, he returned to the plotting room, only to find the way in from the starboard side blocked by twisted metal wreckage and flames. There was an entrance on the port side, and Rairden saw Chief Yeoman Benjamin Sax dash in to pull one of Mullinnix's staff officers—Lieutenant (jg) Robert E. Keeton—from the fiery interior. Sax then returned again to flag plot—other officers were still inside. This time, however, he didn't make it back out. Recognizing that the flag plot had become a death trap, Rairden returned to the catwalk. Once on it, he moved along the side of the ship, looking for injured sailors but wary of the exploding boxes of ammunition all around him. Later he recalled a "terrible feeling of high tension" and the timeless quality of those moments on the deck. "I can't say whether it was three minutes or three hours before I left the ship," he told a reporter weeks later.[23]

Coming to one of the gun positions, Rairden encountered a young sailor, dazed and crying.

"Are you hurt?" Rairden asked.

The seventeen-year-old shook his head "no," but sobbed that he couldn't swim.

Rairden quickly slipped his own life jacket off and fastened it to the sailor. Even then, however, the boy wouldn't jump. Low on patience amid the roaring flames and exploding ammunition, Rairden planted a firm kick in the sailor's rear and sent him tumbling over the side.[24]

No sooner had he done so than another sailor stumbled forward. This man, also without a life jacket, had had both arms broken by the blast across the flight deck, and he couldn't even pull himself over the ship's rail to jump into the water. Scanning the jumbled wreckage around him,

Rairden spotted a spare jacket, pulled it carefully on the wounded sailor, and then helped him over the rail and into the water below.

Meanwhile, Beebe and Crommelin picked their way along the mangled catwalk toward the stern. As they advanced, Beebe also encountered Wiltsie, who fell in beside him. By now the fire engulfing *Liscome Bay* seemed to be spreading even faster, and the search for a route off the ship was becoming more desperate. Beebe, however, hesitated to enter the water without a life jacket or raft. He knew that, true to doctrine, their screening ships had likely scattered at the first recognition of a torpedo attack. There was no telling when they would return to pick up survivors.

As he pondered his predicament amid the rising heat, Beebe recalled that there was a rubber life raft stowed on each corner of the flight deck. He turned and headed for the bow, calling for Wiltsie to join him and Crommelin. There was no response. Beebe didn't realize it at the time, but he was likely the last person to see the ship's captain alive.

Moments later, Beebe located the uninflated life raft near the bow, but the flaming oil in the water prevented an escape from that point. Avoiding the flight deck with its bursting rounds of ammunition, the squadron commander carefully pulled his precious raft back toward the aft section of the ship along a slope of twisted beams. Working his way along the slope, he lost his footing and tumbled downward, still clutching the raft. He smacked into Ensign Daniel Mack, A-V(N), USNR, almost knocking the young officer off the ship and into the flaming water below.

"Excuse me," Beebe said.

"This is no time for excuses, sir," Mack responded.[25]

Mack was right. By now the fire along the flight deck above the men was getting so hot that Beebe felt his face searing. He shielded his face with his left hand as he dragged the raft with his right. Slowly, the officers made it to a point where they were almost abreast of the forward part of the ship's island. At that point, however, they could go no further. Fire was raging ahead and above, and hot flames on the water below licked menacingly along the carrier's port side. They were trapped.

In desperation, Beebe looked into the water for an opening in the flames. His eyes were rewarded with a welcome sight—a light breeze had sprung up along the port quarter and was pushing the flaming oil forward. In a moment, they would be able to slip into the water. Beebe turned to point out the opening to Crommelin.

"We've got to go over here, Captain Crommelin," he called.

There was no response.[26]

Beebe whipped his head around. Crommelin had disappeared. Beebe backtracked, looking for the wounded officer in the fire-kissed darkness, but he was nowhere to be found. Reluctantly, Beebe rejoined Mack and some other sailors who had found the opening in the flames. One by one, they began to clamber down a line hanging from the catwalk into the water. By now, the heat from the deck had become truly unbearable.

As soon as the last sailor and Mack began their descent, Beebe swung out onto the line with his right arm, lugging the life raft with him. As he reached for the line with his left hand, he realized for the first time that his left arm was torn and bleeding from a flying piece of metal shrapnel. There was simply no strength left in it, and no hope that it could hold him on the rope. Beebe fell awkwardly away from the line and into the water below, hitting it hard with a heavy splash. The impact knocked the raft from Beebe's hand, but he was able to grab it as he emerged sputtering on the water's oily surface. Lieutenant Piegari, VC-39's executive officer, had also made it into the water, and he swam over to join his commander. The two men decided against inflating the raft for fear they would be blown into the flames to their right. Kicking vigorously in the dark water, they pushed the heavy raft in front of them, trying to put more distance between themselves and the burning oil. Mack soon joined them, and the three officers pushed and pulled the raft forward until they were nearly exhausted. Only then did they turn around to assess their progress.

They had covered only fifty yards—still far too close to the flaming oil. Furthermore, each of them had heard horror stories about sailors being sucked down into the vortex created by a sinking vessel. With their exhaustion temporarily forgotten, they resumed their kicking, opening the distance another hundred yards. Judging themselves to be at a safe distance, they inflated the raft and started calling for other survivors to join them.

On board, Woodham had spotted Wiltsie and Beebe moving aft on the carrier. Having originally come up on the starboard side of the flight deck, he hesitated to enter the water on that side. The possibility that the carrier would roll over on top of him seemed very real. Ducking low so as to avoid being hit with an errant shell from the exploding ammunition on the flight deck and in the antiaircraft gun tubs, he slipped and slid uphill to the port side of the deck. There, he made a flying forty-foot leap from the port side of the carrier, hitting the ocean surface with a painful slap on his naked rear end. He didn't have a life jacket on, but his teenage years of swimming in the ocean off the southern California coast now paid dividends. With sure, steady strokes, Woodham pulled away from *Liscome Bay,* through some scattered patches of burning oil, and reached the relative safety of the darkness beyond the flames.

In the meantime, Crommelin had escaped the carrier as well. With his right hand burned and useless, he decided against climbing down a rope. Instead, when he saw a patch of sea clear of burning oil, he simply jumped over the side. It was a long plunge, and his bare body smacked painfully into the water below. Ignoring his pain, he started swimming for safety.

Elsewhere on board, men such as Blakley found knotted lines and lowered themselves off. Seaman Leonard Bohm, on the other hand, having escaped from belowdecks, decided to simply leap into the water. As Bohm tensed for his jump, Chief Ashley grabbed his arm and pointed to the chunks of torn wooden flight deck floating beneath them. Smashing into one of those from forty feet up would break a leg, or worse. Ashley directed Bohm to a knotted line a few feet away. Bohm climbed quickly down it, entered the water, inflated his life jacket with four quick puffs, and, relying on the only stroke he knew, backstroked away from the flaming carrier. As he kicked away from *Liscome Bay,* he marveled at the damage. "It looked just like a big saw had cut off the back [*sic*] half of the ship," he later recalled.[27]

As Bohm surveyed the scene, two moderate explosions punctuated the ongoing catastrophe. Those blasts likely marked the detonation of depth-charge bombs stored in the burning Avengers. All the while, smaller calibers of ammunition—notably the 20- and 40-millimeter ammunition and the .50-caliber bullets in the wing-mounted machine guns of the burning planes—continued to cook off.

Meanwhile, officers and sailors continued to hazard this gauntlet of escalating carnage in an effort to escape the carrier's death throes. Ensign Gene Tornquist, one of the VC-39 pilots, had been hurled out of his bunk by the initial explosions but had somehow made his way topside—he couldn't recall how.[28] Clutching a life preserver, he lowered himself down a rope into the water. Once in the ocean, he realized he was surrounded by patches of burning oil. Floating in an oil slick himself, he decided that this was no place to abandon ship and climbed back up the rope.

As Tornquist rejoined the carrier, Storekeeper Clovis Roach picked his way across the flight deck from the flaming starboard side to the port side. He looked out into the sea's gentle swells, and by the light of the burning ship Roach could see heads bobbing in the water. There were, however, no life rafts, at least as far as he could tell. A fellow sailor standing nearby disagreed. "There are three rafts and a floater net way out there," he said to Roach.[29]

That was all the encouragement Roach needed. He walked forward to the ship's anchor chain. Cinching his life jacket tightly around his chest, Roach climbed over the ship's railing and carefully began to lower himself down the chain. He was still wearing only one shoe. Roach had made it about ten feet down when a pair of feet landed heavily on his shoulders, boxing him in his ears. He struggled for a second to maintain his grip. Once he was satisfied that he wasn't going to suffer a backbreaking fall on the anchor below, Roach looked up. Another sailor, apparently more nimble than Roach, had joined him on the anchor chain. His descent was obviously faster than that of the careful Roach.

Slower or not, Roach had no intention of getting kicked again as he negotiated the slippery anchor chain. He reached up and grabbed the sailor's feet. Noting that the sailor wore a life jacket, Roach felt little guilt in hurling him into space. With a curse, the impatient sailor splashed into the dark water below. Free of the pressure from above, Roach continued down the anchor chain. When he was about six feet above the ocean's surface, he let go and dropped easily into the water.

Rairden also decided it was time to abandon ship. Aware that the wind would be pushing the stricken carrier, he first went to the port—windward—side. He saw the ocean full of flames on that side, though, and decided to try his luck on the starboard side. Grabbing a line, he lowered himself hand over hand, dropping the last few feet into the water. Then, with deep, sure strokes, Rairden started swimming away from the carrier. In places he had to dive underwater to swim beneath slicks of burning oil. Behind him, the wind kept pushing *Liscome Bay*'s burning wreck toward him. Working his way diagonally across her advancing path, Rairden eventually made it off to the side of her advance. By then he was only forty feet or so away—still uncomfortably close—and "pretty damned tired."[30]

Meanwhile, on their small catwalk by the gun emplacement, Ensigns Daily and Taylor discussed the prevailing state of affairs.

"They must have ordered 'abandon ship,'" Taylor said. "I guess we didn't hear it."

Daily agreed. Looking around, the two officers spied a frame holding a smashed life raft. It was useless in its wrecked condition, but a long length of coiled rope was attached to it.

"Do you have a knife?" Taylor asked.

Daily pulled a knife from a belt scabbard and handed it to Taylor. With a few frantic saws, Taylor cut loose one end of the rope and dropped it into the water below. He slipped the knife back into Daily's scabbard.

"Lead the men down the rope, Harry," Daily said. "I'll bring up the rear."[31]

With a quick nod, Taylor began leading the sailors in a hand-over-hand descent of the knotted rope. As the men lowered themselves down the rope, Daily stood on the twelve-foot-long catwalk and quickly tied a handkerchief around his hand to avoid a rope burn. As he did, he noticed an object floating in the distance, about a half mile away. Was it an enemy submarine closing in for the final kill? The thought caused Daily to remember that he was standing on top of several hundred thousand gallons of aviation fuel. No doubt the flames would reach the tanks at any moment. A rope burn was probably the least of his worries, he decided. He dropped the handkerchief and moved for the line.

Before Daily could reach it, another explosion detonated on the flight deck above his head. A crewman came sailing out of the darkness and landed, feet first but stunned, on the narrow catwalk beside Daily. Daily grabbed the dazed sailor and pushed him over to the rope.

"Go down the line," Daily ordered.

The sailor needed no further encouragement, and Daily quickly followed him. With knots every two feet, it turned out there was no danger of rope burns. When Daily felt his feet slipping into the warm, dark water, he let go of the rope and began treading water. He looked around for Taylor and the others, but they were nowhere to be seen. Daily felt a brief twinge of surprise. With the ship dead in the water, he had hoped they would be waiting for him. Obviously he had lost them in the darkness.

Back on the ship, Tornquist weighed whether or not it was time to enter the water again. By now the ship was listing dangerously to starboard and sinking further and further beneath the gently breaking waves. He decided it was time to try his luck in the ocean once again and slipped over the side with his life preserver.

Meanwhile, alone in the water, Daily continued to tread water and opened his survival belt. He pulled the life jacket from the belt but didn't inflate it yet, concerned that it might tear on a piece of jagged metal protruding from the ship. As he floated near the carrier, he managed to slip out of one of his shoes. A knotted lace kept the other on his foot. He thought about cutting it away with his pocketknife but hesitated doing so for fear of cutting his leg and nicking an artery in the dark water.

As he floated near the doomed ship, Daily felt his college ring begin to slip off his finger in the oily water. He reached down and pulled the ring off in order to hold onto it, but as soon as he grasped it his life belt came unhooked and started to float off into the darkness. Daily lunged at it, dropping his ring as his hand gripped the life belt. There was no telling how long he would be in the water. The life belt seemed to be the more important of the two, and at any rate, his wedding ring was still securely on his finger. Daily considered it a fair trade-off.

Once he had secured his life belt, Daily looked back at *Liscome Bay*. For a moment, he felt a stab of doubt. Had he abandoned ship prematurely? She was obviously still floating and, despite the list to starboard, didn't seem to be sinking. Daily kicked and stroked away from the ship to get a better perspective. Sixty feet away, he turned to assess the damage to the stern. In shock, he realized that there was simply no stern left to assess. Almost half of the carrier was gone. Daily knew that, every minute, tons of seawater must be pouring into the gaping hole. *Liscome Bay* would go down at any moment.

On the carrier, the badly wounded Bergquist finally staggered onto the flight deck. Looking around, he reached the same conclusion as Daily. With what remained—if anything—of the fantail already submerged and the bow beginning to rise out of the water, *Liscome Bay*'s minutes were numbered. As Bergquist considered his options, an officer appeared beside him.

"Are you okay?" he asked Bergquist.

"I can't use my arm, sir," Bergquist replied, struggling to stand on the listing deck.

"Well, it looks like you and I are the only ones left. Better get off. Ship's going down," the officer said.[32]

Bergquist didn't argue. He limped toward the side of the deck, picking up a foot-long piece of the carrier's wooden deck as he went. Three steps later, Bergquist slipped on a patch of oil, fell on his back, and slid over the side of the deck. He landed in a pack of shipmates who helped to keep him afloat. Choking on salt water and oil, Bergquist—like the others in the water—could only wonder when and if rescue would come.

10
Pacific Dawn

Ensign Frank Daily turned from the carrier and began kicking with all his might, clawing at the ocean with his arms in deep, sure strokes. After a few moments, he turned back to check his progress. He had covered over a hundred yards. He realized that a soft wind was pushing the carrier away from him. It was a lucky break for him—but less lucky for those unfortunate souls who had elected to enter the water off the carrier's starboard side. Those men found themselves swimming in a deadly race with the wind-borne flaming carrier at their backs.

Dr. Rowe and Boatswain Hunt, also fortunate to be on the carrier's port side, were struggling to keep Lieutenant Commander Carroll's head above the oily water. Carroll's condition continued to deteriorate. His eyes, set in a face pale from shock and loss of blood, glazed, and his breath came at short, shallow intervals. There seemed little in the three men's predicament to offer hope for the wounded officer.

Bobbing in the water, Hunt spotted a nearby life raft and left his companions momentarily to try to retrieve it. Reaching it, he began dragging the raft back to the two men. As he swam, Hunt could tell that Carroll must have become unconscious. Rowe was now desperately trying to keep Carroll afloat and administer artificial respiration at the same time. With each swell, oily water broke over Rowe's head. Hunt pulled even harder, trying to get the raft back to the two men.

By the time Hunt reached them, the doctor was simply cradling Carroll in his arms. He looked up at Rowe and locked tired eyes with the boatswain.

"He's dead," Rowe announced.[1]

Reluctantly, the doctor let Carroll's body drift away. As it slipped beneath the waves, Rowe and Hunt clambered into the life raft and broke out the paddles. The two men soon realized that they were floating amid a rapidly developing inferno of burning oil. Trying to stay calm, they paddled away from the burning carrier and into the surrounding darkness.

At about that time, Beasley continued to struggle with the frightened sailor he had rescued from the dangling lifeline. They had only swum a short distance from the ship when the sailor began to panic once again. Fighting loose of Beasley, he floundered and splashed his way back to the lifeline. Despite the oil burning on the water around him and the ever-increasing list of the ship above him, Beasley swam back to the rope.

"Our only chance is to get away from the ship," Beasley told the sailor.

"No, no, no!" he screamed in response. "I can't swim and I have no life jacket."

Floating next to the sailor, Beasley tried for several moments to reason with him—to no avail. Finally, with a worried look at the flaming ship above him and the encroaching oil fires that almost surrounded him, Beasley uttered words that he would remember five decades later.

"I have no choice," he told the sailor clutching the line. "I must leave you—good-bye and good luck." Beasley turned and stroked for safety.[2]

Pausing only to kick off his shoes and dungarees, Beasley pulled away from *Liscome Bay*. But even as he thought he was making it to safety, he heard a distant rumble in the water. Seconds later, the blast from an undersea explosion pummeled him. "Suddenly it felt that pressure inside my body would cause me to explode," he later recalled. "This happened three or four times. I thought for sure I would lose consciousness. I felt sure my ear drums had been damaged and I felt that damage had been caused to my insides. Everything seemed to be closing in on me for the worst."[3]

Bruised by the underwater blasts, and with his head aching painfully where it had been seared by falling gobs of flaming oil, Beasley swam through the darkness. As he pulled through the ocean swells, his lonely state in the dark water weighed heavily on him. "Survive, survive, I must survive," he chanted to himself.[4] After a few more minutes, Beasley looked back, expecting to see that the burning ship had receded behind him. Much to his dismay, he saw that the wind was pushing her toward him. With a sinking feeling, he knew that he couldn't outdistance the ship. His only hope seemed to be to work his way around and let the wind push her away from, rather than toward, him.

Beasley's theory had one major flaw. It required negotiating several flaming oil slicks floating near the stricken carrier. All the while, more giant drops of burning oil fell down on and around him. With grim perseverance, Beasley made it around what was left of *Liscome Bay*'s stern. Tiring, he briefly held onto a large chunk of metal protruding from the stern to catch his breath. Taking a moment to look at the carrier, he thought it looked half-submerged. Time to move on, he thought, as burning ammunition continued to cook off above him.

Pushing away from the ship, Beasley swam through a field of debris partially illuminated by the fires aboard *Liscome Bay*. There was enough light cast on the water for him to find a large piece of cork, three feet square and about six inches thick. He grasped it gratefully and rested as the wind carried his ship further away from him.

A faint cry broke his solitude.

"Help! Help!" a sailor called through the darkness. Away from the light of the burning ship, Beasley couldn't see the man.

"Help! Help me, Lord, help me!" the cry came again. This time, Beasley realized it was mere feet away. He kicked over to where he thought it was coming from.[5]

As he swam through the darkness, someone grabbed Beasley's arm. Sensing that the man was badly injured, Beasley struggled to get him to grasp onto the cork board. Realizing that the wounded sailor was not wearing a life jacket, Beasley locked his legs around the man's waist in case he slipped off the board. For the next several minutes, the delirious sailor prayed, screamed, and called for his mother. He finally calmed down enough for Beasley to ask him his name and what division he had served in.

Smith, the man said. It was Steward's Mate Robert Smith. Beasley realized that there was a very good chance that Smith wasn't going to survive, so he carefully reached over and pulled off his dog tags in order to have them in case the man died and slipped beneath the water.

Meanwhile, Roach, who had been treading water underneath the anchor chain, took off his remaining shoe and began paddling away from the ship. It was a difficult effort in the bulky life jacket, and he made little headway. Roach wasn't concerned at first, but then flames began flicking around the carrier's bow. Oil in the water started igniting. Roach's strokes became more desperate as he struggled to escape the advancing flames. Just as he seemed condemned to being roasted alive, the wind shifted slightly. It pushed the crackling flames back and gave the frightened sailor enough time to splash away from the crippled carrier. Kicking and stroking, Roach made it to a floater net, where he joined about forty other survivors.

Lieutenant Smith faced a similar situation. Adrift in the water off the ship's starboard side, he soon realized that the light ocean breeze was pushing the burning hulk toward him. It was a dangerous predicament. The tremendous heat from the fires burning along the flight deck and in the hangar deck was still cooking off the ammunition stored in the gun platforms ringing the deck. Errant rounds whizzed through the air over Smith's head or plunked into the water around him. A sailor paddled alongside Smith. Together the two men decided to swim aft in order to come around what remained of the ship's stern, but flaming oil off the bow blocked that route. Another sailor joined them as they swam. Skirting the edge of the sinking carrier, Smith felt the bone-rattling rumble of depth charges exploding beneath the surface. The two sailors cried in pain from the explosions, but Smith somehow avoided injury.

Meanwhile, Seaman Edward Jonas, the ship's tailor, struggled by himself in the water. The explosive blasts that had rocked the shipfitters' shop had damaged his eyesight, and he wasn't even sure how he had made it off *Liscome Bay*. Almost blind, Jonas fought to stay afloat until an unknown pilot from VC-39 swam up to him and helped to pull and guide the young sailor away from the sinking carrier. Jonas counted himself doubly lucky—a little over a year ago he had survived the sinking of the cruiser *Quincy* after the Battle of Savo Island.

Beymer was having a slightly easier time of it. He had found a life raft about fifty yards from where he had entered the water and, along with six others, hung onto its side while they floated through a debris field. In the water around them, men began flashing lights to signal their shipmates.

"Cut the lights," someone yelled. They had all heard tales of Japanese submarines surfacing after a successful torpedo strike and machine-gunning the hapless survivors.[6] Despite that fear, the men continued to shine their lights and fish shipmates out of the water. One such sailor had apparently tried to crawl up from the engine room on superheated pipes, thereby burning away most of the flesh on his hands and forearms. Floating in the salt water, he screamed in pain until Beymer and the others pulled him into their raft.

As they did, the shock waves of unseen destroyers depth-charging for *Liscome Bay*'s attacker rolled through the water. Beymer had attended an ocean survival course at Pensacola as part of his flight training and was well aware of the damage an undersea explosion could do to a human body. "Roll over on your back," Beymer told his companions. "Seal your buttocks and ride the percussion out." They all did so and successfully weathered the ensuing blast waves from the depth-charge barrage.

Closer to *Liscome Bay*, Aviation Machinist's Mate Wells and his companions, pushing a life raft of their own, struggled to outdistance the flaming ship and burning oil slicks. No matter how hard they swam, the carrier's fiery silhouette always seemed to be towering above them. Catching the light ocean breeze like a giant sail, she was being pushed through the water. Realizing that they weren't going to outswim the burning hulk while pushing the raft, Wells abandoned the raft and, swimming over alongside a section of the ship that wasn't on fire, grabbed a line. While hanging onto it, he kicked off his shoes and used his pocketknife to cut away his dungarees. Moments later, he felt the carrier begin to rumble and shake. She must be going down, he reasoned, and once again he started kicking away from the ship. When he was about a hundred feet away, Wells felt the impact of an underwater explosion punch at his torso and legs. "It felt like somebody sticking a million needles into my stomach," he later wrote.[7] Nevertheless, he continued to stroke through the darkness, and in the flickering light of burning oil he was able to locate a life raft.

Struggling through heavy crude oil, about two hundred feet from the ship, Seaman Abbott also felt the undersea blast rip into his legs. For a moment he imagined that his legs had been torn off, but a few quick kicks reassured him that he was still okay—at least for the moment. In the dark, without a life jacket, he knew he had to find something to keep him afloat.

The undersea blast pummeled Lieutenant Ries as well. "It felt just like an electric shock, like a million needles poking you all over. It was paralyzing. I sank and then came up again."[8] Several other explosions ripped into Ries, sending him sinking with each blast. But he struggled back to the surface each time, and the underwater detonations soon subsided. He and a sailor found an empty life raft and pulled themselves into it.

Fire Controlman Jenkins also felt the underwater explosions, but he weathered them little the worse for wear. He continued swimming, pulling a wounded shipmate through the water while the man lay on his back in the water, and wondered how long it would take for a rescue ship to arrive. Somewhere beyond the waves, Seaman Jelsema and his raftmate steadily added to the number of men clinging to their raft. If a man was too weak or injured to make it to the raft, Jelsema and the others would swim out and pull him in.

By now, Parachute Rigger James Honold regained consciousness and found himself, much to his surprise, not in the parachute storage room but floating in the water about two thousand feet from *Liscome Bay*. Badly wounded on his left side, he could only move his right arm and leg as he struggled to stay afloat. He flailed about in the ocean, weakening with every second, and had almost given up when his right arm grabbed onto a buoyant seat cushion. Tucking it under his arm, Honold managed to stay afloat. Momentarily, he heard the shouts of a fellow survivor.

"Come on over," Honold yelled. "I have something to hang onto."

The other man joined Honold. Soon, a life raft floated into view about twenty feet away.

"I can't make it to it," the other man said.

Leaving him clutching the seat, Honold struggled over to the raft and pulled it back. Both men hauled themselves into it.

Elsewhere, Maxsy Homec bobbed in the water, thankful for the boatswain who had draped the life jacket over his head. But what of his brother Frank? He tried swimming around the ship's burning hulk, only to encounter impassable patches of burning oil. Treading water, he tried to figure out what to do next. Realizing that he couldn't make it around to the ship's starboard side, and worried that he would be sucked down with her when she sank, Homec reluctantly began paddling away from her.

At about 0533, twenty-three minutes after Tabata's torpedo had punched into her side, *Liscome Bay* gave up her obstinate fight with the seawater flooding her mangled and battered compartments. She made a graceful, quick departure from the surface—keeling over slightly to starboard and then slipping backward, stern first and still burning fiercely, beneath the waves. As the carrier's white-hot metal contacted the cool ocean, a loud hiss rent the early-morning air and a massive cloud of steam veiled the survivors' view of their carrier for a brief moment. When it lifted, *Liscome Bay* was gone, leaving behind an orange glow emanating from the depths. After ten seconds or so, the glow sullenly faded out. Clinging to a life net with a collection of other survivors, Woodward watched with awe as the ship on which he had served as officer of the deck less than thirty minutes earlier disappeared into the Pacific's depths.

Standing on the bridge of the destroyer *Franks*, a crewman watched the carrier's dramatic death in disbelief. "It was just like putting a candle out. The ball of fire was snuffed out as the ship sank. We were just dumfounded. That's the first time we experienced the horrors of war. I think it sort of scared everyone. We just sort of felt, 'My gosh, this is for real.' We knew it was a lot of men lost because of the way the ship blew up into a ball of fire. It happened so fast."[9] Carley, closer to the scene, described the aftermath of the ship's plunge beneath the waves. "A deathly silence hung over the scene, broken only by the cries of frightened and injured men. We saw no life boats, rafts, or nets—only men floating on the surface of the sea, alive and dead," he recalled.[10]

Beasley, still wrapped around the badly wounded steward, also saw the carrier sink. As she gurgled and hissed in her final death throes, Beasley spoke to his companion.

"Smith, there goes the *Liscome Bay*," he said.

"Goodbye," Smith muttered feebly in response.[11]

Lieutenant Smith and the two wounded sailors with him were barely one hundred feet from the carrier when she sank. Despite the tales they had heard about sinking ships dragging shipwrecked men into their vortex, there was no suction as the ship disappeared from view—just a sickly gurgle and a loud, defiant hiss. Rairden was even closer to the ship when it went down. "There was no suction," he recalled, "only a hissing sound as the water came up over the hot steel, silencing the guns which were still going off."[12] In the aftermath of the sinking, he found a wooden section of the flight deck and pulled himself onto it. As he did so he realized, for the first time, that his left collarbone was broken.

Meanwhile, Seaman Whalen awoke to find himself in a patch of oily water with a half-inflated life belt. The last thing he remembered was being rocked by an explosion and chipping his tooth. Another explosion must have blasted him off the ship. Collecting his wits, he began treading water.

Aerographer's Mate Donald Cruse, paddling through the darkness despite his severed Achilles tendon, called back and forth to other swimmers in an effort to maintain as much contact as possible. Some men, fearing the force of underwater explosions from the sunken carrier's munitions or fuel bunkers, warned the others to try to swim as horizontally as possible. They had heard terrible stories of what the shock waves from such explosions could do to swimmers in the water. Seaman Bill Fisher was one such swimmer. Benefiting from a childhood of swimming in the ocean off California, he swam strongly through the easy swells. Spying a life raft, he stroked over to it and clung onto its side with a small group of his fellow survivors.

Elsewhere, Daily inflated his life belt and floated in place for several minutes, contemplating his next move as he bobbed on the ocean swells. The sea was becoming slightly choppy, at least where he was, with two-foot waves. A strange film—a mix of diesel fuel, oil, and butter—polluted the water's surface. From out of the inky darkness, a panicked cry broke the silence: "Shark! Shark!"[13] A chill ran down Daily's spine. For a brief moment he imagined a tiger shark slashing out of the dark depths, rolling over onto its back for a sudden, vicious attack on his dangling legs. Or would it come at him from the surface? He squinted into the early-morning gloom, looking for a dorsal fin slicing through the water.

A second later, Daily's fears of shark attack were interrupted by the rolling shock waves of several underwater explosions. The force of the explosions pushed him up several inches. He knew he was sensing the detonation of depth charges, but he was unsure if they were from ordnance exploding aboard *Liscome Bay* or from depth charges placed by destroyers attempting to avenge her death. Daily rolled onto his back, trying to minimize the exposure of his body to the shock waves. After a few blasts, the unseen explosions subsided. Nor were there any more cries of "shark."

Relieved, Daily floated aimlessly and alone for thirty minutes as he waited for the sun to rise. He knew he was about fifteen miles from Makin, the nearest island. Once the sun came up he would start the long swim to dry land, but at the moment the early-morning world around him was still painted in hues of charcoal gray. It had barely become light enough for Daily to make out a lone figure swimming away from him. The sailor spotted Daily about the same time and stopped swimming.

"Hey, you got a life jacket?" he called over the water.

"No, but I have a life belt," Daily responded.

"I'm tired. You mind if I come over?"

"Sure. Let's see if it'll hold us both."[14]

Daily and the sailor swam toward one another. When they met, they hung onto each other, taking advantage of Daily's life belt's buoyancy. Despite the sailor's exhausting swim, his behavior was surprisingly hyperactive. For three full minutes he let loose a stream of profanity about the Japanese, their submarine, and its torpedo. The sailor, it seemed, was holding every member of the Japanese chain of command, from Emperor Hirohito on down to the lowliest sailor aboard their unseen attacker, responsible for the destruction of his shipboard home and the loss of his prized twenty-dollar "geetar."

Finally, the sailor took a break. Catching his breath, he changed the subject.

"Hey, you got your pants on?" he asked.

Somewhat taken aback, Daily replied that he did.

"Mind putting my wallet in your pocket? I'm stark naked," he explained.[15]

Daily accepted the wallet and slipped it into his trouser pocket, amazed that the sailor had been swimming for a half hour, clutching his wallet the entire time. For the next few minutes they conversed as they floated together, trying to figure out what exactly had happened to *Liscome Bay*.

A distant red light on the water's surface caught Daily's eye and interrupted the conversation. The light was waving back and forth. Daily realized it was a penlight flashlight. He disengaged from the sailor, and they both struck out for the signal.

Five minutes later, after a grueling swim through the increasingly choppy sea, Daily and his companion reached the sailor wielding the flashlight. He had located a floater net—a weblike contraption of cargo nets and block of cork—and was signaling for others to join him. From all points of the compass, exhausted and injured men splashed to the welcome safety of the net.

As Daily drew up, a chorus of happy voices greeted him.

"Hey, Paymaster made it," they called out. Even in the face of the disaster that had befallen them, they were still enthusiastic about the next payday. Daily's arrival reinforced that happy prospect.[16]

When he reached the net, Daily found a rough organizational scheme already in place. With the wounded on top of the net, the rest of the men, including a recently arrived Woodham, clung to its edges in concentric circles several sailors deep, "like mating beetles."[17] Only the badly injured were actually pulled on board. One sailor was so terribly burned that he couldn't even be pulled onto the net. Those around its edges had to force the edges of the net down into the water and let him float atop it. It was a grim sight. Burned chunks of flesh were literally falling off of his arms as he sat in shock.

Crommelin was among the wounded. He lay in the center of the net, tortured by painful burns oozing in the cruel seawater. They ached even more painfully as his skin began to dry.

"I'm dying," he announced to the sailors around him. "Throw me overboard. I'm not going to make it. Make room for someone else."

A nearby sailor responded in a tired but determined voice to Crommelin's entreaty: "Shut up, Captain. You're going to make it."[18]

Crommelin fell silent and kept his place aboard the net.

Not every officer displayed the same courage aboard the crowded net. One clambered frantically on board, pulling his way through the circle of sailors around the net's perimeter. As he scooted into the center, his hand fluttered near the holstered pistol on his belt.

"We're going to have to shoot some people or the net will go under!" he announced in a panic-stricken voice.

Another officer snarled back, "You go for that pistol and you're a dead man."[19] The pistol remained holstered, and the crowded floater net still managed to keep its bedraggled group of survivors on the surface. Other officers paddled around its perimeter, checking on the men and rearranging the survivors as needed to protect the most seriously wounded. Eventually, the number of survivors crowded on and around it swelled to seventy-five or so—far more than the fourteen it was designed to hold.

Elsewhere, Lieutenant Smith and his two companions, after paddling through the oily flotsam, eventually reached a smaller float, where they joined other survivors. Nearly exhausted from their ordeal, they clung to it with aching arms. In the darkness, they heard a nearby voice call out.

"Hey there . . . hey there!"

"What do you want? Are you hurt?" Smith shouted back.

"No. I just want some company."

"We'll be over on the next boat, kid," a chief petty officer answered, prompting a grim laugh from his companions around the float.[20]

Floating in the debris field, Beasley and the steward Smith continued their lonely ordeal. As the skies lightened, Beasley could see the extent of the steward's grim injuries for the first time. Horribly scalded, Smith was in terrible pain. His arms "looked like one big blister full of water. In some places the skin had begun to slip from his flesh. He had a bad cut from his hairline to the bridge of his nose. His skull was visible."[21] Afraid that the steward might slip into unconsciousness and die, Beasley kept talking to him and encouraging him to hang on.

As the morning sun crept into the sky, Beasley spotted another group of survivors—a knot of three swimmers. Calling back and forth, they agreed to swim toward one another. After several hard minutes of swimming, Beasley and Smith finally had some company. Even better, the others had been clinging to a large plank of wood from the flight deck. Breaking Beasley's cork float in half, they were able to put a piece of cork under one of Smith's armpits and the plank under the other. With one man holding Smith's head above the water, the five survivors floated together and hoped for the best.

Meanwhile, Ries was still swimming through globs of oil and batches of flotsam when he heard cries for help from nearby. Stroking over to the man, Ries asked him if he was okay.

"Yeah," he answered.

"Let's save our lungs, then," Ries panted.[22] Fortunately, Ries was able soon thereafter to spot an empty life raft, and he and the sailor pulled themselves into it.

Hidden among the ocean swells, Ensign Robert E. Wall, a Georgia Tech graduate and one of the ship's gunnery officers, was swimming with a fellow officer. The man was so badly burned that he could barely see in front of him. Their choices seemed painfully simple, however—swim or die. The two men kept swimming, until the injured officer's clawing hands slapped down on a small floating box.

"Wait a minute. What's this?" he called to Wall.[23]

Wall splashed over to him and examined the box. It was a pound of butter—just the thing, he thought, for the wounded officer's burns. Wall tore into the box, grabbing handfuls of the butter and smearing it in a protective coating over his companion's burned flesh.

Meanwhile, the aviators Beebe, Mack, and Piegari, clutching their own small raft, called for other survivors to join them. A chorus of voices answered them.

"Hey, have you got an extra life jacket?"

"How you doing? Do you need some help?"

"I've got a man over here that needs something to keep him up."[24]

The three officers began the slow task of collecting the nearby survivors. Leaving the raft, they would splash out to them and drag them back to the comparative safety of the raft. Overhead, gray streaks of dawn brightened the early-morning sky. The extra light made the task of finding shipmates much easier, and soon eight men were clinging to the raft.

Having worked hard to collect survivors, Beebe reached a point in his endurance where he simply couldn't kick anymore. Was this it? he wondered. Then he realized that he still had his marine-issue field shoes on his feet. Dunking his head underwater for a moment, he unlaced the shoes and pulled them off his feet. Tying them back together with their laces, he draped them around his neck. If they made it to shore somewhere, he would likely need them. With the shoes off his feet, Beebe felt like a massive weight had been released. He and the others resumed their rescue work. Three more men were pulled to the raft. A few minutes later, they retrieved a solitary sailor.

Overhead the sky continued to lighten, and now Beebe could make out the faces of his fellow swimmers. To a man, they were virtually unrecognizable. Their dousing in the oily water had left each one with coal-black hair, black eyebrows and eyelashes, and a dark-tan coat on their arms, faces, and torsos. It might have been funny if not for the fact that the same oil had probably choked and gagged fellow sailors to death somewhere beyond the gently rolling swells.

As Beebe contemplated the small raft's crew, he heard another shout in the distance.

"Hey . . . Sis is over here. He needs help badly," Davis called. Beebe didn't need convincing of that—he knew Sistrunk was still recovering from his appendectomy.[25]

Piegari didn't need convincing either. He quickly splashed out from the raft in the direction of Davis's voice. A minute later, a nearly exhausted Davis pulled up alongside the raft. The effort to keep the wounded officer afloat had almost been too much for him. Moments later, Piegari reappeared, pulling Sistrunk behind him. Sistrunk looked like a drowned rat, but at least he was alive. The group of survivors pulled him to safety inside the raft. Davis's and Sistrunk's arrival swelled their group to sixteen, most of whom were paddling in the water and hanging onto the rope along the raft's side.

As the sky brightened further, it revealed to the survivors an unsettling sight. None of the battleships, destroyers, and transports that had surrounded them less than an hour before were visible. It seemed to the men in the water that the other ships had sped out of the area at the first sign of submarine attack. It was a pragmatic decision, but one of little consolation to *Liscome Bay*'s survivors still bobbing in the ocean swells.

In the end, fate seemed content with the deadly hand it had already dealt the escort carrier's crew. At daybreak a squat Wildcat fighter appeared overhead, wagging its square wings to signal to the survivors that it had spotted them. A relieved cheer arose from the ragged pockets of *Liscome Bay*'s men bobbing in the water. Shortly thereafter, a vessel's superstructure appeared on the horizon. Despite the sight of the Wildcat, feelings of unease gripped many of the survivors. Was it an American ship? Could it be the submarine that had sunk them earlier that morning, coming back to finish off the job? The unidentified vessel, with sailors crowding her forward lifelines, pulled closer, and the faces of the sailors and the fluttering Stars and Stripes at the gaff dispelled their fears. It was the destroyer *Morris,* joined moments later by the destroyer *Hughes. Hull* and *MacDonough* (DD-351) would follow later.

Unknown to the men from *Liscome Bay* still struggling in the water at that hour, the first terrible blast on board *Liscome Bay* had sent a swell of confusion rippling through the ships of Task Group 53.13. The fear of imminent follow-on enemy attacks quickly followed. Radio operators repeatedly stepped on one another's transmissions as Rear Admiral Griffin's task group undertook evasive maneuvers. Finally, ten minutes after the torpedo strike, *Hughes* called Griffin. *Hughes* was a hardy ship—one of the first American destroyers to escort a British convoy all the way from the United States to England, a veteran of Midway and the fight for Guadalcanal and of the recapture of the Aleutians. Her crew had helped rescue *Yorktown*'s survivors after she was sunk at Midway. They were familiar with the grim work at hand and were passing near the stricken carrier at the time.

Later, *Hughes*'s commander, E. B. Rittenhouse, described what he saw early that morning: "We were close enough to clearly read the bow number on the port side; *Liscome Bay* apparently having reversed her heading from the time of first explosion. Men were seen jumping off the flight deck into the water, one group of about five men jumping with a rubber boat which tumbled after them. This group appeared to land directly into flaming oil which seemed to cover the area all along the starboard side and around the bow." He went on to describe the damage: "The entire after half of the ship was blazing furiously and smoke and flame poured out of the hangar deck from all directions. The flight deck forward appeared to be the last to go up in flames. Half-way between the island and the stern, there appeared to be a huge hole from flight deck to at least one deck below the hangar deck."[26]

Hughes could spot men bobbing in the dark, oily water. She radioed Griffin: "Chestnut, *Hughes*. Request permission to pick up survivors. Over."

"Negative. Circle and search for submarines," came the response. "Particularly to eastward. Over."

"Wilco. Out."[27]

Moments later, however, Griffin radioed the destroyer *Hull*.

"Proceed to assistance of burning ship. Over."[28]

Again, a flurry of radio transmissions interrupted one another until Griffin was able to make himself heard once again. By that time, eighteen minutes had elapsed since Tabata's attack.

"Destroyers with Africa, this is Chestnut. Three destroyers nearest fire remain vicinity. I say again. Three destroyers nearest fire remain vicinity. Acknowledge. Over."

"*Morris*, Africa. I think this means you and the two nearest you. Go on in."

"Roger. Out."[29]

At 0533, *Liscome Bay*, still burning, had slipped hissing beneath the waves. The task group made another simultaneous turn, this time forty degrees to port, while *New Mexico* assumed the guide position vacated by *Liscome Bay*. The two remaining escort carriers started launching their aircraft for antisubmarine sweeps while *Hull*, *Hughes*, and *Morris* moved in to search for survivors. The other destroyers took up protective screening positions.

Although it seemed much longer in the memories of the surviving crewmen, *Hughes* and *Morris*, with *Hull* trailing behind, reported later that they arrived at the dark oil slick that marked *Liscome Bay*'s demise within seven minutes of her sinking. The destroyers found themselves in a field of violently rent floating debris—splintered wooden flight deck planking, aircraft tires, mattresses, torn life rafts, and floater nets—and quickly went to work. Like those in *Hughes*, *Morris*'s men were familiar with the task at hand. The veteran *Morris* had been on the scene to rescue survivors of *Lexington* at Coral Sea, *Yorktown* at Midway, and *Hornet* at Santa Cruz. Some of *Morris*'s sailors took to the sea in two whaleboats to recover the men in the water, while others threw a pair of life rafts over the side at the packs of oil-soaked men. Still others hurled heaving lines and trailing lines into the sea, using them to drag the shipwrecked sailors over to the side of *Morris*. Once alongside, they could pull themselves up the cargo netting hung over the destroyer's side.

Sistrunk was among the first men rescued. A sailor hurled him a line, but, suffering from a severe knee and leg injury, Sistrunk couldn't make it up the rope. The destroyer's crew lowered a stretcher for him. Once he was on board, however, Sistrunk insisted that *Morris*'s sailors provide him with a rubber raft with which he could go back into the water and rescue other survivors. It was a request that his rescuers wisely chose to ignore as they continued their grim work.

In a remarkably vivid after-action report, *Morris*'s skipper, Commander F. T. Williamson, recalled the scenes confronting his men. *Liscome Bay*'s survivors, he wrote,

> were all very badly shaken up and some them had suffered bad burns, broken limbs, and blast shock. One man died while the medical officer [Lieutenant (jg) H. L. Armentrout] was administering blood plasma while another died in the water before being picked up by the ship's motor whale boat. The other stretcher cases were all in frightful condition with injuries ranging from severe internal hemorrhages to shattered limbs, head concussion and completely disfiguring flash burns. This ship has rescued survivors from the *Lexington*, *Yorktown*, and *Hornet*, but it was agreed unanimously that the sinking of the *Liscome Bay* and the condition of the comparatively few survivors constituted the most heartrending disaster yet seen.[30]

Despite the remnants of tragedy around them, the men of *Morris* and the survivors of *Liscome Bay* rose magnificently to the occasion. Once again, the words of *Morris*'s captain provide the best description:

> Inspiring is no word for the conduct displayed by the men picked up in the water around the *Liscome Bay*. Every time our motor whale boat would approach a man in the water, he would invariably say, "Never mind me, there are others who need the boat because of their injuries." The oil and wreckage was heavy on

> the water throughout the entire area of our rescue operations and many of the men couldn't see for the oil in their eyes. Despite this fact, and many more pressing physical disabilities . . . the absolute courage of these men was electrifying. As one man would be taken aboard, he would turn around and assist the ship's company in getting other of his shipmates out of difficulties.[31]

As his destroyers continued their work, Griffin stood grimly on *New Mexico*'s bridge. Despite the passage of time, he still knew little beyond the fact that one of his carriers had disappeared in a flash of flame. If her attacker was still out there, it had yet to be discovered.

At 0610, the excited voice of the destroyer *Maury*'s radio operator crackled over the airwaves.

"Torpedo wake on 160 off port side of *Maury*!"

"Roger. Out."

"I am running down that torpedo wake now. Over."

"*Maury*, Chestnut. Which way was torpedo heading? Over."

"Torpedo wake was heading 160 coming from 340. Over."

"All ships except *New Mexico* avoid danger area. Danger area is in vicinity of *New Mexico. Mississippi*, *Corregidor,* acknowledge. Over."

"Wilco. Wilco."[32]

Actually, *Maury* had spotted two torpedo wakes. One had missed the destroyer by a scant fifteen yards. The second was slightly farther away. The wakes seemed to solve the mystery of *Liscome Bay*'s attacker, but the idea that an enemy submarine remained in the area only increased Griffin's discomfort. He radioed the destroyers picking up the survivors.

"Report conditions your vicinity. Over."

"About sixty percent of survivors have been picked up. Sixty percent of survivors. Over."

"Roger. Proceed with rescue. Do not make reports. Over."

"Roger. Out."[33]

The rescue work continued while the task group waited for further word from *Maury* regarding the torpedo wake. Minutes later, *Morris*'s sonar operator reported screw noises. The ship was jumpy; it was later determined that she was detecting the sound of *Baltimore*'s engine. By then, *Maury* still hadn't found the source of the torpedo, and *Hull* was dispatched to join the search for the elusive submarine. She carried on board seven survivors whom her whaleboat had plucked out of the oily water. Griffin also ordered *Corregidor* and *Coral Sea* to commence launching aircraft. It was now 0637.

Less than two minutes later, another excited radio operator called in to *New Mexico*.

"Chestnut, *Gridley*. We have sound contact on port bow."

"Roger. Out. Task Group 52.13, Chestnut. Emergency tackline turn six. *Corregidor*, acknowledge. Over."

"Wilco from *Corregidor*."

"*Mississippi* and *Baltimore*, Chestnut. Prepare to launch aircraft for anti-submarine patrol. Over." The battleship and the cruiser both carried catapult-launched float planes.

"Wilco. Out."

"Wilco. Out."

"Chestnut, *Gridley*. We picked up a very good echo fifteen hundred yards. Making an attack. Over."

"Roger. Out. Africa, Chestnut. Send *Hull* to assist *Gridley*. Retain two destroyers with you. Over."

"Wilco."

"*Corregidor*, Chestnut. Resume launching, over."

"Wilco."[34]

Hull diverted from its track toward *Maury* and steamed to join *Gridley*, which was already dropping depth charges. Despite the towering "whooshes" of white foam off her stern marking the depth charges' explosions, there were no indications of any success. Elsewhere, *Maury*'s skipper was also concluding that he was unable to find the origin of the torpedo wakes he had dodged.

The failure to locate or sink the phantom submarine drove the tension on *New Mexico*'s bridge a notch higher. Griffin ordered *Baltimore* to launch her antisubmarine patrol; then he radioed *Maury*.

"*Maury*, Chestnut. Have you had any sound contact? Over."

"Negative. Over."

"How certain were you that it was a torpedo wake? Over."

One can easily imagine the irritation at that moment on *Maury*'s bridge after the two narrow misses. Her captain sent a terse reply: "The wake which was seen was observed by the commanding officer, lookouts, two torpedomen, and some men on the bridge. We are rather certain. Over."

"Roger. Out," came the sheepish reply.[35]

Back at the oil slicks, *Morris* and *Hughes* continued to pluck survivors out of the sea. The destroyer *MacDonough*, reacting to Admiral Turner's orders in Task Force 52, sailed to take *Hull*'s place in the recovery operation. While she was en route to their assistance, the first two destroyers continued their work.

With the sun climbing slowly on the horizon, *Hughes* pulled carefully alongside Daily's crowded floater net. Sailors aboard the destroyer dropped a four-foot-wide rope ladder over *Hughes*'s starboard side. From the waterline it was an eight-foot climb to her deck, although to the men in the water she looked like the Empire State Building looming above them. Many of the survivors, either wounded or exhausted from their ordeal, struggled to make it up the ladder. Nevertheless, with sailors pushing from below and pulling from above, the destroyer men recovered all of the floater net occupants.

As they pulled *Liscome Bay*'s survivors on deck, *Hughes*'s crew gently escorted their new guests over to the port side of the ship. They were a tragic sight—burned, soaked, and covered in oil, many suffered broken bones or deep gashes and cuts from flying debris, while others simply lay quietly on the destroyer's decks, dazed by concussions or post-traumatic shock. *Hughes*'s medical officer and the destroyer's two pharmacist mates worked frantically to triage the survivors and treat the wounded. The ship's small sick bay was overflowed, so the medical officer commandeered *Hughes*'s mess hall, turning it into a makeshift emergency room.

Daily, although burned himself, paced the deck, identifying those who were most badly wounded and directing the pharmacist mates over to them. As he passed one of the wounded baker strikers, Daily saw the man's eyes roll back into his pale head. Shaking uncontrollably, he was going into shock. Daily grabbed the striker and pulled him across the deck, back to the sunlit starboard side of the destroyer. He shoved him up against the ship's hot exhaust stack, counting on it to warm the man. It worked. In a couple of minutes, the striker's tremors subsided. Satisfied, Daily pulled the striker back over to the rest of the wounded men. Lowering the sailor gently back to the deck, Daily noticed the destroyer pulling up alongside a solitary survivor sitting in the middle of a wrecked raft. It was Robert C. Smith, the carrier's lead officers' cook.

"Smitty, Smitty, you made it!" Daily called excitedly.

Smith looked up with an exhausted face and managed a tired wave. As *Hughes* hove into position, he clambered slowly up the ladder. Daily helped pull him up the last few feet. Daily had barely pulled Smith onto the deck when he heard a familiar voice.

"Anybody got my wallet?"[36]

Turning, Daily spied his erstwhile swimming companion. Reaching into his trousers, he extracted the soaked wallet and handed it to the happy sailor. Perhaps it would enable him to buy another "geetar." Meanwhile, *Hughes* and *Morris* continued to pick up survivors. They hauled the bedraggled and oil-soaked survivors up directly from the sea while whaleboats and launches crisscrossed the area, searching for other survivors. One of *Hull*'s rescue crews had plucked Whalen out of the water. As he crawled onto the deck, the exhausted seaman vomited up the sickening mixture of seawater and oil he had swallowed in the water—a vile concoction "as dark as the transmission fluid in a car."[37]

One launch from *Morris,* filled with men, came across Ries, sprawled in a life raft. The launch added Ries's raft to the train of rafts it was towing and dragged them back to *Morris*. Severely burned and unable to use his legs following the concussions from the undersea blasts, Ries couldn't make it out of his raft. Sailors aboard the destroyer hooked him under his armpits and pulled him aboard, where he lay among the wounded. Destroyer men scrambled among them, dressing wounds, sprinkling sulfa powder, and, occasionally, covering the faces of dead men with makeshift shrouds. A whaleboat from *Morris* also rescued Honold, eventually depositing the badly wounded parachute rigger on a sheet of canvas spread out on the destroyer's fantail.

Fireman Phelan Allee, who had been blown off the ship and struggled in the water with a leaking life jacket all morning, watched two of the destroyers with nets over their sides pluck survivors from the sea. His yells and shouts failed to attract their attention, however, and they pulled away from him. Allee was wondering if he had been abandoned when a launch from *Morris* puttered by. Riding up onto the crest of an ocean swell, he waved and yelled at the launch's crew. This time his shouts were heard, and the sailors on the launch pulled him aboard. Motoring back to *Morris*, they worked to stanch the flow of blood from the deep lacerations in Allee's left knee, left thigh, and the left side of his back.

Beasley, Smith, and their three companions had spied the rescue effort early on, but they had drifted away from the site of the sinking and the main cluster of survivors. With increasing frustration, they watched the destroyers and their small boats pull people from the water. None came, and Smith continued to drift in and out of consciousness.

Finally, just as the rescue effort appeared to be winding down, a whaleboat from *Hughes* appeared in front of Beasley. He and the other men helped the crew pull Smith into the boat, and then they joined him. Beasley saw that Smith had lost consciousness as soon as he was in the boat, and a corpsman injected him with a shot of morphine to ease his pain. The corpsman turned to Beasley: "You're next," he said, motioning with his syringe. He could see that Beasley, now wearing only his undershorts, was also in pain. Most of his hair had been burned off by the flaming oil, and each breath brought a fresh surge of pain in his lower ribcage.

"Absolutely not," Beasley snapped. "I'll make it without that stuff." Shrugging, the corpsman returned to his work.[38]

The launch motored back to *Hughes*, pausing only to pull one last man from the water. Beasley was pleased to see that it was Lieutenant Commander Bodler, the ship's gunnery officer, who had ordered him and the others to abandon ship.

As the survivors continued to be pulled aboard, Griffin and Task Group 52.13 still faced the specter of another enemy attack. *Gridley* and *Maury* still hadn't located the Japanese submarine, and at 0717 radar operators reported an unidentified aircraft twenty miles to the north. By now, thirty minutes has passed since Griffin had ordered *Baltimore* to launch her aircraft.

"*Baltimore*, Chestnut. Why haven't you launched? Over."

"We are preparing now."

"Roger. Expedite. Over."[39]

Fortunately, the unidentified aircraft turned out to be an American plane, and when *Maury* reported no sonar contacts, Griffin ordered her to rejoin the task group. Then he tried *Baltimore* one more time.

"When do you expect to launch? Over."

"Wait. Over." A pregnant pause. "One plane will be launched in five minutes and second shortly thereafter. Over."

"Very badly done. Over."

"Roger."[40]

By then, the morning's tension, and the rescue of *Liscome Bay*'s survivors, was winding down. At approximately 0800, *Morris* and *Hughes*, which had been joined by *MacDonough*, and once again by *Hull*, reluctantly concluded their search. They had scoured the area. There just weren't any more men to pull aboard. The destroyers turned to head for Makin's lagoon with their battered human cargo.

While searching for survivors, *Morris* had pulled alongside Chaplain Carley and the two sailors clutching their floating plank. By then, Carley's life jacket was soaked in oil, and its weight made it nearly impossible to climb up the destroyer's cargo net. The chaplain tugged it off and began treading water, his arms and legs seeming impossibly heavy as he fought to keep his gasping mouth and nose above the waves. One of *Morris*'s sailors recognized his distress and threw him a rope. Carley slipped it under his armpits, and with a series of tugs the sailor and his crewmates hauled the tired chaplain aboard. As they pulled Carley up over the gunwale, the sailor recognized that he had rescued a chaplain and smiled irreverently.

"Well, Padre, I see religion paid off."[41]

Carley, exhausted and covered in thick patches of oil, didn't argue. In fact, he couldn't have agreed more.

11
Surviving

Once he reached *Hughes,* Beasley clambered up the cargo net draping her sides. Despite his wounds, he was determined to make it aboard on his own. By the time he pulled himself onto the deck, he realized that he must have presented a strange sight. Clad only in a pair of torn and oil-stained undershorts, he was almost bald where his hair had been burned off. Looking down, he saw that the little toe on his left foot had almost been cut off. It dangled by a small piece of skin and muscle. A corpsman ran over to Beasley and, taking him by the arm, helped him down a ladder to the destroyer's after mess hall, which the crew had converted into a makeshift infirmary. Beasley found the heat and stench in the small, crowded room almost unbearable and decided he would be better off above deck. Moving to leave, he saw a medical team wrapping Steward Smith in gauze from head to toe.

Throughout *Hughes,* the crew worked steadily to tend to *Liscome Bay*'s survivors. The most urgent cases—some twenty in all—were carried to the after mess hall, while those with minor wounds were directed to various cleaning stations where they used diesel fuel and rags to scrub themselves clean of the thick engine oil caking their bodies. The oil was a greater problem for the half-dozen severe burn cases brought on board. Those men, like Smith, suffered second-degree burns over as much as 40 percent of their bodies. The destroyer's medical officer set up two-man "burn teams" composed of nonmedical volunteers. They removed oil from the patients, cleaned burns, and applied sulfa powder or boric ointment dressing. Morphine and plasma was then used to try to stabilize the victims and ward off shock.

As *Hughes* turned to head for Makin, her men stepped among the survivors, handing out water and oranges. The ship's galley worked to provide sandwiches and soup, while the storekeeper started handing out clean shirts, dungarees, and undershorts. No shoes were available—only overshoes. Beasley found himself wearing a pair of size forty undershorts around his twenty-eight-inch waist. On his size eight-and-a-half feet he wore size eleven overshoes held on by rubber bands. He wasn't complaining, though, and soon he found a seat in the shade beneath one of the destroyer's 5-inch guns.

Meanwhile, *Hughes*'s officers gathered up Ensign Daily and other fellow officers and led them to the destroyer's small set of officers' quarters. There, Daily and the others took the only showers available—cold seawater showers with special seawater-type soap. It was enough to remove about 90 percent of the oil encrusting their bodies and hair. Leaving the showers, they discovered that their counterparts in *Hughes* had completely cleaned out their dressers and put all their clothes on top. Gratefully, Daily slipped on a clean khaki uniform. As with Beasley, shoes would have to wait.

Once dressed in his borrowed uniform, Daily padded in stocking feet to the destroyer's wardroom and sank wearily into a chair. Other men joined him. As time passed, a stunned silence settled on *Liscome Bay*'s officers as they realized how few of them were present. It would be a long time before casualty figures were available, but the small number gathered in the wardroom was an ominous sign.

Spirits began to rise as *Hughes*'s mess attendants slid steaming plates of food before the carrier's officers. Over a hearty breakfast, Daily and his companions began comparing notes from the early-morning torpedo strike and sinking. Surely, they assured one another, there must be more survivors on other ships besides the approximately one hundred officers and men who had been dragged out of the sea by *Hughes*.

Tim Woodham and the enlisted survivors experienced similar hospitality. Woodham was so covered in heavy bunker fuel oil that the destroyer crew had to wash him down with diesel fuel just to break up the globs of oil sticking to his skin. It was a painful experience, "like a million needles running down your skin at the same time."[1] Cold saltwater showers finished the job, and then *Hughes*'s crew passed out all the extra clothes they could find.

Shoes were in short supply. Beasley had been fortunate to get a pair of surplus overshoes, but Woodham wasn't so lucky. Instead, he wrapped his feet in engine room rags to protect them from being seared on the destroyer's hot metal decks baking in the tropical sun. Considering what he had just been through, he had no complaints, and he shuffled by a khaki-clad *Hughes* crewman without giving it a second thought. The *Hughes* sailor—Woodham assumed he was a chief petty officer—noticed Woodham's feet.

"They couldn't find any shoes for you?" he asked.

"No."

"What size do you wear?"

"Nine and a half," Woodham responded.

"Come with me. I can get you some shoes."

Woodham followed the *Hughes* crewman toward the bridge. Soon, he realized that they were entering "officers' country" aboard the destroyer. His would-be benefactor was, in fact, an officer.

"Sir, I'm an enlisted man," Woodham told his guide. Woodham received no answer, however, and the two men soon reached a door marked "Captain."

Hughes's khaki-clad captain stepped into his quarters, invited Woodham in, and pulled a brand-new pair of Florsheim leather dress shoes from one of his drawers.

"Take these," he said, giving the pair to Woodham. "And here, take these," he added, handing over a pair of black socks. Woodham started to protest, but the captain cut him off with a wave of his hand. Woodham accepted the gift and left the cabin.[2]

As the destroyers headed for Makin, the shipwrecked sailors tried to piece together who had made it off the sinking carrier and who had not. Abbott, Ashley, Beebe, Blakley, Bohm, Carley, Charters, Davis, Galliano, Honold, Hunt, Mack, Piegari, Rairden, Ries, Rowe, Sistrunk, Tornquist, and Wells were among those aboard *Morris*. Allee and Whalen, who were among the seven survivors picked up by *Hull* and subsequently transferred to *Morris*, were also on that destroyer. *Hughes*'s complement of survivors included Adams, Ames, Beasley, Beymer, Bodler, Bruce, Crommelin, Cruse, Daily, Jelsema, Mahood, Pinder, Roach, Woodham, Woodward, and Youtz.

Fire Controlman Jenkins, after settling on board *Hughes*, realized that he was still carrying a pair of binoculars underneath his life jacket from his battle station as the 40-millimeter fire control director. Although Jenkins wore the binoculars, they were actually signed out from *Liscome Bay*'s storeroom to the officer in charge of the fire control director. Jenkins spotted the lieutenant among the survivors on board *Hughes*.

"Here are your binoculars, sir," Jenkins told the lieutenant.

Smiling, the lieutenant told Jenkins to keep them. "Right of salvage," he explained.[3]

Not all of the survivors were aboard the destroyers. Lieutenant Wells, who had flown with Blair's lost patrol and landed aboard *Lexington*, had been preparing for an early-morning takeoff to return to *Liscome Bay*. The captain's announcement of the sinking of *Liscome Bay* to his crew stopped Wells in his tracks. Paling, he returned to his guest quarters without a word. He wouldn't feel up to flying until the next morning. By then, however, the young aviator had recovered his spirits. Climbing into a Wildcat freshly painted "Baby Airedale" and "Orphan Annie" by *Lexington*'s sympathetic air group, Wells took off and headed back to his original home, the escort carrier *Corregidor*.[4]

Chaplain Carley, on board *Morris*, faced a more solemn duty. Three survivors had died shortly after being pulled from the ocean. *Morris*'s records show them to be Lieutenant Commander Lester H. Kern, DE-V(S), USNR, of Baltimore, Maryland, Seaman Second Class Walter N. Foland, of Mountain View, California, and Chief Yeoman Harold E. Carlson, of Pensacola, Florida.[5] As the destroyer headed toward Makin, her captain ordered a burial at sea. The officer of the deck provided Carley with a copy of the New Testament. Gathering a contingent of *Liscome Bay*'s crew on *Morris*'s fantail, Carley presided over a simple service beside the sailors' shrouded remains. As silence descended over *Morris*, he turned to the fourteenth chapter of John. "Do not let your hearts be troubled," Carley read. "Believe in God, believe also in me. In my Father's house there are many dwelling places. If it were not so, would I have told you that I go to prepare a place for you? And if I go and prepare a place for you, I will come again and will take you to myself, so that where I am, there you may be also."[6]

Early that afternoon, the destroyers bearing *Liscome Bay*'s survivors stood into Makin's lagoon. *Hughes* pulled alongside the U.S. Coast Guard attack transport *Leonard Wood*. Sailors placed a two-foot-wide, fifteen-foot-long wooden plank between *Hughes*'s bridge and an open port in *Leonard Wood*'s side. The ships heaved up and down in opposite directions, which in turn shifted the plank up and down three feet at a time. The *Liscome Bay* survivors viewed the proffered path to *Leonard Wood* with a great deal of skepticism, but somehow all of them managed to make it across and into the outstretched arms of *Leonard Wood*'s waiting sailors. Crewmen transported the more seriously wounded by line and pulley over to the transport's deck.

Woodham lined up to make the awkward crossing and, subconsciously, looked down at his feet. He realized he was still wearing the destroyer captain's shoes. Embarrassed, he paused in line and started to unlace them.

"What are you doing down there?" a familiar voice called from the bridge.

"Forgot to return your shoes, sir," Woodham shouted back.

"Damn it, Woodham, I gave you those shoes," the skipper replied. "Now get out of here." With his blessing, Woodham kept the shoes and headed for *Leonard Wood*.[7]

Once on board, Daily gathered with his fellow survivors in a room that appeared to be one of the transport's mess halls. Shortly thereafter, he felt the ship rumble as it got under way. A moment later, general quarters trumpeted through the ship.

The sounding of general quarters was routine for a ship leaving port in a war zone, but the recent ordeal of *Liscome Bay*'s crew had temporarily wiped the notion of "routine" from their minds. At the first sound of that familiar call, the mess hall emptied as the shell-shocked survivors rushed topside en masse. Once on deck, they realized, sheepishly, that it was just another routine general quarters. Nevertheless, *Leonard Wood*'s captain learned his lesson. For the rest of the voyage, he simply announced general quarters over the ship's loudspeakers. The transport

Neville, also carrying *Liscome Bay* survivors, stood out of the lagoon the same day. Both ships also carried soldiers from the army units that had recently captured Makin.

After the false alarm, *Leonard Wood*'s crew issued Daily and his fellow survivors shoes, shaving gear, toothbrushes, and combs. Combing his hair that day, Daily discovered that, in addition to the burns on his legs and arms, he had suffered a serious gash on his scalp during his escape from the carrier. During a quick trip to the sick bay, his wound was cleaned and dressed.

Later that evening, Daily found an empty bunk in a coast guard officer's room. He tried unsuccessfully to fall asleep and, giving up, wandered into the wardroom to watch a poker game. Tiring of the game, he returned to his bunk. Around 0200 he met his roommate, who had just been cleaned out at the poker table. Daily pulled out his waterlogged wallet, extracted his last twenty dollars—two oil- and water-soaked tens—and handed them to his roommate. Cheered, the officer returned to the poker game. Two hours later he came back, tired but happy, with a handful of cash. He repaid Daily, and both men fell asleep.

The next day was Thanksgiving, November 25, 1943. Before their crews and passengers sat down for the traditional dinner, *Leonard Wood* and *Neville*, now en route back to Pearl Harbor, flashed signals at one another exchanging the names of the survivors each ship carried. Daily kept a nervous tally as *Neville* signaled the names across the waves. He knew that there were approximately 160 survivors aboard *Leonard Wood*, and his pay books tallied the total crew aboard *Liscome Bay*—her own crew, Mullinnix's staff, and the pilots and aircrewmen of VC-39—as over 900. How many of the remainder were in *Neville*?

The signalman slowly but steadily flashed the names, one by one, from *Neville*'s bridge. Ten, then 20, then 50 names flashed across the water. Heads on *Leonard Wood* nodded with satisfaction. So far, so good, they thought. The number eventually grew to 100. At 107, the signals stopped. The survivors stared at *Neville*'s bridge in disbelief. Slowly, the reality sank in as the men on *Leonard Wood* completed the awful arithmetic. Rear Admiral Mullinnix, Captain Wiltsie, and 642 of their shipmates had died.

The massive figure of casualties proved almost incomprehensible to the lost carrier's survivors. Six hundred and forty-four! Some of the sailors came from towns with populations smaller than that. Who had ever heard of the navy losing that many men in a single American warship's sinking?

In fact, *Liscome Bay* had just joined a small, terrible fraternity. Two years earlier, at Pearl Harbor, 1,177 men had died aboard *Arizona* (BB-39) when a Japanese bomb detonated her forward ammunition magazine. That same day, the capsizing of the battleship *Oklahoma* (BB-37) cost 415 lives. The sinking of the light cruiser *Juneau* (CL-52) in the Solomons in 1942 took the lives of 683 of her crew, including the five Sullivan brothers. The carrier *Franklin* (CV-13) lost 724 men following a Japanese air attack the morning of March 19, 1945, although fellow ships towed her safely to port. At the very end of the war, in 1945, a torpedo attack on the heavy cruiser *Indianapolis* (CA-35) killed 803 officers and men. Since *Franklin* did not actually sink, the loss of *Liscome Bay* would stand in the navy's records as the most costly sinking of a carrier. Six hundred and forty-four men had perished in the span of twenty-three minutes.

Around midday, the survivors aboard *Leonard Wood* sat down for supper. As they dined on slivers of turkey and ham with fruit gravy and sweet potatoes, they struggled with emotions of thanksgiving and grief. The casualty figures hung heavy in the air, and the traditional holiday meal served in the strange environment of the transport only reinforced the fact that they were all thousands of miles from home. Chaplain Carley had presided over a Thanksgiving Day service earlier in the day, and as he picked at his turkey and ham his thoughts turned to the twelve hundred pounds of uneaten turkey that had been brought on board *Liscome Bay* for this same meal. He knew that, in hundreds of homes back in the States, families would be celebrating this same meal, completely unaware that a father, son, or husband would never again sit down to share it with them.

Maxsy Homec suffered a special kind of uncertainty. He knew his brother Frank was not on his ship. Jim Honold had similar questions about the fate of his first cousin and fellow shipmate Clayton Rucker.

Learning of the men's predicament, the skippers of *Leonard Wood* and *Neville* exchanged signals. The messages brought good news for Honold but bad news for Homec. Rucker was among the survivors. Frank Homec was not.

On Thanksgiving night, two of the survivors succumbed to their wounds. The next morning, *Liscome Bay*'s crew gathered aft for the funeral service and subsequent burial at sea. Woodham found himself standing in the front row, while Daily stood to the side. They both stared silently at the two canvas sacks lying on wooden slides near the edge of the deck.

The chaplains finished their brief service and, closing their Bibles, gave one of *Leonard Wood*'s officers an almost imperceptible nod. With a quick motion, the slides tilted and the canvas sacks slid off the chute. The sound of the resulting "swoosh" hit Daily's stomach like a punch. It was yet another somber reminder—as if they needed one—of the cost of the ordeal that he and his shipmates had undergone.

For some, the ordeal continued. Honold, the parachute rigger who had been blasted unconscious off *Liscome Bay*, lay in sick bay with two compound fractures in his left leg, burned skin, and lacerations on his head and back. His left leg was in such bad shape that the doctors suggested amputating it.

"Don't cut off my leg," Honold ordered.

"You might get gangrene," a doctor warned. But he heeded Honold's desire and contented himself with sewing up the various cuts. He left the rigger covered in wet gauze from the waist up.

Later in the voyage, a blond-haired sailor approached Honold's bed.

"Were you on a life raft with two guys?" he asked.

"No," Honold mumbled. "I was just with one other guy."

"That's what I meant," the sailor said. "I was that guy. But you were so covered in oil—I thought you might be a black man."

"I thought you were, too," Honold replied. For the remainder of the passage to Pearl, Honold's friend from the life raft stayed by his bunk.[8]

Elsewhere in the ship, Beasley and Steward Smith shared a common compartment. Smith, oftentimes delirious, was completely wrapped in gauze because of his burns. Small slits allowed only his mouth and nose to show. He would awaken at night, screaming in pain. Beasley still had the man's dog tags. He wasn't yet convinced the young steward would pull through.

One day, a visit from Warner Duff shook Beasley even more. According to Duff, only five of the ship's twenty-three signalmen survived—Duff, Beasley, Beasley's boot camp buddy Wally Andrews, Gerald Goss, and Pete Unbehagen. With a start, Beasley realized that they were the same five men from the signal gang who were missing from his friend Chuck Williams's dream about his Alabama wedding.[9]

Meanwhile, life had to go on. Daily's chief enlisted assistant, Fred Sheppard, had also survived the sinking, and the two men began to reconstruct *Liscome Bay*'s pay records. They created a payroll survey sheet and, with the help of three other officers, interviewed the survivors to establish their pay status. Eventually, Sheppard had finished a complete pay record for each man. It was hard, detailed work, but Daily and Sheppard were glad to have something to take their minds off their recent brush with death.

Elsewhere in the crew, Daily observed that his fellow survivors' reaction to the sinking seemed to fall into three distinct demographic groups. The youngest men—those under twenty—accepted their survival with a typical teenager's sense of immortality. They soon returned to their card games or jawing about girlfriends they would soon see again back in port. The men between twenty and thirty seemed more reflective but were also soon ready for duty. The torpedo attack and its aftermath had hit the older men the hardest. Even five days after the sinking, the older survivors were, according to Daily, still stunned by the magnitude of the disaster at sea.

Daily, for his part, simply stayed focused on his work with the pay records. Reconstructing them would enable the men to get paid once the ship made it back to Pearl Harbor, but that was still several days away. In the meantime, practically all the surviving crew were without any cash, rendering them unable to buy cigarettes, candy, cards, and other items from the ship's store to pass the time during their transit back to Hawaii. Aware of the economic problem befalling the crew, Lieutenant Commander Oliver Ames, *Liscome Bay*'s senior surviving officer (not counting Crommelin, who was, as Carrier Division 24's chief of staff, technically not part of the carrier's crew), approached Daily a few days into their voyage.

"Hey, Pay, are these any good?" he asked, pulling from his oily wallet every paycheck Daily had ever issued him. Ames, heir to his Massachusetts family's industrial fortune, always had plenty of money on hand. His navy pay must have struck him as an amusing pittance in comparison, but Ames had accepted his paychecks nevertheless as a polite gesture to Daily. He had just never bothered to cash them.

"Sure, Ollie," Daily answered in amazement. "Just take them to the ship's paymaster, and he'll cash whatever you want."[10]

Smiling, Ames tracked down *Leonard Wood*'s paymaster, cashed his checks, and distributed the proceeds to *Liscome Bay*'s survivors. After that, the ship's store did a brisk business for the rest of the voyage.

Besides his paymaster duties, Daily didn't forget that he was still in charge of the supply division. Every day, he trekked down to *Hughes*'s sick bay to visit the wounded survivors of his division such as Smith. Each one was a burn victim, lying on the deck in a Stokes stretcher and swathed in baking soda–soaked bandages. Daily would kneel beside the burned sailors, their useless arms swaddled in bandages. For some he would light a cigarette and put it carefully between their lips, allowing them to take a few puffs. For others he would simply spend a few moments speaking with them as the painful rasps of labored breathing echoed around him. Every trip to the sick bay ended the same way. Once he had made his rounds, Daily would slip into a quiet corner of the ship's passageways and, out of sight of the rest of the crew, succumb to the horrible sights and sob as quietly as he could. Nevertheless, he would always steel himself and return to visit the wounded men the next day. It was a sad routine he maintained for the rest of *Leonard Wood*'s voyage.

One afternoon, Daily found himself sitting out on deck, enjoying the sea air. The sailors around him began jawing with one another, swapping stories about how they had made it off the carrier and survived in the morning darkness before being rescued by the destroyers. "I'll tell you how I got off," Daily said. Reaching under his T-shirt, he pulled out a neck chain that combined the Miraculous, St. Joseph, Sacred Heart, and St. Christopher medals in the form of a cross. Daily held it up for the others to see. Without a word, seven of the group reached under their shirts and produced the same medal. A strange silence descended on the group.[11]

Back in the States, the silence about *Liscome Bay* had been broken in an awkward manner. Reportedly, the American press agencies, weary of being scooped by their foreign counterparts, had hounded the navy for more timely reports of ship sinkings and other war news.[12] The navy acquiesced to the press's demands, broke with its tradition of not reporting sinkings until all of the crew's relatives had been notified, and announced *Liscome Bay*'s sinking with a terse press communiqué on December 2, 1943, while *Leonard Wood* was still en route to Pearl Harbor. "The *U.S.S. Liscome Bay* (an escort carrier) was sunk as a result of being torpedoed by a submarine on November 24, 1943, in the Gilbert Islands operation," the news release began. "The next of kin of casualties aboard the *Liscome Bay* will be notified as soon as possible."[13]

Newspapers around the country immediately picked up the story, despite the fact that the next of kin had not yet been notified and despite the fact that the survivors, still at sea, were unable to contact their families and reassure them that they were alive. Some papers simply rehashed the news of the sinking, while others made the connection between local boys and the lost ship. "Tim Woodham On Lost Ship; Fate Unknown" announced Woodham's local paper in California.

In Philadelphia, Daily's wife, Gloria, riding home on a train, glanced at a stranger's *Philadelphia Inquirer* and read "*Liscome Bay* Goes Down in Flames." She nearly fainted at the sight, knowing her husband was on the ship in the Pacific. Kindly strangers helped her from the train, and she somehow made it home. For twenty-four hours she placed calls to the Philadelphia Navy Yard, to Washington, to a retired admiral Daily's father knew, and to anyone who might be able to tell her if her husband was alive or dead. She had no luck with any of them. It was a scene being played out across the country.

Leonard Wood was nearing Pearl Harbor when *Liscome Bay*'s survivors heard a broadcast about the sinking on a San Francisco radio station. Incredulous, Daily and his shipmates realized that, with radio silence being strictly enforced, no survivor lists had been communicated back to Hawaii or the States. Consequently, their families and loved ones back home had no idea whether they had lived or died in the sinking. "We just don't need this, too!" the survivors snapped at one another. They were still twenty-four hours out of Pearl, where they would be able to telegram their families that they were still alive.

Following the newscast, fellow ensign Leonard Black sidled up to Daily. Black was one of Captain Wiltsie's two nephews who had secretly served under Wiltsie on board the carrier. Black had survived—his cousin Bill Schmidt had not. He asked Daily the same question that had begun nagging Daily himself—how should they notify their wives? They had all heard the news by now. If they saw a military telegram arrive, they would automatically expect the worst. Black had a triple problem. Not only did he have to send his wife the good news that he was still alive, but he also had to notify his aunt and his cousin's wife that their husbands had not survived. As Daily and Black talked, they hit upon a solution. They would send their telegrams to next-door neighbors or close relatives of all three and let them break the news—good or bad—to the wives. The two ensigns agreed it was the best plan possible under the circumstances.

The next day, *Leonard Wood* stood into Pearl Harbor. Daily turned over his carefully reconstructed pay records to the Pearl Harbor pay office, enabling the survivors to be paid in full the next day. Once that task was complete, Daily fired off a telegram back to his parents' next-door neighbor. "Perfectly all right," it read. "Expect to be home soon. Tell Mother and Dad." Daily didn't realize it at the time, but his and Black's scheme did the trick. "Nothing but jubilation all around," he later noted with satisfaction.[14] Of course, the term "jubilation" certainly didn't apply to the Wiltsie and Schmidt homes.

With the telegram on its way, Daily checked into the bachelor officers' quarters and soaked in the first hot shower he had enjoyed in weeks, scrubbing at the remaining remnants of oil stuck in his hair. After fifty minutes, he was finally clean and heading for the officers' mess for dinner. He and the other *Liscome Bay* officers entered the room to a resounding round of applause from the other officers present.

Beasley and *Liscome Bay*'s other wounded, meanwhile, were transferred to hospitals onshore. Beasley found himself in a hospital in Honolulu and managed a brief visit to check in on Smith. He found the steward still wrapped in gauze but seemingly in better shape and spirits.

"Do you remember Beasley?" Beasley asked.

"No," Smith answered weakly.

"Do you remember anything about being in the water after leaving *Liscome Bay?*"

"Very little. I don't know what happened."

"I just happen to have your ID tags," Beasley told him. "I'll leave them on your night stand. The nurse will put them away for you."

"Okay. Thanks."

"Try and remember my name—Beasley. Maybe we'll meet again someday and have a long talk." With that said, and the dog tags back in their owner's possession, Beasley returned to his bunk.[15]

Honold was also in the hospital. One evening, he awoke with a start. Something was crawling out of his leg cast—a maggot. He yelled for the corpsman, who turned on the light and discovered dozens of maggots seething on the bed. The corpsman raked them off and, the next morning, summoned a doctor.

The doctor began cutting away the cast. Honold kept a careful eye on the doctor's face, wondering what expression it would show.

To his relief, the doctor's face broke into a smile.

"Take a look, sailor," he said. "The maggots have eaten away all the bad stuff." Honold looked. The doctor was right. His leg wound was "pretty and red." An X-ray confirmed that the bones were still in place, and the doctor replaced the cast.

Honold's cousin Clayton Rucker also visited him in the hospital.

"I was up forward on the ship when the torpedo hit," Rucker told Honold. "I ran out onto the catwalk and looked midship where you were stationed. All I could see was a big hole. You could have put an eight-room house in that hole."

Honold asked Rucker to write a letter to his parents. "Just tell them I have a broken finger—that's why I'm not writing," he told his cousin.[16]

A few days later, the carrier *Saratoga*—the same ship that Rear Admiral Mullinnix had so recently commanded—stood into Pearl for a brief stopover. Overdue for stateside repairs, she was leaving for San Francisco the next day. *Liscome Bay*'s survivors received orders to embark in her for transportation back to the West Coast. Before leaving, Daily bought a raincoat in order to be ready for the cold San Francisco weather, and then he made a quick side trip to the base hospital to track down Captain Crommelin.

Finding Crommelin's room, Daily explained to the burned captain that the crew was leaving for California but that his pay records had been given to the appropriate staff at Pearl.

"Pay, thanks for everything," Crommelin said from his hospital bed. "You did a great job."[17] With that simple praise ringing in his ears, Daily reported to *Saratoga*. Most of *Liscome Bay*'s other survivors, Beasley among them, also made it on board the carrier for the trip back to the States.

The old carrier made the five-day unescorted run to San Francisco at top speed through rough weather. One night, Bergquist recalled later, the rolling ship pitched sailors from their bunks as waves broke over the flight deck. For a man with multiple compound fractures in his left leg, it was a painful and frightening evening.

Beasley spent the voyage in a makeshift collection of cots on the ship's hangar deck. Rough weather aside, he had no complaints about his accommodations—he was happy to be back with Andrews, Goss, and Unbehagen from the signal gang. His uniform—if one could call it that—was another matter. He was still wearing his size forty undershorts and the overshoes donated by *Hughes*. Since the rescue, he had only managed to add a hospital gown to his ensemble. One of *Saratoga*'s storekeepers had located an extra pair of dungarees, but as luck would have it, they were also too large. Beasley had to use a rope to keep them up.

Arriving on a night of seventy-mile-per-hour gale winds and seven-foot waves in the bay, *Saratoga* was unable to moor. Instead, a seagoing tug took off *Liscome Bay*'s ambulatory survivors and transported them to Alameda NAS. The men on stretchers had to wait until *Saratoga* could moor at Hunters Point Naval Shipyard in order to be lowered by yard cranes off the flight deck.

Upon arriving at Alameda, Daily learned that the navy had convened an investigative board to examine the ship's sinking. The board, which met initially on December 9, included representatives from the Commander in Chief, U.S. Fleet; the Chief of Naval Operations; the Bureaus of Aeronautics, Ships, and Ordnance; the Commander Fleet Aircraft—West Coast; and the Maritime Commission. That evening its members met with the ship's two surviving officers from *Liscome Bay*'s company—Lieutenant Commanders Ames and Adams. Captain Crommelin was still waylaid in the Pearl Harbor hospital recovering from his wounds.

For the next two days, the board interviewed twenty-five other survivors, trying to speak with someone from each section of the ship. Daily appeared on December 10. He found the assembled officers, as well as the two civilians from the Maritime Commission, to have little interest in placing blame for the sinking. Instead, their attention focused on the specifics of *Liscome Bay*'s damage, the escape of her survivors, and the manner of her sinking. It was clear to Daily that they were intent on identifying whatever engineering steps to take on *Liscome Bay*'s sister ships to reduce future casualties and damage in the event of similar torpedo attacks. To help understand the survivors' descriptions of the sinking and their escapes, the board visited *Wake Island*, one of *Liscome Bay*'s sister ships, which was in port at the time.

Once the survivors' testimony was complete, the officers sifted through the occasional minor contradictions as they analyzed the causes of the disaster and the conditions that had exacerbated it. Although the board did not issue its official findings until March 10, 1944, it provided an initial memorandum to the navy on December 22, 1943. "The principal conclusion reached," the memo read, "was that the primary cause of the loss of the vessel was the mass detonation of aircraft bombs stowed in the hold . . . as a result of heavy fragment attack produced by a contact torpedo explosion in way of, or very near, this magazine."[18] The memorandum also noted that the unfortunate timing of the torpedo attack—when so many of the crew were at flight quarters or manning exposed antiaircraft gun positions along the flight deck and gallery walkways on the aft section of the ship—undoubtedly contributed to the heavy loss of life.

In the meantime, the shipyards of Henry Kaiser were still building escort carriers in a headlong rush to reach their goal of constructing fifty carriers within a year. With the ongoing construction in mind, and more escort carriers destined to sail into harm's way, the board recommended that "the best practicable protection against fragments resulting from a contact underwater explosion . . . be provided for the aviation bomb stowage."[19] Not "the best possible," but "the best practicable." Such were the exigencies of war. To a large degree, the navy's conclusions regarding Kaiser's escort carriers echoed the earliest concerns of the sailors assigned to crew the baby flattops. The carriers, as constructed, were distressingly vulnerable to the rigors of combat. The thin hulls and bulkheads, while economical, left the ships ill-prepared to withstand a torpedo attack. The board's report acknowledged these shortcomings with an almost fatalistic acceptance.

The objective of Kaiser's escort carrier program, the board noted, "was to provide a large number of small escort carriers in the shortest possible time by following mass production methods. It is well known that all classes of escort carriers, as well as other naval ships converted from merchant types, do not have armor protection against direct hits by bombs and projectiles, and do not have torpedo protection systems such as those provided in large carriers."[20]

After analyzing the disaster, the navy instituted a number of changes to the design of *Liscome Bay*'s surviving and future sister ships. Emergency lighting was improved. Certain interior doors and bulkheads that had proven prone to being mangled from shipboard explosions and thus hindering escapes were removed or modified. The most dramatic alteration, however, was to add a liquid-filled blister, or bunker, on those portions of the hull that shielded bomb storage magazines. The added thickness reduced the amount of ordnance an escort carrier could carry, but it provided needed reassurance to other escort carrier sailors familiar with the fate of *Liscome Bay*.

That was in the future, however. By now, Daily was far more concerned with getting back home to Gloria. The band of survivors remained in San Francisco awaiting orders to send them on their thirty-day survivor's leave. Daily and Black holed up in a San Francisco hotel, bought new uniforms, and reported daily to the 12th Naval District as they awaited the coveted orders.

At least one sailor didn't wait around for orders. Tim Woodham had never been able to get a telephone call or telegram off to his parents, who were now living inland in Barstow, California. The threat of the brig seemed laughable compared to what he had just been through, and Woodham, determined to get word of his safe return to his parents, went

AWOL for the first and only time in his military career. He hitchhiked his way southeast, eventually arriving in the dusty Mohave Desert town at 5:30 A.M. Like so many of his fellow survivors' families, Woodham's parents had feared the worst. His arrival at the doorstep at that early-morning hour seemed akin to a miracle to his stunned, but overjoyed, father and mother.

The survivors who lay wounded in Oak Knoll Naval Hospital didn't enjoy such freedom of action, but they had a special treat one afternoon when they were paid a visit by Admiral Chester W. Nimitz, the Pacific Fleet's commander in chief, and movie star Joan Crawford. Don Cruse felt himself being shaken awake by the beautiful brunette actress.

"Wake up, sailor, and stand up if you can," she warned Cruse.[21]

Cruse's severed Achilles tendon was in a soft cast, and he quickly swung out of his bunk as Nimitz worked his way through the ward. The admiral pinned Purple Hearts on skivvy shirts and shook hands with the survivors.

Beasley, hospitalized with his friend Andrews at Alameda NAS, did not share in such a visit. In fact, as he and Andrews tried to find someone to issue them a decent uniform, the signalman became convinced that they were lost in the navy bureaucracy. Like Beasley, Andrews also wore a makeshift uniform—a borrowed shirt and pair of dungarees and a set of hospital slippers. By the second day in the hospital, Beasley had had enough.

"I'm going to sneak out and find someone that can help us," he told Andrews.

"You're going to get us in trouble," Andrews warned.

"That might be an improvement," Beasley replied. "Come on, go with me."[22]

Andrews allowed himself to be convinced, and shortly after lunch the next day the two sailors slipped out of the hospital. Looking back on the moment, Beasley recalled that they looked like "anything but sailors—overshoes held on with rubber bands, pants without a belt, a split-tail gown, bareheaded and all the hair burned off, and a pair of bedroom shoes." Years later Beasley would laugh about the incident, but at the time he meant business.[23]

Once outside the hospital, they spied a building a short distance down the street. Above it, a pennant fluttered.

"Andrews, there is our man," Beasley announced. "That flag means there is a rear admiral in that building."

Standing in his makeshift uniform and bedroom slippers, Andrews looked even paler than normal.

"Sam," he said, "we are heading for trouble, but let's go."

The two sailors made it to the front entrance of the building and were halfway down the hall toward the admiral's office when the chief master-at-arms and a member of the shore patrol intercepted them.

"We're here to see the admiral," Beasley announced.

The chief answered with a stream of profanity, threatening to throw the two men in the brig if they didn't return to the hospital immediately. Temporarily chastened, Beasley and Andrews withdrew.

"Sam, we'd better get back before we get into serious trouble," Andrews warned.

By now, though, Beasley's blood was up. "No," he replied. "While we were in there I noticed a back entrance. We'll go in that way."

The sailors slipped around the building's corner and into its back door. Finding the admiral's hallway once more, they flapped and flopped hurriedly down it in their overshoes, slippers, and oversized clothes. Upon reaching the admiral's office, they darted in without a second thought. Their sudden appearance surprised a yeoman and a lieutenant, and although the yeoman stood speechless, the lieutenant yelled for the shore patrol. Once again the chief and the patrolman burst onto the scene, but this time a shouting match ensued. So close to their goal, Beasley and Andrews were no longer willing to back down.

The chief grabbed Andrews, the patrolman grabbed Beasley, and both men started dragging the two sailors out of the office. At that moment, the door to the admiral's inner office flew open. Out stepped the admiral.

"What's going on out here?" he demanded.

The chief began to explain, but Beasley quickly interrupted with his version of events. Each man shouted to be heard over the other while the admiral simply stared in amazement.

"You two men come into my office," he finally said to Beasley and Andrews.

"Yes, sir!" they responded triumphantly. They followed the admiral into his office, where he bid them to sit down. For the next few moments, the two sailors related their story and frustration to the admiral. Throughout their tale, he simply sat silent behind his desk.

Once Beasley and Andrews finished speaking, the admiral remained quiet. To Beasley, the silence seemed to stretch into minutes. Finally, the admiral reached across his desk for a pen and paper. With quick, sure strokes, he penned a note, handed it to Beasley, and called for the chief.

"Take these two men to the PX in the jeep," he ordered the chief. "Then you go to the hospital and see to it that each *Liscome Bay* survivor is issued a full complement of clothing, bed gear, toilet articles, and other basic issue equipment."

The admiral turned his attention back to Beasley and Andrews. "As for you two men, take that note to the Storekeeper and I am sure he will issue you a full complement of your needs."

Beasley and Andrews sprang to their feet. "Yes, sir, and thank you, sir!" they said before following the chief—now with a noticeably improved attitude—to his jeep. Within an hour, the two sailors had a new issue of equipment and a seabag to carry it in. Beasley never learned the admiral's name, but fifty years later he still had the seabag.[24]

A few days later, a hospital orderly delivered Beasley money for a train ticket and a brown envelope containing a set of navy orders. According to the orders, Beasley had thirty days of survivor's leave, after which he was to report back to Portland, Oregon, for assignment with an outgoing unit. Wasting no time, he caught an eastbound train cross-country back to Mount Airy, North Carolina. He arrived home on Christmas Eve.

Elsewhere in San Francisco, orders filtered in sending the other survivors off on leave. One set was addressed to Daily's assistant, Sheppard. Sheppard paid a quick visit to Daily before heading out.

"Mr. Daily, wherever you go, send for me," he told Daily.[25] It was the best compliment Daily had received in his navy days, and in a quick breach of naval discipline the officer and enlisted man exchanged a fierce hug. Then Sheppard was homeward bound.

Orders then arrived for Daily's friend Black, sending him on his way home. Now Daily was left alone, but he soon received his leave orders as well. He placed a quick call to his wife, booked a ticket on a United Airlines DC-3 for the twenty-three-hour journey from San Francisco to Newark, and was soon winging his way eastward. Home lay ahead, and *Liscome Bay* was already nothing more than a memory.

A train ride took Daily from Newark to his in-laws' house in Stafford, Pennsylvania. It seemed like another age when he had last seen his wife, and the ensign bounded up the back steps into her parents' kitchen. Gloria met him there, grabbing her husband as soon as he stepped through the back door. The young ensign and his wife clung to one another, motionless and speechless, for nearly twenty minutes.

12
Aftermath

Japan eventually lost six of the nine submarines it sortied against the U.S. forces operating in the Gilberts. Despite *I-175*'s success against *Liscome Bay*, this devastating loss ratio rattled the nerves of the Japanese admirals. They aborted the Imperial Navy's submarine operations in the Gilberts on December 4, and the three surviving subs headed home. In total, the submarine counteroffensive had only been able to claim credit for sending *Liscome Bay* to the bottom. A few months later, when the Americans moved further west and invaded the Marshalls, Japan dispatched to the islands only two submarines—*RO-39* and Tabata's *I-175*. Rather than conduct offensive operations, they were assigned lifeguard duties to rescue downed aviators.

In the end, however, it was *RO-39* and *I-175* that needed rescuing. On February 1, 1944, the destroyer *Walker* (DD-517) sunk *RO-39*. Sixteen days later, sonar operators in the destroyer *Charrette* (DD-581) detected *I-175*. Joined by the destroyer escort *Fair* (DE-35), *Charrette* attacked Tabata's submarine with a new type of weapon—the hedgehog. The hedgehog enabled a destroyer to hurl depth charges over two hundred yards forward of her bow rather than simply projecting depth charges off the side. It proved its effectiveness for the first time against *I-175*, destroying the I-boat and exacting revenge for the sinking of *Liscome Bay* four months earlier.[1]

The U.S. Navy's admirals also learned a lesson in caution from the events in the Gilberts. Acting on the information received as a result of the board convened at Alameda in December 1943, the navy began implementing changes to improve the survivability of *Liscome Bay*'s sister ships. In the meantime, Henry Kaiser's shipyards continued to crank out *Casablanca*-class carriers and delivered to the navy the fifty promised within the span of a year.

Kaiser's baby flattops, and those of the other classes, served in every theater of the war and remained an integral part of American convoys and amphibious assaults. They paid a price for their utility, however. By the end of the war, of the seventy-six escort carriers that had been commissioned, six had been lost to enemy action. In addition to *Liscome Bay*, these included *Block Island* (CVE-21), lost in the Atlantic to a German U-boat on May 29, 1944; *St. Lo* (CVE-63) and *Gambier Bay* (CVE-73), sunk by the Japanese during the brutal Battle of Leyte Gulf on October 25, 1944; *Ommaney Bay* (CVE-79), mortally wounded by kamikazes in Lingayen Gulf on January 2, 1945, and scuttled by U.S. forces two days later; and *Bismarck Sea* (CVE-95), destroyed by a kamikaze while supporting the landing of marines at Iwo Jima on February 21, 1945.

The sinking of *Liscome Bay* remains the most controversial of these losses. The conventional wisdom has become that the green army troops on Makin took far too long to finish off the small group of Japanese on the tiny island. Their tentative attacks were frequently delayed by individual snipers or isolated pockets of defenders. Rather than press home their assaults, they were too often content to wait for poorly coordinated tank, artillery, or air support to dislodge enemy troops. At the time, the tactics seemed guaranteed to minimize American casualties. These tactics may have succeeded onshore; it was a different matter entirely once *I-175* arrived on the scene.

Naval historian Samuel Eliot Morison, comparing the performance of the army's 165th Regimental Combat Team on Makin to that of the marines at Tarawa and elsewhere, lambasted it as a "miserable, dilatory performance, giving the enemy ample time to reorganize and dispute every step."[2] His implicit conclusion was that the army's tardiness in securing Makin kept the vulnerable carriers offshore far too long. William T. Y'Blood, in *The Little Giants: U.S. Escort Carriers against Japan*, drew the same conclusion.[3]

To a large extent, even the U.S. Army's official history of its role in the war agrees with this argument, sympathizing with "Howling Mad"

Smith's characterization of Makin's seizure as "infuriatingly slow": "Considering the size of the atoll, the nature of the enemy's defenses, and the great superiority of force engaged by the attacking troops, [Smith's] criticism seems justified. It is all the more so when to the cost of tardiness is added the loss of a valuable escort aircraft carrier—along with more than half her hands aboard."[4]

There are, of course, two sides to every story. Edwin P. Hoyt, in *How They Won the War in the Pacific: Nimitz and His Admirals*, recognized the army's slow pace in capturing Makin but hesitated to lay all the blame at the army's—or anyone's—doorstep. "Some of the carrier men claimed that the loss of the *Liscome Bay* . . . [was] the direct result of keeping the carriers as 'sitting ducks,'" he wrote. "But that was the job of the escort carriers, as would be shown beyond doubt at Leyte."[5]

To an extent, both sides are right. Had the army secured Makin a day earlier, *Liscome Bay* might have slipped out of the Gilberts before *I-175* arrived on the scene. But Hoyt's words ring with a cold logic—the same logic that enabled President Roosevelt and the navy to conclude that the nation's need for fifty escort carriers in 1943 and 1944 justified sending the thin-skinned ships and their crews so quickly into harm's way. In the end, the army worked on its island-fighting tactics, the navy installed another layer of protection on the vulnerable jeep carriers, and both continued to carry the fight to the Japanese.

In the meantime, the brutal Pacific conflict continued for another twenty-one months. The fight for Makin and the sinking of *Liscome Bay* receded into the American public's memory as other islands—Saipan, the Philippines, Okinawa, and Iwo Jima—took an even higher toll in American lives. With each battle the U.S. military rolled inexorably toward Japan, until, on September 2, 1945, American warships rode majestically at anchor in Tokyo Bay and accepted the Japanese surrender. Three carrier escorts—one American and two British—participated in that historic moment.

Today, no *Casablanca*-class carrier escort survives—not even as a museum or memorial. They have long since been dismantled and sold for scrap. The Chapel of St. Cornelius at the Valley Forge Military Academy in Wayne, Pennsylvania, commemorates *Liscome Bay* with a set of two stained-glass windows and the words of the Navy Hymn. One reads, "In memory and in honor of the gallant men of the *U.S.S. Liscome Bay* CVE 56 and the aircraft squadron VC-39 and especially in honor of the men of the V-4 Division and their loved ones. 'Eternal father, strong to save, hear us when we cry to thee. For those in peril on the sea.' Presented by Lieutenant (jg) Samuel S. Rickley—V-4 Division Officer and his son George Robert Rickley, Class of 1965." The inscription on the other window simply reads, "*U.S.S. Liscome Bay*. November Twenty-Fourth 1943. Gilbert Islands." Below those words, the window depicts a small, sinking carrier and men sitting in a life raft or clinging to wooden flotsam.[6]

Another small memorial exists on the hangar deck of the aircraft carrier *Yorktown*, moored permanently as a floating naval museum and memorial at Patriot's Point, South Carolina, just outside Charleston. Thanks to the work of survivors Machinist's Mate Second Class Albert G. Stoner, Torpedoman's Mate Third Class Donald C. Walz, and Seaman Second Class Leonard J. Bohm, and with the generous financial support of the family of *Liscome Bay*'s executive officer, Commander Finley E. Hall, a set of commemorative plaques was dedicated in a dignified ceremony on board *Yorktown* on October 22, 1990. A memorial service on her flight deck followed three days later, attended by survivors Fireman First Class Phelan E. Allee, Seaman First Class James C. Beasley, Seaman Second Class Leonard Bohm, Seaman Second Class Kenneth J. Harris, Seaman First Class James D. Honold, Radioman's Mate Second Class Tony A. Kehl, Shipfitter Third Class Joseph P. Lennon, Machinist's Mate Second Class Albert Stoner, and Seaman First Class Teofilo T. Trevino.

This book was not, of course, simply the story of the construction, deployment, and destruction of *Liscome Bay*. Nor was it intended to be an analysis of the United States' carrier escort program, or of the capture and cost of Makin. Rather, it was written to tell the story of the men whose paths crossed the decks of *Liscome Bay*. Their stories continued long after Tabata's torpedo ripped her decks asunder. Among those men:

Seaman First Class Richard L. Abbott Jr. Lieutenant Commander Oliver Ames recommended that Abbott receive a letter of commendation for his heroic efforts on board *Liscome Bay* in aiding the ship's wounded. Inexplicably, the recommendation was denied.[7]

Fireman First Class Phelan E. Allee. After convalescing in stateside hospitals from the deep cuts on his left torso and leg, Allee received orders to ship out on one of the navy's attack transports. He saw further action supporting the invasions of Iwo Jima and Okinawa. By November 1945 he had accumulated enough points to be discharged. He made his way back to Texas, where he was discharged on December 1, 1945—nearly three years to the day after he enlisted.

Lieutenant Commander Oliver Ames. Ames ended the war commanding Carrier Aircraft Service Unit 22 at NAS Atlantic City, New Jersey, where he was commended for "able leadership, sound judgment, and outstanding performance of duty."[8] Upon leaving the navy, he returned to Massachusetts.

Seaman First Class James C. Beasley. After taking his survivor's leave in North Carolina, Beasley returned to the West Coast and shipped out on the attack transport *Alpine* (APA-92), commissioned on April 22, 1944. There he joined fellow *Liscome Bay* signalmen Pete Unbehagen and Jerry Goss and Quartermaster's Mate Second Class Dale Wilker, another of his friends from his former carrier. In that ship they saw further action off New Guinea, Guam, the Philippines, and Okinawa. After the war, Beasley completed his college degree and eventually earned a master's degree as well. He eventually retired as a public school system administrator in North Carolina.

Lieutenant Commander Marshall U. Beebe. Beebe lost fourteen of VC-39's twenty-nine pilots in the sinking of *Liscome Bay*. He remained in the Pacific for the subsequent Marshall Islands campaign. Returning stateside, he took command of fighter squadron VF-17, the "Jolly Rogers," flying F6F Hellcats from the carrier *Hornet* (CV-12). His squadron flew strikes against Okinawa, Iwo Jima, and the Japanese home islands, and by the end of the war it had shot down 313 enemy planes, making it the most deadly navy fighter squadron in the Pacific.

Beebe eventually became an ace with ten and one-half kills, and on a single mission over Japan, on March 18, 1945, he shot down five enemy aircraft.

Following World War II, Beebe remained in the navy, eventually commanding Air Group 5 on board the carrier *Essex* (CV-9) during the Korean War. While serving in *Essex* he met author James Michener, who dedicated his book *The Bridges of Toko-Ri* to "Marshall U. Beebe—Jet Pilot." Beebe later served as the technical adviser for (and briefly appeared in) the film of the same name. He concluded his career in 1963, following command of the carrier *Bon Homme Richard* (CVA-31), by commanding the 7th Fleet's Task Group 77.4. Beebe died on March 18, 1991, at the age of seventy-seven.

Seaman Second Class Raymond J. Bergquist. After the sinking of *Liscome Bay*, Bergquist spent a month in the hospital, took thirty days of survivor's leave in Kansas, and then returned to sea with *Salamaua* (CVE-96), one of the last Kaiser-built carrier escorts, as part of her commissioning crew. He spent the rest of the war on her. *Salamaua* suffered a kamikaze strike in Lingayen Gulf on January 13, 1945, but after repairs in San Francisco she returned to the war zone to support the landings on Okinawa. Later she escorted the convoy that landed American occupation troops in Yokohama, Japan, joined the "Magic Carpet" fleet, and made several runs returning American veterans home from the Pacific.

Aviation Machinist's Mate Second Class John T. Beymer. Following a stint at Oak Knoll Naval Hospital, Beymer took his survivor's leave and then reported for further sea duty with Air Group 14 on board the aircraft carrier *Wasp*. Later service included shore duty at Corvallis, Oregon, before he mustered out of the navy in January 1946. Using the GI Bill, he obtained his undergraduate degree in 1949 and began a teaching career. After earning a master's degree in education administration, Beymer spent twenty-eight years as an elementary school principal. He retired in 1985, a proud husband, father, and grandfather. Looking back on *Liscome Bay*, he wrote decades later, "It is my fervent hope that my children [and] grandchildren never have to go through seeing your only home sink beneath the waves and so many of your shipmates' lives destroyed."[9]

Lieutenant Foster "Crud" Blair. Blair, the leader of the patrol that escaped the torpedoing of *Liscome Bay*, remained in the navy until he retired in 1966. He died three years later.

Seaman Second Class Leonard J. Bohm. Bohm had seen enough of sea duty, and upon returning to the West Coast he took up residence in a shore billet at Santa Rosa NAS. Today he is the president of *Liscome Bay*'s survivors' association.

Lieutenant Robert H. Carley. Chaplain Carley spent the months following the sinking of *Liscome Bay* sending out personal letters to each of the next of kin of the 644 men who had gone down with the ship. Some families he visited personally. Over four hundred replies came back to Carley. Overwhelmingly, he noted, the respondents were "comforted by faith in God, by the knowledge of the fact that their loved ones had been doing what he thought to be right in his own heart, or by belief in the cause for which we were fighting."[10]

Lieutenant Commander Wells W. "Buzz" Carroll. Carroll was awarded the Navy Cross for his actions on board *Liscome Bay*. "Lt. Comdr. Carroll was loved by the officers and men of the Liscome Bay. His enthusiasm, energy, and courage offered an example of the highest traditions," Oliver Ames later wrote.[11]

Yeoman First Class Robert J. Charters. Charters returned to the States and, on Christmas Eve of 1943, married the girl he had left behind in San Diego. Afterward, he managed to find a comfortable shore billet at the San Diego NAS.

Captain John G. Crommelin. Crommelin spent several months recuperating from his burns and wounds before returning to duty on the staff of Carrier Division 12, serving in one of *Liscome Bay*'s sister ships, *Gambier Bay* (CVE-73). In August 1944 he returned to the

West Coast to serve as director of training for Fleet Air, West Coast, where he remained for the duration of the war. His departure meant that he was not on board *Gambier Bay* two months later when she was sunk by Japanese shellfire in a desperate battle off Samar.

Although newspapers delighted in describing John and his brothers as "the Indestructible Crommelins," fate proved the moniker wrong. Middle brother Charles, who had fought and connived his way back from the career-threatening injuries he suffered in his attack on Mille Atoll during the invasion of the Gilberts, died in a midair collision during the invasion of Okinawa. Three months later, Richard, the fourth brother and a survivor of the Battles of Coral Sea and Midway, met a similar fate during an air raid on the Japanese mainland.

After the war, John became embroiled in the bitter bureaucratic infighting that plagued the postwar unification of the armed services into the modern Department of Defense. He took a lead role in the ultimately successful battle to preserve naval aviation and its aircraft carriers, but his belligerent advocacy eventually became too much for even the navy, which furloughed Crommelin, sending him home to Alabama for retirement in 1950. Thanks to his war record, he was promoted to rear admiral upon his retirement. Back home, he ran, unsuccessfully, as an independent candidate for Congress. As the years progressed, Crommelin became a perennial political candidate, even considering a run for president at one point, but his increasingly extremist campaign rhetoric marred the proud memory of his long naval career. He died in 1996.

Ensign Francis X. Daily. Promoted to lieutenant (jg), Daily was assigned to the Field Branch of the Bureau of Supplies and Accounts in Cleveland, Ohio, following his thirty-days survivor's leave. In the weeks and months that followed, Daily maintained a steady stream of correspondence with the families of the men listed as missing in action from *Liscome Bay.*

Daily knew that his best friend, Lieutenant (jg) Thomas W. Roche of the ship's engineering department, had been from Cleveland. Roche had been stationed in the engine room in the after section of the ship and had no doubt died instantaneously in the first explosion. One day, Daily picked up a phone book and called the only Roche in the book. A man answered.

"Is this the home of Lieutenant Tom Roche of the *U.S.S. Liscome Bay*?" asked Daily.

The man on the other end hesitated, then, gruffly, answered, "Who wants to know?"

Daily identified himself, explaining that he had been a close friend of Roche's and was checking to see if there was anything he could do for his parents.

"How am I supposed to know you're telling the truth?" the man demanded.

"Probably by meeting with me and letting me talk to you about Tom."

Daily didn't have a chance to say any more. The man on the other end dissolved into sobs. "I'm sorry, son; I believe you, but if you only knew what we've been through since this happened. Crank calls laughing at us, people saying they knew where Tom was, requests for money for memorials. Of course we want to see you."[12]

For the rest of Daily's time in Cleveland, the Roches were like a second set of parents to Daily and his wife, Gloria. Years later, after Daily had left the navy, Mrs. Roche called Daily to tell him that her husband had died. The official cause was heart failure. "But, Frank, you and I know what he really died of," she added. Daily knew—the lingering effects of a father's broken heart.

Looking back on the dramatic events surrounding the sinking of *Liscome Bay*, Daily wrote simply, "There wasn't a man who made it off that ship who wasn't a hero."[13]

Seaman First Class William L. Fisher. Fisher, like Beasley and several other *Liscome Bay* crewmen, served aboard the attack transport *Alpine* for the duration of the war. After the war he returned to his job with the Western Pacific Railroad, where he worked for the next forty-one years.

Rear Admiral Robert M. Griffin. In the months that followed the loss of *Liscome Bay*, Griffin's Battleship Division 3 supported amphibious operations in the Marshalls and on New Ireland. Returning to the States in 1944, Griffin took command of the Puget Sound Navy Yard. Following Japan's surrender, he became Commander, Naval Forces Far East.

Commander Finley E. Hall. The navy awarded Hall the Silver Star for his valor on board *Liscome Bay*. The citation read: "Although able to leave the ship, he chose to make a more thorough inspection for wounded and trapped personnel at the cost of his own life. His actions were in keeping with the highest traditions of the naval service and proved a great inspiration to those who saw him."[14]

Fireman Third Class Robert E. Haynes. After recuperating in naval hospitals, Haynes returned to sea on board the amphibious attack transport *Bottineau* (APA-235) in 1944. She supported the invasions of Saipan and the Philippines and landed occupation troops on Japan. After a short postwar stint as a civilian, Haynes enlisted in the marines. Upon retiring from the corps as a gunnery sergeant, Haynes took a more sedate job with the U.S. Post Office. Today, retired, he lives in Colorado.

Seaman Second Class Maxsy T. Homec. Homec returned to Hudson, Wyoming, on his survivor's leave to find it a ghost town. Practically all the young men were away at war. Offered a chance to be discharged, Homec declined and shipped out once again, this time on board the hospital ship *Bountiful* (AH-9). *Bountiful* supported landings on Saipan, Peleliu, Iwo Jima, and Okinawa in waters where even a hospital ship was at risk of Japanese air attack. The navy honorably discharged Homec following Japan's surrender. He returned to Hudson, where he eventually took a job as the elementary school's custodian and coached the boys' basketball team to many years of success. Today, retired, he lives in Lander, Wyoming.

Seaman First Class James D. Honold. Honold, the Arkansas teenager who had been so young when he tried to enlist that his parents had to sign his enlistment papers for him, spent nineteen months in hospitals recovering from his wounds. Even light duty proved too much for his badly injured left leg, and the navy discharged him on May 29, 1945.

Seaman First Class Edward Jonas. The ship's tailor, temporarily blinded by the explosions that wracked *Liscome Bay* and then saved in the water by an unknown pilot from VC-39, reflected on his experience nearly fifty-one years later. "If the pilot who let me hold on to him reads this and remembers it," Jonas wrote, "I say thank you in capital letters: THANK YOU."[15] Jonas later served in the destroyer *Mansfield* (DD-728) and barely weathered Typhoon Cobra in December 1944. Injured in that storm, he spent the remainder of the war stateside.

Fireman Third Class James L. King. The Birmingham, Alabama, fireman eventually received his electrician's rating and served in the attack transport *Alpine* for amphibious actions off New Guinea and the invasions of Guam, the Philippines, and Okinawa. King survived a kamikaze attack on *Alpine*, left the navy in 1945, and returned to Birmingham, where he worked in the steel industry.

Cook Third Class Doris Miller. Miller's body, like those of the other 644 casualties from *Liscome Bay*, was never recovered. In honor of his memory, the navy named the *Knox*-class destroyer escort *Miller* (DE-1091) after him in 1973. Later reclassified as a frigate, *Miller* served the navy for nearly two decades before being decommissioned in 1991.

Rear Admiral Henry M. Mullinnix. The loss of Mullinnix left a tragic gap in the ranks of the navy's World War II "air admirals." In honor of his service, the navy christened the destroyer DD-944 *Mullinnix* in 1958. Mullinnix's widow, Kathryn, served as the ship's sponsor. *Mullinnix* served the navy until decommissioning in 1983, seeing duty in the Cuban missile crisis and providing naval gunfire support during the Vietnam War. Her final mission came as a target ship. In 1993 a torpedo sent Mullinnix's namesake to a watery grave during a live-fire training exercise.

Lieutenant Commander John B. Rowe. Rowe received the Navy Cross for his courageous actions on board *Liscome Bay*. "The conduct of Lieutenant Commander Rowe was an inspiration to all," his citation read.[16]

Ensign Frank Sistrunk. Upon recovering from his wounds, Sistrunk rejoined Beebe when Beebe took command of fighter squadron VF-17, the "Jolly Rogers." In February 1945, during the massive carrier raids on Tokyo, he was shot down by Japanese antiaircraft fire near Hammamatsu. Forced to ditch at sea, Sistrunk suffered another impromptu swimming lesson before being rescued by an American submarine.

The submarine returned Sistrunk to Pearl Harbor, where he begged to be allowed to rejoin Beebe and VF-17. When the navy refused, Sistrunk—without orders, money, or even a duffel bag—hopped an ammunition ship bound for the carrier *Hornet*, on which VF-17 was based. He finished the war still flying with the Jolly Rogers, having shot down five enemy aircraft and achieving ace status.

Following the surrender of Japan, Sistrunk left the service, earned his college degree, married, and fathered two children. When war broke out in North Korea, he again volunteered for active duty. Coincidence brought him back together with Beebe aboard the carrier *Essex*, flying with Air Group 5. In Korea, however, Sistrunk's luck finally ran out. During a bombing raid on the North Korean bridges at Toko-Ri, his Skyraider suffered extensive damage. Wounded himself, Sistrunk was unable to nurse his aircraft back to *Essex*, and he crashed outside Wonsan. His decorations included the Distinguished Flying Cross with three Gold Stars, the Air Medal with seven Gold Stars, and the Purple Heart.

Lieutenant Gardner Smith. Liscome Bay's communications officer earned the Navy and Marine Corps Medal for towing a wounded shipmate to safety from the sinking carrier. He later served as the communications officer on the staff of Commander, Service Squadron, South Pacific Force and then as the communications officer for Commander, South Pacific Area and Force.

Major General Ralph C. Smith. During the bitter fighting on Saipan in June 1944, Smith and his division found themselves under the command of the marines' "Howling Mad" Smith. Infuriated with the slow pace of the army division's advance, Howling Mad relieved Smith. The marine general's abrupt treatment of Smith forever tainted his relations with his army counterparts, and in the end their confrontation on Saipan damaged the professional reputations of both men.

Rear Admiral Richmond K. Turner. Turner later commanded the navy's amphibious assaults on Kwajalein, Saipan, Tinian, Guam, Iwo Jima, and Okinawa. By the end of the war, the hard-drinking, abrasive "Terrible Turner" was nevertheless regarded as the navy's foremost expert on amphibious operations. Retired from the navy in 1947, the man *Time* called "one mean son of a bitch" spent his last four years tending to his invalid wife—his former high school sweetheart. He died six weeks after her in 1961.

Seaman Second Class Lloyd D. Whalen. After his thirty days of survivor's leave, Whalen happily found a billet on board the hospital ship *Hope* (AH-7), on which he spent the rest of the war before returning to Texas.

Captain Irving D. Wiltsie. Wiltsie received the Navy Cross for his heroism on board *Liscome Bay*. The navy also honored him by naming the destroyer DD-716 *Wiltsie* on August 31, 1945. His widow, Helene—the same woman Ensign Daily had witnessed waving goodbye to her husband on the dark San Diego dock—christened the vessel. Following distinguished service in the Korean War and Vietnam, *Wiltsie* was decommissioned in 1976 and subsequently transferred to the Pakistani Navy. Pakistan renamed her *Tariq*, after a legendary Arab warrior.

Aviation Machinist's Mate Third Class Tim Woodham Jr. Following his survivor's leave, the navy assigned Woodham to NAS Santa Rosa, where he served with Carrier Aircraft Service Unit 36. There he worked with an F6F Hellcat training unit and met the woman who would become his wife of fifty-five years. Later, Woodham went back to sea attached to Air Group 6 in the carrier *Hancock* (CV-19), barely survived a kamikaze strike on her off of Okinawa, and ended the war with the carrier in Tokyo Bay.

Ensign William J. Woodward Jr. After the war, Bill Woodward, Daily's fellow "bull" ensign from the ship and the officer of the deck when the torpedo first hit, returned to the high-society life of Long Island to succeed his father as the owner of Maryland's Belair Stables—an operation that produced Triple Crown winners Gallant Fox and Omaha. In 1955, Woodward's wife, Ann, mistaking him for an intruder, shot him dead in their Oyster Bay, Long Island, home. Two novels, including Truman Capote's *Unanswered Prayers*, were reportedly based on the tragedy. Although Ann was acquitted of the homicide charges following a much-publicized trial, the rumor and innuendo weighed on her, and eventually she took her own life.

The Aerology Gang. Lyle Blakley retired as a chief warrant officer following a full naval career and died in Tacoma, Washington, in 1981. Perry L. Bruce Jr. retired as a chief aerographer's mate after twenty years and went to work for the National Security Agency. Williard L. Pinder also spent a career in the navy, retiring from the Naval Reserve as a master chief aerographer's mate. After the war, Russell J. Mahood became a journalist with the *Chicago Tribune*. Donald A. Cruse completed thirty years of naval service in 1968, attained the rank of commander, retired, went to work briefly for Pan American Airways as a meteorologist, and then reenlisted once again in the navy. Today he resides in Arlington, Virginia.

One might be tempted to end the story of *Liscome Bay* with some piece of florid prose about the heroism and sacrifice of her crew. I think it is better to allow a fellow sailor to offer his simple commentary.

One day after the loss of *Liscome Bay*, the skipper of the destroyer *Morris*, Commander F. T. Williamson, prepared his ship's after-action report. As he sat in his cramped cabin, the images of the rescue operation in the foul, oily waters off Makin were still fresh in his mind as he wrote the following conclusion to his statement: "Inspiring is no word for the courage displayed by the men picked up in the water around the *Liscome Bay*. . . . [T]he absolute courage of these men was electrifying. . . . The glowing performance of all hands concerned displays clearly the spirit of America in this war—the indomitable spirit of righteousness it takes to win a war."[17]

Six decades later, the words of *Morris*'s skipper still ring true.

Notes

PROLOGUE

1. James C. Beasley, "The *U.S.S. Liscome Bay*—(CVE 56)" (unpublished memoirs, November 1994), 6 (hereafter cited as Beasley memoirs), copy in author's possession.

CHAPTER 1

1. Scot MacDonald, *Evolution of Aircraft Carriers* (Washington, D.C.: Office of the Chief of Naval Operations, 1964), 49.
2. Ibid., 49–50.
3. Ibid., 50.
4. Ibid., 52.
5. Doris Kearns Goodwin, *No Ordinary Time* (New York: Simon and Schuster, 1995), 318.
6. Norman Friedman, *U.S. Aircraft Carriers: An Illustrated Design History* (Annapolis: Naval Institute Press, 1983), 176.
7. William T. Y'Blood, *The Little Giants: U.S. Escort Carriers against Japan* (Annapolis: Naval Institute Press, 1987), 42.
8. Ibid.
9. Ibid., 35.
10. Ibid.
11. Goodwin, *No Ordinary Time,* 319.
12. MacDonald, *Evolution of Aircraft Carriers,* 53.
13. Clark G. Reynolds, *The Carrier War* (Alexandria, Va.: Time-Life Books, 1982), 132.
14. Donald A. Cruse, "Back to Sea in *U.S.S. Liscome Bay*" (unpublished memoir, January 1987), 2 (hereafter cited as Cruse memoirs), copy in author's possession.

This misspelling haunts *Liscome Bay* to this day; many histories of World War II use the incorrect spelling "Liscombe" or "Liscomb."

CHAPTER 2

1. Francis X. Daily, "The Forgotten Flattop: *U.S.S. Liscome Bay*—CVE 56" (unpublished memoirs, 1998), 1 (hereafter cited as Daily memoirs), copy in author's possession.

2. Beasley memoirs, 2.

3. Letter of commendation citation for Commander Irving D. Wiltsie. Award citations are from the files of Robert Cressman, Ships' History Branch, Naval Historical Center, Washington, D.C. (hereafter abbreviated NHC).

4. U.S. Navy biography sheet for Captain Irving Wiltsie (December 12, 1943), NHC.

5. Ibid.

6. Ibid.

7. Ibid.

8. Daily memoirs, 1.

9. "Finley E. Hall," *The Lucky Bag* (Annapolis: U.S. Naval Academy, 1929), 268.

10. Daily memoirs, 1.

11. Ibid., 2.

12. Robert Schwartz, "The Sinking of the *U.S.S. Liscome Bay*." Originally published in *Yank*, June 11, 1944; reprinted in *Yank: World War II from the Guys Who Brought You Victory*, ed. Steve Kugler (New York: St. Martin's Press, 1990), 127–29.

13. Figures for the number of the *Liscome Bay*'s total crew, including the staff of Carrier Division 24 and the men of VC-39, range from 911, according to the ship's official navy history (Ships' Histories Section, "History of the *U.S.S. Liscome Bay* [CVE 56]" [November 1950], NHC), to 948, as reported by Lieutenant Commander Oliver Ames ("Action Report of the *U.S.S. Liscome Bay* [CVE-56]," December 16, 1943, Modern Military Records Branch, National Archives, College Park, Maryland [hereafter abbreviated NA]). Because it is clear that Ames's report includes the Carrier Division 24 staff and the men of VC-39, I use the larger figure.

14. Clifford M. Drury, *The History of the Chaplain Corps, United States Navy*, vol. 2, *1939–1949* (Washington, D.C.: Government Printing Office, n.d.), 185.

15. James Michener, *Tales of the South Pacific* (New York: Macmillan, 1947), 79.

16. "Navy Officer Gives Life Aiding Other Wounded," *New York World Telegram*, December 14, 1943.

17. Letter of commendation citation for Lieutenant John B. Rowe.

18. William Fisher, *U.S.S. Liscome Bay* Association survivor's statement, 1.

19. Raymond J. Bergquist, *U.S.S. Liscome Bay* Association survivor's statement, 1.

20. Maxsy Homec, telephone interview by author, January 10, 2003.

21. Ibid.

22. "Ship's Cook Third Class Doris Miller, USN," www.history.navy.mil/faqs/faq57-4.htm (visited April 3, 2001).

23. Gail Buckley, *American Patriots: The Story of Blacks in the Military from the Revolution to Desert Storm* (New York: Random House, 2001), 275.

24. *Pittsburgh Courier,* mail-in coupon available on website, www.nara.gov/exhall/people/11e.jpg (visited April 3, 2001).

25. Navy Cross citation for Mess Attendant Second Class Doris Miller, www.history.navy.mil/faqs/faq57-4a.htm (visited April 3, 2001).

26. "Ship's Cook Third Class Doris Miller, USN."

27. Francis Daily, telephone interview by author, July 17, 2001.

28. Beasley memoirs, 2.

29. Daily memoirs, 3.

30. David Nichols, *Ernie's War: The Best of Ernie Pyle's World War II Dispatches* (New York: Random House, 1986), 386.

31. Bureau of Ships, "Loss of *Liscome Bay,*" war damage report no. 45 (March 10, 1944) (hereafter cited as *Liscome Bay* war damage report), 11.

32. Beasley memoirs, 2.

33. Daily memoirs, 4.

34. Y'Blood, *Little Giants,* 35.

CHAPTER 3

1. Daily memoirs, 4.

2. Beasley memoirs, 5.

3. Daily memoirs, 5.

4. William B. Allmon, "Enemy's Perfect Hit," *World War II,* July 1992, 32.

5. Beasley memoirs, 4.

6. Richard Thruelsen, *The Grumman Story* (New York: Praeger, 1976), 103.

7. Reynolds, *The Carrier War,* 67.

8. Eric Bergerud, *Fire in the Sky* (Boulder, Colo.: Westview Press), 252.

9. John B. Lundstrom, *The First Team: Pacific Naval Air Combat from Pearl Harbor to Midway* (Annapolis: Naval Institute Press, 1984), 445.

10. James F. Dunnigan and Albert A. Nofi, *Victory at Sea: World War II in the Pacific* (New York: William Morrow, 1995).

11. Lundstrom, *The First Team,* 454.

12. Marshall U. Beebe, "Sis—Liscome Bay and Toko-Ri." *Naval Aviation Museum Foundation,* Spring 1984, 4.

13. "*Liscome Bay* Survivor Home for Christmas," *Des Moines Register,* December 17, 1943.

14. Ray Parr, "City Airman Survives Two Lost Carriers," *Daily Oklahoman,* December 21, 1943.

15. Daily memoirs, 5.

16. Reynolds, *The Carrier War,* 100.

17. James King, telephone interview by author, July 30, 2001.

18. Naval Aviation Accident Report 44-9123. Beasley seemingly recalls this accident as well in his memoirs (4), although he places it later in *Liscome Bay*'s voyages. Interestingly, VC-39's muster rolls do not show Castello as a member of the squadron. He may have been based on another carrier, or perhaps his absence reflects an error in the records.

19. Tim Woodham to author, e-mail correspondence, July 25, 2001.

20. Ibid.

CHAPTER 4

1. Daily memoirs, 6.
2. Ibid.
3. Beasley memoirs, 3.
4. Daily memoirs, 5; Cruse memoirs, 2.
5. Ibid.
6. Allmon, "Enemy's Perfect Hit," 32.
7. Paolo E. Coletta, "Richmond K. Turner," in *Men of War: Great Navy Captains of World War II*, ed. Stephen Howarth (New York: St. Martin's Press, 1993), 373.
8. Y'Blood, *Little Giants*, 42.
9. William B. Allmon, "Gilbert Islands Campaign: Takin' Makin," *World War II*, November 1999, 30–36.
10. Daily memoirs, 7.
11. Ames, "Action Report of the *U.S.S. Liscome Bay.*"
12. Ibid.
13. *Cincinnati Star*, December 11, 1943.
14. Ames, "Action Report of the *U.S.S. Liscome Bay.*"
15. Beebe, "Sis—*Liscome Bay* and Toko-Ri," 3.
16. Oliver Ames, "Report of War Operations—*U.S.S. Liscome Bay*" (December 8, 1943), NA.
17. James Horan, "Witness Tells Gallant End of Flat-Top," *New York Journal-American*, December 20, 1943.

CHAPTER 5

1. Joseph Alexander, "The Turning Points of Tarawa," in *No End Save Victory: Perspectives on World War II*, ed. Robert Cowley (New York: Putnam, 2001), 293.
2. Jon Guttman, "More on Lieutenant Blair," *Aviation History*, May 2001.
3. Philip A. Crowl and Edmund G. Love, *The U.S. Army in World War II: The War in the Pacific—Seizure of the Gilberts and Marshalls* (Washington, D.C.: Office of the Chief of Military History, 1955).

4. James Horan, "Witness Tells Gallant End of Flat-Top," *New York Journal-American*, December 20, 1943.

5. Ibid.

6. Merle Miller, "Makin Taken." Originally published in *Yank*, December 12, 1944; reprinted in *Yank: World War II from the Guys Who Brought You Victory*, ed. Steve Kugler (New York: St. Martin's Press, 1990), 143.

7. Crowl and Love, *U.S. Army in World War II*, 77.

8. George C. Dyer, *The Amphibians Came to Conquer: The Story of Admiral Richmond Kelly Turner*, vol. 2 (Washington, D.C.: Department of the Navy, 1972), 681.

9. Homec, interview.

10. Tim Woodham to author, e-mail correspondence, May 14, 2002.

11. Horan, "Witness Tells Gallant End of Flat-Top."

12. Y'Blood, *Little Giants*, 41.

13. Daily memoirs, 9.

14. Beasley memoirs, 6.

15. Ibid., 7.

16. Ames, "Report of War Operations—*U.S.S. Liscome Bay*."

17. James Michener, *The Bridges at Toko-Ri* (New York: Random House, 1953), 146.

18. Daily memoirs, 9.

19. Beebe, "Sis—*Liscome Bay* and Toko-Ri," 4.

20. Guttman, "More on Lieutenant Blair," 75.

21. Y'Blood, *Little Giants*, 42.

CHAPTER 6

1. Malcolm W. Cagle, "The Crommelin Brothers Five," *Naval Aviation Museum Foundation* 2 (Fall 1988): 13.

2. "John G. Crommelin," *The Lucky Bag* (Annapolis: U.S. Naval Academy, 1923), 145.

3. Cagle, "Crommelin Brothers Five," 14. The Vindicator vibrated so violently in flight that pilots nicknamed it the "Vibrator."

4. "Richard Crommelin," *The Lucky Bag* (Annapolis: U.S. Naval Academy, 1938), 293.

5. "Five Members of Crommelin Family Are Officers in Navy," *Montgomery (Ala.) Advertiser*, January 23, 1941.

6. John B. Scott Jr., "The Crommelin Brothers," *Alabama Heritage*, Fall 1997, 6.

7. Eric Hammel and John E. Lane, *Seventy-Six Hours: The Invasion of Tarawa* (Pacifica, Calif.: Pacifica Press, 1985), 44.

8. Ibid.

9. Alexander, "Turning Points of Tarawa," 302.

10. Silver Star citation for Commander Henry Crommelin.

11. Oliver Jensen, "Carrier War," *Life*, March 26, 1945, 88.

12. Scott, "The Crommelin Brothers," 6.

13. Gold Star citation for Commander Charles Crommelin.

14. Cagle, "Crommelin Brothers Five," 13.

CHAPTER 7

1. Samuel Eliot Morison, *History of United States Naval Operations in World War II*, vol. 3, *The Rising Sun in the Pacific* (Boston: Little, Brown, 1948), 23.

2. Ibid.

3. Carl Boyd and Akihiko Yoshida, *The Japanese Submarine Force and World War II* (Annapolis: Naval Institute Press, 1995), 57.

4. Talk between Ships log of USS *Idaho*, included as an enclosure to Robert M. Griffin, "Report of Loss of *U.S.S. Liscome Bay*," submitted by Commander Task Group 52.13, December 11, 1943 (hereafter cited as "TBS log"), NA.

5. Ibid.

6. Ibid.

7. Beasley memoirs, 8.

8. Schwartz, "Sinking of *Liscome Bay*," 126.

9. Ibid.

10. Harold Smith, "Admiral's Aide Tells How Baby Flat Top Sank," *Chicago Tribune*, December 11, 1943.

11. Schwartz, "Sinking of *Liscome Bay*," 126.

12. TBS log.

13. Samuel Eliot Morison, *History of United States Naval Operations in World War II*, vol. 7, *Aleutians, Gilberts, and Marshalls, June 1942–April 1944* (Boston: Little, Brown, 1948), 139.

14. TBS log.

15. Daily memoirs, 9; Ships' Histories Section, "History of the *U.S.S. Liscome Bay* (CVE 56)," 2.

16. E. M. Zacharias, "*U.S.S. Liscome Bay* (CVE 56), Sinking of," after-action report, November 30, 1943, NA.

17. J. L. Hunter, "The Sinking of the *U.S.S. Liscome Bay*," after-action report, December 5, 1943, NA.

18. Beasley memoirs, 8.

19. TBS log.

20. "Mishap Saves Baltimorean from Sinking," *Baltimore Sun*, December 14, 1943.

21. "Baby Carrier Sinking Told," *Los Angeles Times*, December 20, 1943.

22. Zacharias, "*U.S.S. Liscome Bay* (CVE 56), Sinking of."

CHAPTER 8

1. Schwartz, "Sinking of *Liscome Bay*," 125.

2. Ibid., 127.

3. Richard Weicker, "*Liscome Bay* Sinking 'Living Hell,'" *Decatur Herald and Review*, January 1, 1944.

4. Ibid.

5. Glenna Elledge, "Bruce Returns with Compelling Stories to Civitan Clergy Appreciation Dinner," *Smyth County (Va.) News and Messenger*, February 28, 1998.

6. *Liscome Bay* war damage report, 5.

7. Robert E. Haynes, *U.S.S. Liscome Bay* Association survivor's statement, 1.

8. Ships' Histories Section, "History of the *USS Liscome Bay*," 4–5.

9. *Liscome Bay* war damage report, 6.

10. Drury, *History of the Chaplain Corps*, 184.

11. Schwartz, "Sinking of *Liscome Bay*," 126.

12. James D. Horan, "Witness Tells Gallant End of Flat-Top," *New York Journal-American*, December 20, 1943.

13. Daily memoirs, 10.

CHAPTER 9

1. Drury, *History of the Chaplain Corps*, 185.

2. Ships' Histories Section, "History of the *USS Liscome Bay* (CVE 56)," 2.

3. William J. Woodward Jr., *U.S.S. Liscome Bay* Association survivor's statement, 1.

4. John Jenkins, *U.S.S. Liscome Bay* Association survivor's statement, 1.

5. Tim E. Woodham, *U.S.S. Liscome Bay* Association survivor's statement, 2.

6. Lloyd Whalen, telephone interview by author, 11 April 2002.

7. Beasley memoirs, 9.

8. Ibid.

9. James D. Horan, "Witness Tells Gallant End of Flat-Top," *New York Journal-American*, December 20, 1943.

10. Beasley memoirs, 9.

11. Ibid.

12. Ibid., 10; author's review of ship's survivor lists, NA.

13. Beasley memoirs, 9.

14. "Montgomery Naval Captain Tells Story of *Liscome Bay*," *Montgomery (Ala.) Advertiser*, December 13, 1943.

15. Beebe, "Sis—*Liscome Bay* and Toko-Ri," 62.

16. Woodward, survivor's statement, 1.

17. Homec, interview; "Survivor of *Liscome Bay* Gives Account of Sinking," *Riverton (Wyo.) Review*, January 6, 1944.

18. Richard Weicker, "*Liscome Bay* Sinking 'Living Hell,'" *Decatur Herald and Review*, January 1, 1944.

19. King, interview.

20. Beebe, "Sis—*Liscome Bay* and Toko-Ri," 64.

21. Schwartz, "Sinking of *Liscome Bay*," 125.

22. "Admiral's Yen for Coffee Saved Sailor's Life," *Seattle Times*, December 24, 1943; "Crew Member Relates Death of *Liscome Bay* from Torpedo Blasts," *Portland Oregonian*, January 7, 1944.

23. "Admiral's Yen for Coffee Saved Sailor's Life."

24. Ibid.

25. Beebe, "Sis—*Liscome Bay* and Toko-Ri," 63.

26. Ibid.

27. Leonard Bohm, telephone interview by author, July 9, 2001.

28. "*Liscome Bay* Survivor Home for Christmas," *Des Moines Register*, 17 December 1943.

29. Schwartz, "Sinking of *Liscome Bay*," 126.

30. "Admiral's Yen for Coffee Saved Sailor's Life."

31. Daily memoirs, 11.

32. Bergquist, survivor's statement, 2.

CHAPTER 10

1. Schwartz, "Sinking of *Liscome Bay*," 126.

2. Beasley memoirs, 10.

3. Ibid.

4. Ibid.

5. Ibid., 11.

6. John T. Beymer, *U.S.S. Liscome Bay* Association survivor's statement, 2.

7. Ray Parr, "City Airman Survives Two Lost Carriers," *Daily Oklahoman*, December 21, 1943.

8. Richard Weicker, "*Liscome Bay* Sinking 'Living Hell,'" *Decatur Herald and Review*, January 1, 1944.

9. Gerald Astor, *The Greatest War: Americans in Combat, 1941–1945* (Novato, Calif.: Presidio Press, 1999), 411.

10. Drury, *History of the Chaplain Corps*, 184.

11. Beasley memoirs, 11.

12. "Admiral's Yen for Coffee Saved Sailor's Life," *Seattle Times*, December 24, 1943.

13. Daily memoirs, 12.

14. Ibid., 13.

15. Ibid.

16. Ibid.

17. Ibid., 14.

18. Ibid.

19. Ibid.

20. James D. Horan, "Witness Tells Gallant End of Flat-Top," *New York Journal-American*, December 20, 1943.

21. Beasley memoirs, 12.

22. Weicker, "*Liscome Bay* Sinking 'Living Hell.'"

23. "Pound of Butter Provides Ointment to Save Officer's Life in South Pacific," *Atlanta Constitution*, December 24, 1943.

24. Beebe, "Sis—*Liscome Bay* and Toko-Ri," 64.

25. Ibid.

26. E. B. Rittenhouse, "Operations Incident to Sinking of *U.S.S. Liscome Bay*—Report of," after-action report, November 26, 1943, NA.

27. TBS log.

28. Ibid.

29. Ibid.

30. F. T. Williamson, "*U.S.S. Liscome Bay*—sinking of," after-action report, November 25, 1943, NA.

31. Ibid.

32. TBS log.

33. Ibid.

34. Ibid.

35. Ibid.

36. Daily memoirs, 15.

37. Whalen, interview.

38. Beasley memoirs, 12.

39. TBS log.

40. Ibid.

41. Schwartz, "Sinking of *Liscome Bay*," 128.

CHAPTER 11

1. Daily, interview.

2. Tim Woodham, telephone interview by author, July 9, 2001.

3. Jenkins, survivor's statement, 2.

4. Y'Blood, *Little Giants*, 42.

5. *Morris*'s after-action report (Williamson, "*U.S.S. Liscome Bay*—sinking of") identifies the buried yeoman as H. E. Coulson. This was likely Harold E. Carlson, as identified on *Liscome Bay*'s muster roll.

6. Drury, *History of the Chaplain Corps*, 185.

7. Woodham, interview.
8. James D. Honold, *U.S.S. Liscome Bay* Association survivor's statement, 2.
9. Beasley memoirs, 13.
10. Daily memoirs, 17.
11. Ibid., 23.
12. Ibid., 18.
13. Ships' Histories Section, "History of the *USS Liscome Bay* (CVE 56)," 5.
14. Daily memoirs, 19.
15. Beasley memoirs, 14.
16. Honold, survivor's statement, n.d.
17. Daily memoirs, 19.
18. C. M. Bolster et al., "*U.S.S.* Liscome Bay (CVE 56)—Loss of. Report of Investigation Board," December 22, 1943, NA.
19. Ibid.
20. *Liscome Bay* war damage report, 2.
21. Cruse memoirs, 2.
22. Beasley memoirs, 15.
23. Ibid.
24. Ibid., 16.
25. Daily memoirs, 20.

CHAPTER 12

1. Boyd and Yoshida, *Japanese Submarine Force*, 126. Boyd and Yoshida's account is based on Japanese war records and is thus due great credence. It also comports with Robert J. Cressman's *The Official Chronology of the United States Navy in World War II* (Annapolis: Naval Institute Press, 2000). Nevertheless, other World War II historical literature reveals some uncertainty regarding the identity of *I-175*'s killer. The entries for *Charrette* and *Fair* in the *Dictionary of American Naval Fighting Ships*, for example, report that the two ships destroyed not *I-175* but *I-21*. Boyd and Yoshida claim, however, that *I-21* was reported missing in the Gilberts in November 1943. Wilfred J. Holmes, in *Undersea Victory: The Influence of Submarine Operations on the War in the Pacific* (Garden City, N.Y.: Doubleday, 1966), credits *I-175*'s sinking to *Charrette* and *Fair* in February 1944 in the Marshalls. One competing claim is found in Walter J. Boyne's *Clash of Titans: World War Two at Sea* (New York: Simon and Schuster, 1995), which claims that McCoy *Reynolds* sank *I-175* in February 1944. This claim is doubtful; according to the *Dictionary of American Naval Fighting Ships*, *McCoy Reynolds* had not yet been commissioned at that time and was still on America's East Coast. Samuel Eliot Morison, in volume 7 of *History of United States Naval Operations in World War II*, simply reports that *I-175* was lost in the Marshalls in February 1944. Another view of *I-175*'s demise comes from correspondence between Albert Stoner, one of *Liscome Bay*'s survivors, and the

Suikokai Foundation of the Japan's Imperial Navy Association. According to a letter sent by Yorimasa Inoue, chief clerk of the foundation, dated May 15, 1990, *I-175* was sunk by the U.S. destroyer *Nicholas* on February 17, 1944, east of the Marshall Islands. This date comports with those provided in the foregoing texts, but the *Dictionary of American Naval Fighting Ships* does not list an attack on a submarine by *Nicholas* that corresponds with that time frame. In fact, Cressman reports that *Nicholas* sank *I-11* on that date. Regardless of such discrepancies, all seem to agree on one fact—*I-175* did not survive the war.

2. Morison, *History of United States Naval Operations*, 7:132.

3. Y'Blood, *Little Giants*, 1.

4. Crowl and Love, *U.S. Army in World War II*, 126.

5. Edwin Palmer Hoyt, *How They Won the War in the Pacific: Nimitz and His Admirals* (New York: Weybright and Talley, 1970), 310.

6. Daily memoirs, 26.

7. Letter of commendation citation for Seaman Second Class Richard L. Abbott Jr.

8. Letter of commendation citation for Commander Oliver Ames.

9. Beymer, survivor's statement, 3.

10. Drury, *History of the Chaplain Corps*, 185.

11. Navy Cross citation for Lieutenant Commander Wells Worth Carroll, USNR—File CVE13/P15, letter, March 20, 1944.

12. Daily memoirs, 21–22.

13. Francis Daily, telephone interview by author, August 17, 2001.

14. Silver Star citation for Commander Finley E. Hall.

15. Edward Jonas, *U.S.S. Liscome Bay* Association survivor's statement, 3.

16. Navy Cross citation for Lieutenant Commander James B. Rowe.

17. Williamson, "*U.S.S. Liscome Bay*—sinking of."

Bibliography

PRIMARY SOURCES

Interviews

Bohm, Leonard. Telephone interview by author, July 9, 2001.
Daily, Francis. Telephone interviews by author, July 17, 2001, and January 6, 2002.
Fisher, William. Telephone interview by author, April 11, 2002.
Haynes, Robert E. Telephone interview by author, October 10, 2002.
Homec, Maxsy. Telephone interview by author, January 10, 2003.
King, James. Telephone interview by author, July 31, 2001.
Whalen, Lloyd. Telephone interview by author, April 11, 2002.
Woodham, Tim. Telephone interview by author, July 9, 2001.

Survivors' Statements Collected by U.S.S. Liscome Bay *Association*

Bergquist, Raymond J.
Beymer, John T.
Bohm, Leonard.
Fisher, William.
Haynes, Robert E.
Honold, James D.
Jelsema, Carl, 1998.
Jenkins, John.
Jonas, Edward.
Woodham, Tim E.
Woodward, William J., Jr.

Unpublished Memoirs

Beasley, James C. "The *U.S.S. Liscome Bay*—(CVE 56)." November 1994. Copy in author's possession.

Cruse, Donald. "Back to Sea in *U.S.S. Liscome Bay*." January 1987. Copy in author's possession.

Daily, Francis X. "The Forgotten Flattop: *U.S.S. Liscome Bay*—CVE 56." 1998. Copy in author's possession.

National Archives, Modern Military Records Branch, College Park, Maryland

Ames, Oliver. "Action Report of the *U.S.S. Liscome Bay* (CVE-56)." December 16, 1943.

———. "Report of War Operations—*U.S.S. Liscome Bay*." December 8, 1943.

Beebe, Marshall U. "Comments of Commanding Officer of Composite Squadron Thirty-Nine Re: Operation of Aircraft Aboard *U.S.S. Liscome Bay*." December 16, 1943.

Bolster, C. M., et al. "*U.S.S. Liscome Bay* (CVE-56)—Loss of. Report of Investigation Board." December 22, 1943.

Bureau of Ships. "Loss of *Liscome Bay*." War damage report no. 45, March 10, 1944.

Calhoun, Walter C. (commanding officer, USS *Baltimore*). "*U.S.S. Liscome Bay*—Report On." After-action report, December 10, 1943.

Commander in Chief, United States Fleet. "*U.S.S. Liscome Bay* (CVE 56)—Loss of." Memorandum to commanders in chief, Pacific and Atlantic Fleets, December 30, 1943.

Griffin, Robert M. "Report of Loss of *U.S.S. Liscome Bay*." Commander Task Group 52.13 action report (Serial 0034), December 11, 1943.

Hunter, J. L. (commanding officer, USS *Mississippi*). "The Sinking of the *U.S.S. Liscome Bay*." After-action report, December 5, 1943.

Koenig, J. W. (commanding officer, USS *Maury*). "*U.S.S. Liscome Bay*, Loss of, *Maury* Account of." After-action report, December 2, 1943.

Motes, J. L. (commanding officer, USS *Gridley*). "Action Report." After-action report, November 26, 1943.

Naval Aviation Accident Report 44-9143 (accident of October 16, 1943).

Naval Aviation Accident Report 44-9577 (accident of November 9, 1943).

Rittenhouse, E. B. (commanding officer, USS *Hughes*). "Operations Incident to Sinking of *U.S.S. Liscome Bay*—Report of." After-action report, November 26, 1943.

Solomons, E. A. (commanding officer, Destroyer Division 2). "Action Report, Sinking of *U.S.S. Liscome Bay*, 24 November 1943." November 30, 1943.

Talk between Ships (TBS) log, USS *Idaho*. November 24, 1943.

Taylor, H. W. (commanding officer, USS *Coral Sea*). "Sinking of *U.S.S. Liscome Bay* on 24 November 1943—Report on." After-action report, December 3, 1943.

"*U.S.S. Liscome Bay* (CVE 56)—Loss of." Memorandum report prepared by Department of the Navy's Damage Investigation Board, December 22, 1943.

Williamson, F. T. (commanding officer, USS *Morris*). "*U.S.S. Liscome Bay*—sinking of." After-action report, November 25, 1943.

Young, A. L. "Sinking of *U.S.S. Liscome Bay*." Memorandum, December 10, 1943.
Zacharias, E. M. (commanding officer, USS *New Mexico*). "*U.S.S. Liscome Bay* (CVE 56), Sinking of." After-action report, November 30, 1943.

Naval Historical Center, Washington Navy Yard, Washington, D.C.

Gold Star citation for Commander Charles Crommelin.
Letter of commendation citation for Commander Oliver Ames.
Letter of commendation citation for Commander Irving D. Wiltsie.
Letter of commendation citation for Seaman Second Class Richard L. Abbott Jr.
Letter of commendation citation for Lieutenant John B. Rowe.
Navy and Marine Corps Medal citation for Lieutenant Gardner Smith.
Navy Cross citation for Lieutenant Commander Wells W. Carroll.
Navy Cross citation for Mess Attendant Second Class Doris Miller.
Navy Cross citation for Lieutenant Commander John B. Rowe.
Navy Cross citation for Captain Irving D. Wiltsie.
"Ship's Cook Third Class Doris Miller, USN." www.history.navy.mil/faqs/faq57-4.htm (visited April 3, 2001).
Ships' Histories Section. "History of the *U.S.S. Liscome Bay* (CVE 56)" (November 1950).
Silver Star citation for Commander Henry Crommelin.
Silver Star citation for Commander Finley E. Hall.
Silver Star citation for Captain Irving D. Wiltsie.
U.S. Navy biography sheet for Vice Admiral Robert M. Griffin (February 12, 1964).
U.S. Navy biography sheet for Rear Admiral Henry M. Mullinnix (December 2, 1943).
U.S. Navy biography sheet for Captain Irving Wiltsie (December 12, 1943).

United States Naval Academy, Annapolis, Maryland

"Finley E. Hall." *The Lucky Bag*. Annapolis: U.S. Naval Academy, 1929.
"Irving D. Wiltsie." *The Lucky Bag*. Annapolis: U.S. Naval Academy, 1921.
"John G. Crommelin." *The Lucky Bag*. Annapolis: U.S. Naval Academy, 1923.
"Richard Crommelin." *The Lucky Bag*. Annapolis: U.S. Naval Academy, 1938.
U.S. Navy biography sheet for Commander Charles L. Crommelin (November 7, 1951).
U.S. Navy biography sheet for Vice Admiral Henry Crommelin (November 24, 1959).
U.S. Navy biography sheet for Rear Admiral John G. Crommelin Jr. (January 9, 1966).
U.S. Navy biography sheet for Captain Quentin C. Crommelin (May 22, 1968).
U.S. Navy biography sheet for Lieutenant Richard G. Crommelin (November 12, 1942).

SECONDARY SOURCES

Alexander, Joseph. "The Turning Points of Tarawa." In *No End Save Victory: Perspectives on World War II*, edited by Robert Cowley, 292–305. New York: Putnam, 2001.

Allmon, William B. "Enemy's Perfect Hit." *World War II*, July 1992, 30–36.

———. "Gilbert Islands Campaign: Takin' Makin." *World War II*, November 1999, 30–36.

Astor, Gerald. *The Greatest War: Americans in Combat, 1941–1945*. Novato, Calif.: Presidio Press, 1999.

Barlow, Jeffrey G. *Revolt of the Admirals: The Fight for Naval Aviation, 1945–1950*. Washington, D.C.: Naval Historical Center, 1994.

Beebe, Marshall U. "Sis—*Liscome Bay* and Toko-Ri." *Naval Aviation Museum Foundation*, Spring 1984, 2–5, 62–66.

Bergerud, Eric. *Fire in the Sky*. Boulder, Colo.: Westview Press, 2000.

Boyd, Carl, and Akihiko Yoshida. *The Japanese Submarine Force and World War II*. Annapolis: Naval Institute Press, 1995.

Boyne, Walter J. *Clash of Titans: World War Two at Sea*. New York: Simon and Schuster, 1995.

Buckley, Gail. *American Patriots: The Story of Blacks in the Military from the Revolution to Desert Storm*. New York: Random House, 2001.

Cagle, Malcolm W. "The Crommelin Brothers Five." *Naval Aviation Museum Foundation* 2 (Fall 1988): 11–19.

Coletto, Paolo E. "Richmond K. Turner." In *Men of War: Great Navy Captains of World War II*, edited by Stephen Howarth, 363–79. New York: St. Martin's Press, 1993.

Cressman, Robert J. *The Official Chronology of the United States Navy in World War II*. Annapolis: Naval Institute Press, 2000.

Crowl, Philip A., and Edmund G. Love. *The U.S. Army in World War II: The War in the Pacific—Seizure of the Gilberts and Marshalls*. Washington, D.C.: Office of the Chief of Military History, 1955.

Dictionary of American Naval Fighting Ships. Edited by James L. Mooney. Washington, D.C.: Naval Historical Center, 1991.

Drury, Clifford M. *The History of the Chaplain Corps, United States Navy*. Vol. 2, *1939–1949*. Washington, D.C.: Government Printing Office, n.d.

Dunnigan, James F., and Albert A. Nofi. *Victory at Sea: World War II in the Pacific*. New York: William Morrow, 1995.

Dyer, George C. *The Amphibians Came to Conquer: The Story of Admiral Richmond Kelly Turner*. Washington, D.C.: Department of the Navy, 1972.

Evans, David C., and Mark R. Peattie. *Kaigun: Strategy, Tactics, and Technology in the Imperial Japanese Navy, 1887–1941*. Annapolis: Naval Institute Press, 1997.

Friedman, Norman. *U.S. Aircraft Carriers: An Illustrated Design History*. Annapolis: Naval Institute Press, 1983.

Goodwin, Doris Kearns. *No Ordinary Time*. New York: Simon and Schuster, 1995.

Guttman, Jon. "More on Lieutenant Blair." *Aviation History*, May 2001, 74–75.

Jensen, Oliver. "Carrier War." *Life*, March 26, 1945, 77–95.

Hammel, Eric, and John E. Lane. *Seventy-Six Hours: The Invasion of Tarawa*. Pacifica, Calif.: Pacifica Press, 1985.

Holmes, Wilfred J. *Undersea Victory: The Influence of Submarine Operations on the War in the Pacific*. Garden City, N.Y.: Doubleday, 1966.

Hoyt, Edwin Palmer. *How They Won the War in the Pacific: Nimitz and His Admirals*. New York: Weybright and Talley, 1970.

Keegan, John. *The Second World War*. New York: Viking, 1990.

Lundstrom, John B. *The First Team: Pacific Naval Air Combat from Pearl Harbor to Midway*. Annapolis: Naval Institute Press, 1984.

MacDonald, Scot. *Evolution of Aircraft Carriers*. Washington, D.C.: Office of the Chief of Naval Operations, 1964.

Michener, James. *The Bridges at Toko-Ri*. New York: Random House, 1953.

———. *Tales of the South Pacific*. New York: Macmillan, 1947.

Miller, Merle. "Makin Taken." In *Yank: World War II from the Guys Who Brought You Victory*, edited by Steve Kugler, 142–44. New York: St. Martin's Press, 1990.

Morison, Samuel Eliot. *History of United States Naval Operations in World War II*. Vol. 3, *The Rising Sun in the Pacific*. Boston: Little, Brown, 1948.

———. *History of United States Naval Operations in World War II*. Vol. 7, *Aleutians, Gilberts, and Marshalls, June 1942–April 1944*. Boston: Little, Brown, 1948.

Newell, Clayton. *Central Pacific, 1941–1943 (CMH Pub 72-4)*. Carlisle, Pa.: U.S. Army Center for Military History, n.d.

Nichols, David. *Ernie's War: The Best of Ernie Pyle's World War II Dispatches*. New York: Random House, 1986.

O'Leary, Michael. *United States Naval Fighters of World War II in Action*. Dorset, U.K.: Blandford Press, 1980.

Perret, Geoffrey. *Winged Victory*. New York: Random House, 1993.

Prange, Gordon. *December 7, 1941: The Day the Japanese Attacked Pearl Harbor*. New York: McGraw-Hill, 1988.

Reynolds, Clark G. *The Carrier War*. Alexandria, Va.: Time-Life Books, 1982.

Schwartz, Robert. "The Sinking of the *U.S.S. Liscome Bay*." Originally published in *Yank*, June 11, 1944. Reprinted in *Yank: World War II from the Guys Who Brought You Victory*, edited by Steve Kugler, 123–29. New York: St. Martin's Press, 1990.

Scott, John B., Jr. "The Crommelin Brothers." *Alabama Heritage*, Fall 1997, 6.

Spector, Ronald H. *Eagle against the Sun: The American War with Japan*. New York: Free Press, 1985.

Thruelsen, Richard. *The Grumman Story*. New York: Praeger, 1976.

U.S. Army. *The Capture of Makin, 20–24 November 1943*. Washington, D.C.: Center of Military History, 1990.

U.S. Navy. *The Glossary of U.S. Naval Abbreviations (OPNAV 29-P1000)*. Washington, D.C.: Government Printing Office, 1949.

———. *Register of the Commissioned Officers, Cadets, Midshipmen, and Officers of the United States Naval Reserve, January 1, 1943*. Washington, D.C.: Government Printing Office, 1943.

Y'Blood, William T. *The Little Giants: U.S. Escort Carriers against Japan*. Annapolis: Naval Institute Press, 1987.

Index

www.ingramcontent.com/pod-product-compliance
Lightning Source LLC
LaVergne TN
LVHW100818200826
845923LV00028B/249
* 9 7 8 0 8 1 7 3 5 6 0 3 3 *